Indian Literature in English

General Editors: David Carroll and Michael Wheeler
University of Lancaster

Longman Literature in English Series

General Editors: David Carroll and Michael Wheeler
University of Lancaster

For a complete list of titles see pages x and xi

Indian Literature in English

William Walsh

Longman

London and New York

Longman Group UK Limited
Longman House, Burnt Mill, Harlow,
Essex CM20 2JE, England
and Associated Companies throughout the world.

*Published in the United States of America
by Longman Inc., New York*

First published 1990

BRITISH LIBRARY CATALOGUING IN PUBLICATION DATA
Walsh, William, *1916–*
   Indian literature in English. – (Longman literature in
English series).
   1. English literature. Indian writers, to 1977 –
Critical studies
   I. Title
   820.9′954

**ISBN 0-582-49479-6 CSD
ISBN 0-582-49480-X PPR**

LIBRARY OF CONGRESS CATALOGING-IN-PUBLICATION DATA
Walsh, William, 1916–
   Indian literature in Englsh/William Walsh.
     p.   cm. – (Longman literature in English series)
   Bibliography: p.
   Includes index.
   ISBN 0-582-49479-6. – ISBN 0-582-49480-X (pbk.)
   1. Indian literature (English) – History and criticism. I. Title.
II. Series.
PR9484.4.W35   1990
820.9′954–dc20

89-34271
CIP

Set in Linotron 202 9½/11pt Bembo

Produced by Longman Singapore Publishers (Pte) Ltd.
Printed in Singapore

Contents

PR
9484.4
.W 35
1990

Acknowledgements vi

Author's Foreword vii

Editor's Preface ix

Longman Literature in English Series x

1 **Introduction** 1

2 **Prose: Sages and Autobiographers** 31

3 **Fiction: The Founding Fathers – Mulk Raj Anand, Raja Rao and R. K. Narayan** 62

4 **The Succession: From Khushwant Singh to Salman Rushdie** 98

5 **Poetry: Ezekiel, Parthasarathy, Kolatkar, Ramanujan and Others** 125

6 **India in English Fiction: Kipling, Thompson, Myers, Forster, Scott and Farrell** 159

Chronology 187

Select Bibliography 196

Individual Authors 203

Index 215

209303

Acknowledgements

We are grateful to the following for permission to reproduce copyright material:

William Heinemann Ltd for an extract from 'Fiction: The Founding Fathers' in *R. K. Narayan: A Critical Appreciation* (1982) by William Walsh; the Author, Arun Kolatkar for parts of his poems 'The Boatride' (12 lines), 'The Bus' (16 lines) & 'Chaitanya' (6 lines); the Author, Professor Shiv. K. Kumar for part of his poem 'Days in New York' (5 lines); Oxford University Press for part of the poems 'Snakes' (21 lines) & 'The Striders' (15 lines) from *The Striders* by A. K. Ramanujan (© Oxford University Press 1966) and 'Of Mothers' (11 lines) & 'Small-scale Reflections on a Great House' (6 lines) from *Relations* by A. K. Ramanujan (© Oxford University Press 1971); Oxford University Press, New Delhi for part of the poems 'Homecoming' (26 lines) by R. Parthasarathy, 'The Epileptic' (10 lines) & 'Ruminations' (12 lines) by Keki Daruwalla, 'The Sale' (23 lines) & 'Remarks of an Early Biographer' (17 lines) by Arvind Mehrotra from *Ten Twentieth Century Indian Poets* ed. R. Parthasarathy (OUP 1976); Oxford University Press, New Delhi & the Author, Nissim Ezekiel for parts of his poems 'Background Casually' (10 lines), & 'Island' (20 lines) from *Hymns in Darkness* by Nissim Ezekiel (OUP 1976), 'In India' (10 lines), 'Night of the Scorpion' (17 lines), 'Very Indian Poem in English' (20 lines) & 'Poet, Lover, Birdwatcher' (10 lines) from *Latter-Day Psalms* by Nissim Ezekiel (OUP 1982); the Author, R. Parthasarathy for part of his poem 'Stairs' (13 lines).

We have unfortunately been unable to trace the copyright holders of the poems 'Engraving of a Bison on a Stone' by Arvind Mehrotra & 'What's in and Out' by Gieve Patel, and would appreciate any information that would enable us to do so.

Author's Foreword

This book is based firmly in the relationship between India and Britain which has in different forms lasted for well over two hundred years. It began with British commercial exploitation, was followed by political suzerainty and then by the incorporation of India into the British Empire. During the final three quarters of a century of British Imperial rule the increasing and eventual irresistible determination of Indians to achieve independence and national sovereignty, together with the weakening of the British will to preserve their imperial pretensions, led to a new and calmer relationship of two separate powers – the one the most numerous democracy in the world, the other a middling power by world standards, and the two still joined by a peculiarly intimate attachment.

Another basis on which this study rests is the position of the English language in India which, during the British period in India, had become the medium of higher education and the *lingua franca* of intellectual, administrative and political life. The English language has continued to be even more significant in these respects, sometimes in the face of stiff and natural opposition since the conclusion of British Rule in India in 1947. The continued and extended use of English in a country with its own ancient, sophisticated and richly inclusive civilization and with its emphatically individual and sensitive ethos and sensibility is an extraordinary fact of national and linguistic life. It is also a powerful testimony to the expressive and creative capacities of the English language itself. One stresses the creative capacity because, where language exists on this scale among educated and gifted people, there will also be, indeed there *must* also be, literature. This is a stroke of good fortune for the English reader who is given access to an age-old and robustly alive and contemporary civilization, of singular individuality, which has fundamental categories of thought and modes of feeling deeply different from his own, and yet, as he recognizes at once, displays a profound, universal and attractive humanity.

The treatment of the book falls into six parts and I have followed a generally chronological pattern while keeping the *genres* separate from each other. I begin with a rapid personal excursus which touches fleetingly on the several major influences that compose this intricate, enigmatic civilization, from external invasion to land tenure, from religion to politics, from caste to climate. No one is more aware than I of the subjectivity of the effort to lay out the context of Indian literature in English.

It was in a society showing the influence of different rulers – Rajput, Mogul and British – of their very different cultures – Hindu, Muslim, Western – that Indian writing in English began at the end of the eighteenth century and developed more strongly and characteristically during the nineteenth. As in England with Carlyle, Mill and Ruskin, so in India with Ram Mohan Roy, Vivekananda, Tagore (more significant to the modern reader as a thinker than as a Victorian poet) and Aurobindo Ghose, a more impressive mind and a sharper writer, this line of prose writers continues down to today with the amazing, sometimes bizarre, Nirad C. Chaudhuri. His most impressive work is autobiographical and I also consider under this heading writings by Gandhi and Nehru.

It was in the nineteen-thirties that genuine Indian novelists began to write in English. Some of the most important of them were Mulk Raj Anand, who wrote indignantly of the Indian poor (but also about the princely caste), Raja Rao, who wrote about an intellectual upper class (but also about the villages) and R. K. Narayan, who wrote of the middle classes. These men established the Indian English literary world and indicated many of the main themes of Indian fiction in English. They were succeeded by other, younger, novelists, many of them women, who brought a nimbler modern spirit, new tracts of experience and new subject matter into the fiction. In the nineteen-fifties a number of gifted poets began to write in English, in spite of its being a learnt tongue unsupported by a living language. This is a further demonstration of the extraordinary capacity of the English language to embody sensibilities immensely remote from its origins and daily use. India has been a significant fact in British life, politics and imagination for many generations and I conclude by examining the experience and image of India as they have appeared in the work of a handful of distinguished English novelists during the last hundred years. I have concentrated here, as throughout, on a few truly gifted and creative writers for reasons of particularity and significance.

I am grateful to the Leverhulme Foundation for an Emeritus Fellowship during the period I was engaged on this work and to the Brotherton Library of the University of Leeds for generous help throughout.

William Walsh.
Leeds.

Editors' Preface

The multi-volume Longman Literature in English Series provides students of literature with a critical introduction to the major genres in their historical and cultural context. Each volume gives a coherent account of a clearly defined area, and the series, when complete, will offer a practical and comprehensive guide to literature written in English from Anglo-Saxon times to the present. The aim of the series as a whole is to show that the most valuable and stimulating approach to literature is that based upon an awareness of the relations between literary forms and their historical context. Thus the areas covered by most of the separate volumes are defined by period and genre. Each volume offers new informed ways of reading literary works, and provides guidance to further reading in an extensive reference section.

As well as studies on all periods of English and American literature, the series includes books on criticism and literary theory, and on the intellectual and cultural context. A comprehensive series of this kind must of course include other literature written in English, and therefore a group of volumes deals with Irish and Scottish literature, and the literatures of India, Africa, the Caribbean, Australia and Canada. The forty-seven volumes of the series cover the following areas: pre-Renaissance English Literature, English Poetry, English Drama, English Fiction, English Prose, Criticism and Literary Theory, Intellectual and Cultural Context, American Literature, Other Literatures in English.

David Carroll
Michael Wheeler

Longman Literature in English Series

General Editors: David Carroll and Michael Wheeler
University of Lancaster

Pre-Renaissance English Literature

★ English Literature before Chaucer *Michael Swanton*
English Literature in the Age of Chaucer
★ English Medieval Romance *W. R. J. Barron*

English Poetry

★ English Poetry of the Sixteenth Century *Gary Waller*
★ English Poetry of the Seventeenth Century *George Parfitt*
English Poetry of the Eighteenth Century 1700–1789
★ English Poetry of the Romantic Period 1789–1830 *J. R. Watson*
★ English Poetry of the Victorian Period 1830–1890 *Bernard Richards*
English Poetry of the Early Modern Period 1890–1940
English Poetry since 1940

English Drama

English Drama before Shakespeare
★ English Drama: Shakespeare to the Restoration, 1590–1660
   Alexander Leggatt
★ English Drama: Restoration and Eighteenth Century, 1660–1789
   Richard W. Bevis
English Drama: Romantic and Victorian, 1789–1890
English Drama of the Early Modern Period, 1890–1940
English Drama since 1940

English Fiction

★ English Fiction of the Eighteenth Century 1700–1789 *Clive T. Probyn*
★ English Fiction of the Romantic Period 1789–1830 *Gary Kelly*
★ English Fiction of the Victorian Period 1830–1890 *Michael Wheeler*
★ English Fiction of the Early Modern Period 1890–1940 *Douglas Hewitt*
English Fiction since 1940

English Prose

English Prose of the Renaissance 1550–1700
English Prose of the Eighteenth Century
English Prose of the Nineteenth Century

Criticism and Literary Theory

Criticism and Literary Theory from Sidney to Johnson
Criticism and Literary Theory from Wordsworth to Arnold
Criticism and Literary Theory from 1890 to the Present

The Intellectual and Cultural Context

The Sixteenth Century
* The Seventeenth Century, 1603–1700 *Graham Parry*
* The Eighteenth Century, 1700–1789 *James Sambrook*
The Romantic Period, 1789–1830
The Victorian Period, 1830–1890
The Twentieth Century: 1890 to the Present

American Literature

American Literature before 1880
* American Poetry of the Twentieth Century *Richard Gray*
American Drama of the Twentieth Century
* American Fiction 1865–1940 *Brian Lee*
American Fiction since 1940
Twentieth-Century America

Other Literatures

Irish Literature since 1800
Scottish Literature since 1700

Australian Literature
* Indian Literature in English *William Walsh*
African Literature in English: East and West
Southern African Literature in English
Caribbean Literature in English
* Canadian Literature in English *W. J. Keith*

* *Already published*

For Tim and Christina

Chapter 1
Introduction

1. Notes on Background and Context Origin

In this introductory chapter I want to indicate some of the many influences that have gone into the composition of the ancient, elaborate and mysterious civilization of India: which is itself the background for, and the context of, Indian literature in English. If one interprets this phenomenon somewhat loosely to incorporate certain nineteenth-century writers in India, it might be said to be the product of the last hundred years. On a stricter and more contemporary understanding – which is what I should prefer to take here, though it is not always possible to observe such severe lines of demarcation – Indian literature in English is the product of the last fifty years; the period, one notes, when for the most part the British were no longer governing India. But whether one takes the longer or shorter view and however much importance one attaches to the medium, Indian literature in English has an Indian soul and expresses a sensibility drawn from the same sources as the other embodiments of the Indian spirit and the Indian tradition.

To begin with, then, there is the physical configuration of the land itself; the sheer size and geographical variety of the sub-continent where everything is on a colossal scale, from the Himalayas in the far north, the Indo-Gangetic plain, the three great rivers – so significant also in Indian iconography – the Indus, the Ganges, the Brahmaputra, to a second hilly and tribal area and to the southern cities of the coastal area. In the countless villages with a climate invariably difficult and often oppressive there evolved over some six thousand years a distinctive, independent and coherent manner of life. The aboriginal population suffered the incursions of Greeks, Persians, Moguls, Europeans, all of whom deeply affected, without substantially altering, the nature of Indian culture, which has throughout its history shown a genius for absorption and persistence. No one has given a more dramatic and impassioned account of the origins and growth of Indian civilization than the cultural historian Nirad C. Chaudhuri (b. 1897) whose masterpiece in another genre, *The Autobiography of an Unknown Indian* (1951), I shall speak of in a different context. In *The Continent of Circe* (1965) Chaudhuri has evolved, as much from imagination as from history, a theory of Indian development which, he is satisfied, provides him with a casual explanation of the character and failures of his society. We may not agree with what is a passionately subjective and intuitive explanation of the origins of Indian society. But Chaudhuri's sharp, unforgiving eye, natural audacity and impatient, intellectual edge – while they may not qualify him as an unfailingly objective analyst of national life – do offer what impresses as a pure intensity of perception. The evidence for, or perhaps I should say the source of Chaudhuri's theory or conviction about, the shaping of Indian society by immigration is, first, the undoubted fact of the diffusion of the Indo-European languages and, secondly, his own interpretation of the early Indian epics, supported thirdly by a method of extrapolating backward into history and pre-history the logic of his observations of contemporary Indian society. And when I say 'logic' I do not mean to omit feeling. Chaudhuri is a man lacerated by the present and by scorn for the poverty and degradation he sees in every corner of contemporary society and powerfully impelled to find in the past a coherent explanation for the chaos and despair that surround him.

The core of the doctrine of *The Continent of Circe* is that the Hindus are of European stock, immigrant Aryans from Mitannian-Mesopotamia, who colonized the Indo-Gangetic plain and parts of South India. They were a complete society with a triple structure: an aristocracy composed of priests and fighters, and then the general body of the community carrying on normal economic activities as peasants, traders, cattle-raisers, artisans, to which they added a caste of lower workers, the Indras (who were not, however, the primitive dark autochthonous population) to make the four-caste society that the Hindu community has remained ever since – at least in theory. The Aryan settlement was complete in its essential form by the end of the seventh century B.C., and with it the basic ethnic pattern of India firmly established – the outstanding feature of which is the ferocious opposition between the civilized community of the Aryans and the indigenous primitive population, or any other, which threatened it. This Aryan civilization was affected by later invasions of Persians and Greeks, which were culturally though not ethnically important, and later by incursions of barbarian nomads from Central Asia. These later invasions meant that the Hindus had to fight for the survival of their society on two fronts: against the internal proletariat of the indigenous folk and an external proletariat of Asian nomads. The Hindus in consequence became a closed society based on birth, and was self-conscious, colour conscious and violently xenophobic.

The Islamic expansion in India, gradual in its first phase and overwhelming in its second, brought into India the propagators of a new aggressive culture who had an absolute conviction of the superiority of their culture and a religious duty to spread it. It was a well-established and mature society with a fully developed way of life. In the north it displaced the Hindu ruling class and lodged in the Indian consciousness the conviction of an irreconcilable conflict between Hindu and Muslim. There could be no question of absorbing the Muslims, and Hindu society on its side lost what power of assimilation and adaptability it had once possessed. The bulk of the new Islamic population were Hindu converts, but this fact made no difference to the sense of solidarity among themselves or to their feeling of oneness with the Islamic world outside.

The psychological experience of the British in India, first as traders, then as rulers, closely repeated, according to Chaudhuri, that of the Hindus themselves. A people of temperate climate, at a period of great vitality in their national life, with a strong disposition in favour of the fascinating, richly promising East, became, under the brutalities of a tropical climate and among a potentially hostile population, horribly demoralized. Their sense of proportion broke down. They lost their usual equability in human relations. They became extreme and strident. They were outraged by the lack among the Hindus of the European virtues of 'reason' and 'measure': everything appeared inconsistent and extravagant, lush and awry. They were continually oppressed by the possibility of submergence in a lower culture. Their pride in race intensified. Their sense of colour became neurotic. They grew increasingly unwilling to share their culture. 'The British in India . . . paraded a racial arrogance, whose mildest form was a stony silence' (p. 122).

In repeating the psychological development of the Hindus, the history of the British in India helped to harden the Hindus in their own strong bias as confirmed believers in blood and birth. The repetition enforced the original disposition. The Hindus remain, in Chaudhuri's judgement, a people divided against themselves, suffering an exhaustion of vitality and an ever-present maladjustment with the tropical environment. What happened to the Hindus happened to the British, and what happened to the British made any modification of the Hindu nature still more unlikely. It was the excruciatingly cruel country which had the same effect on both peoples. 'Western scholars', writes Chaudhuri, 'have sometimes made Buddhism or Vedanta responsible for the apparent indifference of the Hindus to the things of the world, especially for their disinclination to mental and bodily exertion and attributed to us a world-negation which we never had. The philosophies did not make our life what it is; it was the life which made the philosophies what they are' (p. 144).

There are personal and psychological undertones in Chaudhuri's reading of the origins of Indian culture. And yet in the end he comes down unambiguously on an impersonal and objective influence as the key item, namely the brutalities of life in a tropical climate. To ignore the geography is to misconceive the history. Life and climate in a subcontinent of quite harsh extremes are, except to a tiny favoured few, incomparably hard.

2. Caste and Religion

If the extraordinary nature of the Indian past, a set of the sharpest physical antitheses, and the national history of invasion, resistance, absorption and survival are potent influences on the character of Indian civilization, no less significant are the principle of caste on which society was organized and the Hindu religion which the system embodied and confirmed. The beginnings of caste are lost in millennial obscurity. But it is clear that it is linked to Aryan conceptions of racial and personal purity and pollution, by the division of labour on the grounds of efficiency in a primitive society and by the conviction of *dharma* – the absolute acceptance of one's lot in a stratified, hierarchical society. Caste is a principle of order which differentiates among mankind in a way that is both intrinsic and tyrannical; it is also seen as a cohesive force binding the various parts of society together. Orthodox scholars make much of this paradoxical point. For example, R. P. Masani writes in *The Legacy of India* (1937):

> The end of the sciences, according to Hindu philosophy is
> the realization of the unity of everything that exists. The
> scheme of social policy, based on caste, recognized such
> unity; at the same time it took into account the diversity
> of temperament and the complexity of the needs and
> processes of human life. . . . The concept of organic unity
> and interdependence ran through the whole system. Even
> when it has sought to deduce divine sanction for the
> ascendency of the superior orders on the hypothesis that
> the four castes had emerged from four different limbs of
> the Creator of the Universe, the underlying idea was not
> one of detachment but of union.[1]

The fourfold division of caste referred to in R. P. Masani's strongly favourable account of caste was into: the Brahmins, who represented and operated spiritual power; the Kshatriyas, who were the aristocracy of warriors and administrators – this last a curiously contemporary touch; the Vaisya, who are the ordinary general mass of the people; and the Indras, the underclass or untouchables, whose appallingly deprived and ignoble existence cannot be justified by any argument, religious, political or historical. As R. P. Masani claims in the essay just quoted, caste gave every member of society a place, a function and support, mitigating unrestrained competition and maintaining social tranquillity. Of course the rigidity of the fourfold division was blurred in time. There were innumerable divisions and sub-divisions of caste, class, families and guilds. Nevertheless the concept of a system based on caste lasted for thousands of years and is evident still in democratic India in its caste-determined, innumerable, stringent regulations on food, marriage, social custom, the role of women in the family and society.

The classic Aryan pattern of caste, the basic fourfold division already in being in the third century B.C., was loose enough to permit the growth of lesser groups or Jatis, such as family or occupational groups, as well as myriad regional variations. The caste system has served India for over two thousand years as a formative and integrating system, bringing about social coherence and helping to ensure in daily life the dependence of each part of the population on the other parts. But caste was also a medieval tyranny using religious sanctions and psychological imprinting to preserve the fundamental *status quo* and for the lowest of the castes abolishing the essential sense of individual esteem and personal dignity. It is this aspect of caste which is exposed in V. S. Naipaul's mordant, irritable but acutely observant study of his travels in India, *An Area of Darkness* (London, 1964). Naipaul was born in Trinidad in 1932 to a Hindu family. His grandfather, an indentured worker, was from Uttar Pradesh and the family was of pure Brahmin descent – an illustration of how one could be of the highest caste and the poorest class. The modes and forms of family life were profoundly Indian and Naipaul has retained in his adult life Brahmin delicacies and repugnancies about food and cooking, although he was also an agnostic in a devout, orthodox family. What Naipaul is shaken by when he visits India, and what he returns to again and again in an almost compulsive way, is the condition of squalor, the state of public lavatories, the crude ways of a fundamentally rural society. His attitude has something of a Brahmin's horror of the unclean and something of Swift's microscopic scrutiny and appalled recoil. Here is his description of four men washing down the steps of a seedy Bombay hotel. It shows Naipaul's care for exactness in defining atmosphere and action and his capacity to outline a scene so that it stands there, after a few spare strokes, solid and complete. The scene also implies a final moral comment on the caste system, although characteristically Naipaul has no touch of pity for the humiliated men, only contempt for them and disgust with the system.

> The first pours water from a bucket, the second scratches
> the tiles with a twig broom, the third uses a rag to slop
> the dirty water from the steps into another bucket, which
> is held by a fourth. After they have passed, the steps are
> as dirty as before; but now above the blackened skirting-
> tiles the walls are freshly and dirtily splashed. The
> bathrooms and lavatories are foul; the slimy woodwork
> has rotted away as a result of this daily drenching; the
> concrete walls are green and black with slime. You cannot
> complain that the hotel is dirty. No Indian will agree with
> you. Four sweepers are in daily attendance and it is
> enough in India that the sweepers attend. They are not
> required to *clean*. That is a subsidiary part of their
> function, which is to *be* sweepers, degraded beings, to go
> through the motions of degradation. (p. 79)

Naipaul, in spite of his Brahminical background, cannot understand the religious consciousness or give even a provisional acceptance to the religious view of life. This is a peculiar disadvantage for the observer of the Indian scene because so much that is essential in India is consti-tuted by religion. In India, religion enfolds body and soul from conception to dissolution. It is the secret premise of family thought and action. It saturates the speech, the hymns, the myths and stories and the idiom of daily life. It exists in forms accessible to the most sophis-ticated as well as to the least educated, to the austere moralist and the frenzied terrorist. It is the mysterious element in Indian life to which I referred at the beginning of this chapter. And yet Hinduism is religious in a sense that it is hard for Jews, Christians or Muslims to grasp. It has no dogma, no core of doctrine, no code of law, no clergy or ecclesiastical administration.

Here are two passages, one British, the other American, which offer contrasting and complementary accounts of the nature of Hinduism. The first is from *Modern India* (1985) by Judith M. Brown:

> . . . in the Hindu context religion is not basically
> 'something to be believed' but 'to be done'. There is no
> central revelation of the nature of God to which each
> individual must respond, and on which response his

temporal and eternal destiny depends. Rather, religion is concerned with *dharma*; the fundamental laws of existence, to which men and women must conform through performance of their own *dharma* or religious duty. The context of this conformity is the whole community; and the precise prescriptions of personal *dharma* are known to the individuals through the norms of their particular caste's behaviour.[2]

The second passage is from Sir Percival Griffith's *The British Impact on India* (1952):

Hinduism on the other hand, is infinitely complicated, luxuriant in its forms and ideas and abounding in symbols. The Creator and his creations are one and indivisible, as we have seen in an earlier chapter; there is no limit to the possible manifestations of the all-pervading spirit, and a new God may therefore turn up at any time or place. The individual matters little, for he, after all, is but one link in an endless chain beginning and ending in a somewhat nebulous merging with the all-pervading spirit. As for equality, it is a concept necessarily foreign to Hinduism, with its highly stratified society. It is important to emphasize the fundamental difference between the psychological foundations of the two religions – Islam, clearcut, individualistic, democratic, simple – Hinduism, abstruse, caring little for the individual, essentially un-democratic and extremely complicated.[3]

If Hinduism has no corpus of doctrine, no code of law or definitive scriptures, it has its sacred, ancient, authoritative writings, the Veda and the later Epics, and in these works is implied a most distinctive, complex and inclusive vision of human life and destiny, which is neither messianic, progressive, triumphalist or millennial. As in the cluster of ideas which compose the notion of 'caste' there is a biological connection with purity and pollution, so in the Hindu conception of existence and destiny there is an organic parallel with creation and destruction. Existence is constituted by cycles of creation and decay. Just, as in nature, forms and substances decay and are transformed into other forms and other substances, so the bodies and souls of men decay and are reborn in other modes of existence. The forces of creation and destruction are deified as Brahman the creative power and Shiva the destructive power, which are not utterly opposed principles of a Manichean kind but are complementary aspects of the Godhead, having their own echo or analogue in the souls of men. There is no absolute distinction, we remember, between creator and creation in Hindu thought. This is the meaning of the remark in the Bhagavad-Gita: 'When we consider Brahman as lodged within the individual being, we call him the Atman.' The purpose of human life is to bring about by discipline and renunciation the union of the soul with the divine or the recognition of their identity. This is the state called Nirvana, the obliteration of the limited imperfect self. Those who fail in this duty condemn themselves 'to a prolongation of their state of separation and misery, and perhaps to an intensification of it in another existence or series of existences'.

I mentioned the Bhagavad-Gita, the Lord's Song, which is a marvellous religious poem, composed about 200 B.C., and is itself an episode in a Sanskrit epic *The Mahabharata*. It brings warmth, humanity and grace to the teachings of the Veda, which I have been attempting to sketch, turning the abstract figure of Brahman into the appealing God-man Krishna. At the same time the Bhagavad-Gita illustrates vividly the strength and permanence of Hinduism which come from its being planted firmly in the common facts of ordinary life as well as in its capacity to ascend to sublime heights of spirituality. The embodiment of religious truths in poems, hymns, stories and drama is one of the most effective ways in which Hinduism is made an intimate and functional part of the consciousness and conscience of young and old. In his introduction to his elegant translation of a Tamil version of another Sanskrit epic poem, *The Ramayana* (1973), R. K. Narayan writes: 'It may sound hyperbolic, but I am prepared to state that almost every individual among the five hundred million living in India is aware of the story of *The Ramayana* in some measure or other.' Children are told the story at bedtime. Others will have studied it and learnt stanzas by heart. Others will have heard it from a traditional story-teller or seen it on the stage as a dance-drama. It pervades religious, cultural and home life.

In fact the whole social context serves to instil and enforce Hindu beliefs and Hindu feelings. There may be no official Hindu church and clergy appointed to guard faith and morals but spiritual authority does exist and is widely disseminated throughout a tissue of agencies. The father, the head of the family, the mother in domestic life, the priestly caste – the Brahmins – in the conduct of ritual and the solution of ethical problems, the guru, the holy man, the ascetic who has renounced the world, the keeper of the temple, all have some measure of religious authority and work for the diffusion of Hindu values and the ordering of behaviour.

I want to pause here amid this welter of unavoidable generalities to give one or two concrete instances, not of the religious spirit but rather of the naturalness of religion in India. Here is my first example taken from R. K. Narayan's novel, *Mr. Sampath* (1949), in which a pure religious experience is focused in a common homely object, a sandal-wood image found in a packet of saffron from the grocer. It gives a new meaning to the words 'an object of sentimental value':

> He prayed for a moment before a small image of Nataraja, which his grandmother had given him when he was a boy. This was one of the possessions he had valued most for years. It was of sandal wood, which had deepened a darker shade with years, just four inches high. The carving represented Nataraja with one foot raised and one pressing down a demon, his four arms outstretched, with his hair flying, the eyes rapt in contemplation, an exquisitely poised figure. His grandmother had given it to him on his eighth birthday. She had got it from her father, who discovered it in a packet of saffron they had bought from the shop on a certain day. It had never left Srinivas since that birthday. It was on his own table at home, or in the hostel, wherever he might be. It had become part of him, the little image. He often sat before it, contemplated its proportions and addressed it thus: 'Oh God, you are trampling a demon under your feet, and you show us a rhythm, though you appear to be still. May a ray of that light illuminate my mind.' He silently addressed it thus. He never started the day without spending a few minutes before this image.

We live in utterly different conditions where nobody could worship an image handed down by his grandmother and discovered by her father in a packet from the grocer, and probably like Srinivas, the young man in the passage, we 'grasp the symbol but vaguely' as he says of himself. Nevertheless as we contemplate the image and the scene through Narayan's cool, undistracted art we are not, I think, deceived in detecting beneath the apparently exotic and even alien the common and extraordinary rhythm of life and the special beat given to that rhythm by an intense, unaffected and unquestioning religious spirit.

My second example of the religious spirit is taken from the other end of the social scale – if I may use such an inappropriate British phrase. It is from *The Hill of Devi* (1953), E. M. Forster's record in letter and reminiscences of his service as Private Secretary to an Indian Prince or Princeling, H. H. Sir Rukoji Rav III, who ruled a population of eighty thousand over some four hundred and forty-six square miles.

His territory was inextricably mixed with that of a junior branch of the family so that the Senior Ruler might raise taxes on one side of the street and the Junior Ruler on the other: an example of administrative confusion by no means rare in India, at least during the British Raj. The two states had together signed a treaty of friendship with the Honourable East India Company in 1818 confirming them in their states and possessions. The rulers were Marathas, that is, descended from the caste of the medieval aristocracy, although they also claimed a Rajput inheritance through marriage – an unconvincing claim Forster considered. Forster had a deep affection and admiration for the ruler who was a most generous, sensitive and charming man. It is a testimony to the warmth of their friendship that Forster should have even sympathized with the ruler's religious convictions, Forster himself a liberal, secular humanist, being pretty well bereft of any religious feeling or sympathy except perhaps of an animistic and vaguely numinous kind, and that only in an Indian context, as we can tell from *A Passage to India* (1924).

The excerpt I have chosen from *The Hill of Devi* comes from a letter dated 24 August 1921. It is part of the description of Gokul Ashtami, the eight days of fasting in honour of the birth of Krishna.' It was hard to say how much of what had happened was traditional and how much should be attributed to the Ruler. What is clear, however, is that any conception of ritual that is based on form, dignity and taste is wholly at odds with the Hindu style, which is to blend fatuity with philosophy and vulgarity with mysticism:

> The noise is so appalling. Hymns are sung to the altar
> downstairs without ceasing. The singers, in groups of
> eight, accompany themselves on cymbals and a
> harmonium. At the end of two hours a new group pushes
> in from the back. The altar has also a ritual which is
> independent of the singing. A great many gods are on
> visit and they all get up at 4.30 a.m. – they are not
> supposed to be asleep during the Festival,. which is
> reasonable considering the din, but to be enjoying
> themselves. They have a bath and are anointed and take a
> meal, which is over about 9.00 a.m. At 12.00 is another
> service, during which three bands play simultaneously in
> the little courtyard, two native bands and the European,
> affecting a merry polka, while these united strains are
> pierced by an enormous curved horn, rather fine, which is
> blown whenever incense is offered. And still I am only at
> the beginning of the noise. Children play games all over
> the place, officials should . . . what troubles me is that

every detail, almost without exception, is fatuous and in
bad taste. The altar is a mass of little objects, stifled with
rose leaves, the walls are hung with deplorable oleographs,
the chandeliers, draperies, everything bad. Only one thing
is beautiful – the expression on the faces of the people as
they bow to the shrine, and he himself [the Ruler] is as
always successful in his odd role. I have never seen
religious ecstasy before and don't take to it more than I
expected I should, but he manages not to be absurd.
Whereas the other groups of singers stand quiet, *he* is
dancing all the time, like David before the ark, jigging up
and down with a happy expression on his face, and
twanging a stringed instrument that hangs by a scarf
round his neck. At the end of his two hymns he gets
wound up and begins composing poetry which is copied
down by a clerk and yesterday he flung himself flat on his
face on the carpet. Ten minutes later I saw him as usual in
ordinary life. He complained of indigestion but seemed
normal and discussed arrangements connected with the
motor cars. I cannot see the point of this, or rather in
what it differs from ordinary mundane intoxication. I
suppose that if you believe your drunkenness proceeds
from God it becomes more enjoyable. Yet I am very
muddled in my own mind about it all for H.H. has what
we understand by the religious sense and it comes out all
through his life. He is always thinking of others and
refusing to take advantage of his position in his dealings
with them; and believing that his God acts similarly
towards him. (pp. 105–6)

India has been as rich in religious experience as that other great
source of religion, the Eastern Mediterranean. Hinduism itself
produced its own reforming movements: Janism in the sixth century,
Sikhism in the sixteenth. Janism was Hinduism with a more rigorously
ascetic ethic and a stronger reverence for every form of life, however
humble. Sikhism was a monotheistic reformation of Hinduism, much
influenced by Islam. It grew up as a struggle against the religious
dominance of Hinduism and against the political dominance of the
Muslims, and it gave the Sikhs that vivid sense of independent identity
which is at the root of so much religious and political travail in India
and particularly in Bengal, the Sikh heartland, to this day. India has
also received over the centuries modest religious infiltrations from Jews
and Parsees, another monotheistic religion of Zoroastrian origin,
whose members were expelled by the Muslims from Persia in the

eighth century. Christianity, always as a minority religion, has existed in India almost from its beginnings, brought to India from Syria according to legend by the apostle St Thomas and revived and strengthened by St Francis Xavier in the sixteenth century. Christianity received the support of the British Raj and of the British Protestant missionaries – to which the admirable hymns of Bishop Heber of Calcutta stand as a permanent witness. But Christianity has never made much advance against the immense authority of the Hindu tradition.

By a paradox of religious history, India was also the cradle of another great religion, Buddhism, which, immense in its influence outside India, dwindled away to nothing in its place of origin. Buddha, it is now accepted, was a historical personage, born of a noble family at Lumbiai, in the Sakya republic. His career has parallels with that of Christ. At twenty-nine he became an itinerant preacher and at thirty-five he had the experience of receiving enlightenment. He recruited disciples from all parts of society throughout South Bihar and eastern Uttar Pradesh and founded an order of monks and nuns to continue his mission. Their monasteries, like those of the medieval monks, became centres of spirituality, culture and art. Buddhism is a non-theistic religion. Its supreme value is enlightenment and the Buddha's claim is to be not a god but a fully enlightened human being, which to Buddhists is an attribute superior to any sort of divinity. One can see the point of this in a world where gods thronged every village and every mind as well. Buddhism, this calm and wonderfully mature religion, like the personality of Buddha himself, was carried along the Indian trade routes by Indian merchants and monks into China, Japan and Ceylon and most of Eastern Asia. In India itself Buddhism simply vanished back into the Hinduism from which it came. According to the distinguished scholar, the former President of India and Professor of Eastern Religions at Oxford, Dr Sarvepalli Radhakrishnan, Janism, Buddhism and Sikhism were 'creations of the Indian mind [which] represent reform movements from within the fold of Hinduism put forth to meet the special demands of the various stages of the Hindu faith'.[4]

The other great religion that has had overwhelming effects on the life and history of India is Islam. It was brought to India by the Arabs who conquered Sind in the seventh and eighth centuries A.D. and, later, by the Arabs who came across the North West frontier. Muslims then began to settle in the country and spread their religion. In the Mughal period several dynasties of kings extended the rule and influence of Islam which became the dominant force under the Mughal emperors and, although deeply affected by Persian culture, was made an essential element of Indian civilization. It is almost impossible to exaggerate the degree of 'foreignness' of Muslim belief and practice to the original Hindu culture, and despite centuries of common life it has never been eradicated – indeed, at many times and in many places hardly mitigated. For the Muslim belief is as essential as right practice. Muslims are passionately monotheistic, and are ferociously obedient to the will of Allah as revealed in the Koran, which is preached and defined by the alema, the trained Muslim clergy. They insist on congregational worship, a strongly unifying influence for Muslims living in a Hindu universe. Politics for Muslims have always been shaped by, and subordinated to, religious belief, and their distinctive political theory has always made them troublesome settlers in the host country. Moreover, as J. M. Brown writes:

> . . . observation of Indian society shows that, despite the absence of caste Islam regulates Muslim social behaviour in many ways as finely and in as great detail as do the conventions of caste. Food and drink, dress, marriage, burial rather than cremation (the Hindu custom), the veiling of women and their subordination to men are a few of the many aspects of life which are ordered by convention and law to enable men and women to respond correctly to ultimate reality, which is Allah.[5]

Islam insists on the absolute separation of the divine and the human; Hinduism abolishes the distinction and makes everything human part of the divine. Islam concentrates the divine; Hinduism distributes it. Such a profound difference in the ruling values of life and so sharp an antithesis in its purpose assumes that there will never be an ultimate reconciliation between Hindu and Muslim and incorporates in the stuff of the Indian polity an inescapable and even threatening tension. It shows itself regularly in communal strife, political antagonism and movements towards the disintegration of the State, and most calamitously in the savagery between the communities at the time of the modern foundation of the Indian State, which signalled the demise of a United India before it was ever born.

3. Architecture, Art and Sensibility

I turn now to what is perhaps the greatest expression in art of the complex Indian *persona* and the variety of religious belief sketched above. If Buddhism left only a trace of its presence as a religious force

– and that only the contemplative element in religious life – it exercised a stronger influence on Indian art and architecture. Some of the more spectacular expressions of the Buddhist spirit in India were created during the reign of the great emperor and convert Ashoka, an Indian Constantine who reigned for some forty years between 273 and 232 B.C. They include the smoothly polished sandstone columns, erected at places connected with the Buddha's life, which were often carved with intricately worked symbolic capitals, the *stupas*, mound-shaped structures like the Great Stupa at Sanchi in Central India which has beautifully carved gates, a gallery and an ambulatory passage at the base for the ritual of circumambulation; and *chaitya* halls, sometimes associated with monasteries, long apsed and columned chambers designed for worship and often cut from the living rock. In these works of art of the Manryan period – further developed and refined under the Shunga, Kushan and Gupta – sculpture emerged as the preferred medium of Indian artists and to what a pitch of eloquence they brought it! These forms of sculpture were used to express not only Buddhist but also Brahman and Jain spirituality. In the Gupta period of the fifth century A.D., we see not only powerful, mobile and sensuous examples of Hindu myth in sculpture but also the earliest surviving examples of Indian painting. These are in the sanctuaries and caves of Ajanta, a sequence of wall paintings, the finish and excellence of which testify to their being part of a tradition of painting. The paintings show both Buddhist images and Hindu scenes, some of the latter touched with the erotic feeling of later Indian miniature painting. 'Ultimately,' writes Roy Craven in *A Concise History of Indian Art*, 'Buddhism became so interwoven with Brahminical practices that it is difficult to define the dividing line between the two. Late in the twelfth century, when Islam devastated Northern India, it was a dominant and thriving Hindu culture which received the greatest shock, while remnants of a dying Buddhism were finally snuffed out.'[6]

Muslim art in India blended the Indian and Arabian cultures in a manner which is distinct from its original elements. The Muslim invaders of the tenth and eleventh centuries were far more cultivated than the earliest Arabian settlements in Sind and they brought with them a sharper and clearer theology, a new style of architecture, a new kind of music and different musical instruments, a different mode of painting and an exquisite calligraphy. Their architecture in contrast to the darkness and floridity of the Hindu art was characterized by restraint, openness and the rational disposition of material and purpose. Images were banned by Islam and it was on architecture rather than sculpture that they concentrated their gifts: on mosques, palaces, houses, towns and monuments. Most of the greatest specimens of its lucid and beautiful buildings were erected in the north-west at Delhi,

Agra, Fatehpur-Sikri and Allahmabad. Many were surrounded by
formal and elaborately contrived water gardens. In *The Legacy of India*,
M. S. Briggs states that most of this work was distinguished by the
'dignity of its grouping and disposition, in the masterly contrast
between the central dome and the slender minarets, in the chaste refine-
ment and painstaking craftsmanship of its details, and above all in the
splendour of its materials'.[7]

The qualities of classical and medieval Indian sculpture ('medieval
sculpture was Brahminical in essence and also founded upon a rock-
cutting technique worked out at Ajanta, Badami, and Ellora'[8]), 'lonely
sublimity, physical grandeur and technical mastery', make it one of the
wonders of the world. Indian painting, which itself started with the
wall paintings in the sculptured caves, has almost as long if not as
splendid a major tradition. Whether of the Gujarati school – which
links the wall paintings with later developments, Rajput, Mughal and
Deccani – this painting, while it has qualities of brilliance, wit, observation and vigour, is a more limited and local art. But both forms
bring home to us once again the age, continuity, reach and sophistication of this extraordinary civilization. Moreover, a point I emphasize
again, India keeps an unbroken connection with its origins more
naturally and more effectively than most other contemporary societies.
This is a fact that could be illustrated with innumerable examples. I
choose one from the novels of R. K. Narayan, fiction which illustrates
and embodies whole areas of Indian life, experience and belief. At the
conclusion of *The Sweet Vendor* (1967) Jagar, the protagonist, suddenly
determines to detach himself from, 'a set of repetitions performed for
sixty years' in order to spend the rest of his life helping a stonemason
to carve a pure image of the goddess for others to contemplate. His
decision, which is of course in the classical Indian line, requiring that
'at some stage in one's life one must uproot oneself from one's accustomed surroundings so that others can continue in peace', is in Jagar's
case charmingly blemished with an appealing human flaw. He does not
neglect to take his cheque book with him. The sculptor and servant
of the goddess with whom Jagar proposes to finish out his days
explains in words which beautifully blend the Buddhist and the
Brahmin that the perfection in stone at which he is aiming must still
contain a deliberate fault:

> I always remember the story of the dancing figure of
> Natsuj, which was so perfect that it began a cosmic dance
> and the town itself shook as if an earthquake had rocked
> it, until a small finger on the figure was chipped off. We
> always do it; no one even notices it, but we always create
> a small flaw in every image; it's for safety.

In stressing yet again the continuity of the Indian tradition, I do not for a moment suggest that it is something explicitly conscious and deliberately passed on from generation to generation. The tenacity of the Indian mind and sensibility is not the same as the retentiveness of conscious memory; and the forms it receives are not the bright, summonable images of memory. Rather they are the perspectives from which it sees the frame that stabilizes and orders its experience. They are not ideas but the grounds of ideas. Too important to be biddable by consciousness they are the preliminaries and premises of all consciousness.

We can distinguish in this complex thought and feeling at least three notes, just as we can in another ancient tradition, the Jewish, although the Indian sensibility is less dogmatic and committed than the Jewish. First there is the sense of the divine as the unqualified and absolute ground of being; second, the enjoyment of a rich immediacy of life even in the most meagre of conditions, of custom, habit, rite, symbol, food, dress, of innumerable significant particulars; and, third, stretching between the sense of the first and the living of the second a vital feeling of a continuous tradition.

4. The Foreign Response

This age-old settlement of religious belief, thought-pattern, emotional system and symbolic pattern produces an unusually coherent, undivided and confident personality, at least as it is manifested in art and literature. (I do not speak of the incidence of neurotic illness among the population.) It is a property of the Indian temperament which often proves infuriatingly recalcitrant to the understanding of even sympathetic foreigners. I have referred to V. S. Naipaul's attitude to India. In spite of all its advantages of inheritance, creative power and penetrating intelligence, he found the Indian scene and Indian people fundamentally distasteful and incomprehensible, surely the consequence of his markedly Western and contemporary kind of thought. Another foreign writer with a longer experience of India, and closer ties, is Ruth Prawer Jhabvala, who is Polish by birth, English by education and Indian by marriage. Most of her work is laid there and she expresses with something of the same exhausted anger an almost despairing realization of the sheer, ungraspable strangeness of India and Indians. This occurs not in the fiction but in the introduction to her 1966 volume of short stories called appropriately enough *An Experience of India*. She makes us see how the conditions of life in India induce

n an admittedly tense, self-analytic East European a state of angry,
mpotent lassitude: conditions like the intolerable climate and the
unbearable sights – people dying of starvation in the streets or children
kidnapped to be sent out begging. She is driven in on herself because
of the hollowness of wealthy, Westernized Indians with their party-
chat of Godard, Becket and ecology or by the absence of any social
life in Western terms among ordinary Indians, who simply wish to be
together as family or clan members, doing nothing, thinking nothing,
just being. There is much to be said for this kind of relaxed adaptation
to Indian conditions. But it is impossible for a foreigner who, to
survive, needs to be a strong patient person with a cause – a doctor,
a social worker, a missionary:

> So I am back again alone in my room with the blinds
> drawn and the airconditioner on. Sometimes when I think
> of my life, it seems to have contracted to this one point
> and to be concentrated in this one room, and always a
> very hot, very long afternoon when the airconditioner has
> failed. I cannot describe the *oppression* of such afternoons.
> It is a physical oppression – the heat pressing down on me
> and pressing in the walls and the ceiling and congealing
> together with time which has stood still and will never
> move again. And it is not only those two – heat and time
> – that are laying their weight on me but behind them, or
> held within them, there is something more which I can
> only describe as the whole of India.[9]

This painful, personal statement tells us something about India
(though perhaps more about the writer). But India is also the country
which enabled another foreigner and novelist, E. M. Forster, to write
so lyrically in *The Hill of Devi* towards the end of his two-year stint
in Dewas State Senior:

> Chatarpur was wilder, smaller and weaker than Dewas,
> and far more picturesque. Hidden away in the jungles, it is
> indeed one of the most romantic places I have ever seen.
> The Guest House stood on a steep ridge close outside the
> city, and as the morning mists thinned, the spires of
> Hindu and Jain temples appeared through the white and
> the treetops resembled green cushions. Beyond the city
> were hills. Monkeys scampered up and down the slope –
> black-faced because they had not helped Rama in his wars
> – tigers and leopards were near. No industries. No
> railways. Agriculture as normal, but more diversified; for
> instance, betel-leaf was cultivated – delicate creepers

twined round strings in a walled enclosure. And there was
wonderful sightseeing: the great temple-group of
Khajraho, which is one of the glories of India, and nearer
at hand the lyrical beauties of Mau. Mau is a half-ruined
palace by the side of a lake. One passes through a pillared
hall on to a terrace and the water is reached by steps at
the roots of a great tree. The water is full of growth but
clear, and when the sun sets ducks fly over and hundreds
of fowl beat the surface with their wings far away,
making thunder. On the further side are tombs; a nymph
haunts one of them; she used to eat lotus and walk on the
lotus leaves. The Maharajah told me this and much more:
once he brought a sorcerer to Mau to make the walls
speak by some incense but the man was a 'quack', he
forgot the incense, and the walls have never spoken.
(pp. 128–29)

One thing ought to be said at once about the two passages quoted.
Each is in an important respect out-of-date. The princely order is now
no more than a lingering ghost with no substantial presence, and India,
in spite of vast areas of impoverished, eroded land, has managed to
feed its own people and with the help of the rich bread-basket of the
Punjab has even exported grain. Both pieces certainly witness to the
impact of India and to the extremes of bias the experience of India can
induce. Ruth Prawer Jhabvala's piece is so self-regarding and so
tunnelled in vision that while it records a convincingly personal and
not altogether uncommon experience, it leaves India itself as no more
than a set of feelings and cloudy images. The piece from Forster, on
the other hand, with a greater degree of modesty – or perhaps one
should say more fittingly, of humility – an eye bent more attentively
on the object and on a larger sense of range gives a firmer and fuller
reading of the Indian experience. Both together add to one's feeling
of the complexity of India, the country of classical art, Mughal
splendour, physical beauty, authentic individuality and serene self-
possession but also of an intolerably oppressive environment, mendicant children, poverty, superstition and caste.

5. The British Connection

The British connection with India derived from the early British genius
for trade rather than from the later imperial instinct to rule, although

the latter was probably latent in the former. At the start, from 1600 to 1612 each voyage for the East India Company was an independently funded venture; then several ventures were covered by a Joint Stock, and finally the Merchant Venturers merged into a group with its own capital. This powerful, and profitable conglomerate was given a Crown Charter in 1600. Cromwell supported the Company and Charles II enlarged its authority and equipped it with many of the rights of a true state with powers of ruling – at first over British subjects only – of administration and of taxation. In its first hundred years it grew by skilful negotiation with the native rulers and by careful observance of its strictly commercial function. This was the burden of the advice given by the admirable Sir Thomas Roe who was sent to India in January 1614 by King James as his ambassador. He was one of the many admirable Englishmen who served both India and his own country well. He wrote to the Company before he left India in 1619, enunciating in vigorous Jacobean English the doctrine that was to govern its actions for the best part of a century:

> It is the beggaring of Portugal, notwithstanding his many
> rich residences and territories, that he keeps soldiers that
> spends it; yet his garrisons are mean. He never profited by
> the Indies since he defended them. Observe this well. It
> hath been also the error of the Dutch, who seek planation
> here by the sword. They turn a wonderful stock, they
> prowl in all places, they possess some of the best; yet their
> dead payes consume all their gain. Let this be received as a
> rule: that if you will profit, seek it at sea, and in quiet
> trade: for without controversy it is an error to affect
> Garrisons and land Wars in India.[10]

In the last quarter of the seventeenth century a different view of the Company's policy and function began to emerge. It was provoked by anarchy among the indigenous authorities, with disorder and violence in the north of India and upheavals in Bengal and Bombay. A despatch in 1686 starts roundly 'The Moghul officers are trampling on us and extorting what they please of our estate from us, by the besieging of our Factories and stopping of our boats upon the Ganges; they will never forbare doing so until we have made them as sensible of our Power, as we have of our truth and justice.'[11] The governor of the Company, Gerald Aungier, now believed its servants should go about their business sword in hand. The new pugnacious policy, which often led to humiliating defeat at the hands of the Muchals and the Marathas and to severe damage to the Company's ships from the Malabar pirates, created a wholly new conception of the Company's ultimate aim in India. It was given official expression by another Governor, Sir Joshua Child, in 1687, a fact of singular significance in that he had once adhered strongly to the trade-not-conquest doctrine of Sir Thomas Roe. The Company must establish 'such a politie of civil and military power, and create and secure such a large revenue to maintain both . . . as may be the foundation of a large, well-grounded, sure English dominion for all time to come'.[12]

With this new philosophy, with trade guaranteed and protected by force and with competition increasingly diminished, the Company went from strength to strength becoming an effective instrument of the developing imperialist drive, to which in the course of time the interests of the proprietors were wholly subordinated. In the course of this development the Company had elaborated a strong central administration and a network of British collectors and Indian agents and servants throughout India. It was, therefore, fully prepared to be the organ of government which it became after the Sepoys' Revolt of 1857–58 – a transformation which was natural enough, given the conception and energy of the imperialist philosophy dominant in the nineteenth century. Some have argued that the Mutiny of 1857 in Northern India was the product of growing nationalist feeling and that the high caste sepoys of the Bengal army were the forerunners of the freedom fighters of the twentieth century. Against this it can be contended that there were manifold and complex causes for the Mutiny, religious, economic and social, and while a sense of alienation may have been among them, it was never a leading nor even an ever-present cause.

Nonetheless the Mutiny was as deeply significant an event for the British as for the Indians. It signalled the transfer from Company to Government suzerainty, a better organized army, a more professional civil service and more opportunities in both for Indians if only in subordinate positions. It also shattered the conviction – illusion as it turned out – that the British had a special relationship with and a peculiar understanding of the Indians, especially of the peasants, and of that part of the population incorporated into a British institution, the army. The brutality with which the Mutiny was suppressed with soldiers brought from Britain is a measure of the shock the Mutiny was to the British consciousness. From then on began that distance, coldness and sense of intense racial superiority of which Chaudhuri speaks in *The Continent of Circe*.

The particularly blinding irrationality, hardening with time, persisted as we see in E. M. Forster's *A Passage to India* (1924) and Paul Scott's *The Raj Quartet* (1966–75) almost to the end of British rule. It was met on the Indian side by an attitude which had not existed in the eighteenth century when Englishmen might have Indian wives and

families or, for most of the nineteenth century, when the leaders of
the movement for Indian rights were constitutional in their aims and
methods and more than willing to maintain the British connection.
Indian attitudes in the twentieth century were more and more predi-
cated on the conviction that the British were not just another intrusive
ruler, a milder and more efficient successor to the Rajputs and the
Muslims, but an alien force hostile to the essence, values and idioms
of Indian civilization itself.

6. Inherited and Present Problems

In general the Princely Order – to begin with a marginal matter – had
been supporters of the British power in the time of the East India
Company and throughout the British Raj, each party acting in what
it saw as its own interests. The independent Indian government dealt
more peremptorily with the Princes. As a secular, unitary, new-born
power it found this collection of semi-autonomous authorities distrib-
uted throughout its territory medieval and intolerable, and after what
seems to a foreigner to be adroit and reasonable negotiations the
Princely States were incorporated into the Republic. (The issue of the
Princely purse – their state incomes, that is – was not settled finally
till the middle of the nineteen-eighties.) The skill and toughness with
which the Indian government managed the affair of the Princes testifies
to the political capacity and the administrative talent of its senior
politicians and civil servants – this latter, like the country's infra-
structure of roads, railways and communications, itself a witness to the
positive side of the British Raj. But there were other more stubbornly
intractable problems defying solution by the British and the Indians:
the grinding poverty of the villages in a largely agricultural population
and the calamitous destitution of the big cities, the position and the
rights of women, the ever-increasing population and the condition of
the Untouchables. These are all fundamentally the consequence, first,
of an absolute paucity of economic resources and then of values and
assumptions existing to serve a primitive society in utterly different
circumstances. But these are still today moral and psychological
suppositions drawn from the most ancient times, potent in shaping the
attitudes of society and the responses of individuals. It is hard for a
member of a younger society to grasp the extraordinary age and
continuity of Hindu civilization. In Chaudhuri's *The Autobiography of
an Unknown Indian* (1951), for example, we see a high-minded, respon-

sible and self-improving middle-class engaged naturally and intimately with a culture as old and strange as *Lear*, in which priests with scimitars sacrifice goats and garlanded buffaloes to the music of drums, cymbals and gongs while the worshippers smear themselves with the animals' blood and pelt each other with a dough made of blood and dust.

It is hardly surprising, therefore, that the rights of women were appallingly circumscribed in a society in which *suttee* was abolished only in 1830, and in which cases still occur. Indeed *The Times* reported in 1988 a movement among the Rajputs of Rajasthan to revive the practice of *suttee* on the grounds of tradition, Rajput identity and religious freedom. It may be that these motives are tainted by commercial exploitation since the victims are venerated as goddesses and bring pilgrims and prosperity to the villages where their shrines are erected. It is true that in contemporary India some educated middle-class women have made their way in certain professions and that there are far more women members in the Lok Sahba than in the House of Commons, but it is also true that for many generations the vast majority of women have had few if any rights. They are regarded – and often regard themselves – as inferior to men; their marriages are arranged for them, often in childhood; if they are widows remarriage is made intolerably difficult; women's property rights are set about with limitations, while they are expected to perform labouring work of the heaviest sort on the farms, on the roads and in the cities. Nor again, given the Hindu conviction or instinct about caste and pollution, is it altogether unexpected that in the world's most populous democracy, and despite the efforts of government and the persuasion of moral leaders both before and after Independence, there should still exist the class of the Untouchables, despised, neglected and oppressed.

A profound and significant continuity links ancient and contemporary India. But there are more immediate and practical continuities, particularly between pre- and post-Independence India. For example, India maintained the British tradition of well-trained military forces attending strictly to their own business. It kept up a senior civil service marked by capacity and integrity even if the bureaucracy lower down was packed with officious functionaries. It has retained an independent judiciary which has proved itself able and willing to act as a curb on official excesses. Above all it has an effective, well-organized and cherished democratic system, based on the British model, which has on occasion dismissed the most powerful ministries, as happened to that of Indira Gandhi in 1977 when the nation became alarmed at the brutalities associated with the government's Emergency Powers, and in particular with Sanjay Gandhi's vasectomy campaign. (The over-readiness of Indian governments to assume emergency powers was another practice inherited from the British, who too often and too easily found themselves settling political problems and especially problems of unrest in this particular way.) Again, as one would expect, in the field of foreign affairs British and Indian policies were by no means dissimilar, each having an essential reference to the constants supplied by China and Russia, powers seen even now as enigmatic or dangerous and far more proximate. The Indians have shown as much diplomatic and political skill in playing off China and Russia as they have in balancing Russia and the United States. At the same time they have made themselves the universally recognized leaders of the non-aligned nations while they have persuaded the United States and Western Europe to allocate by far the largest share of aid to India itself. For many years, particularly under Nehru, India assumed even when it was not willingly accorded, an attitude of distinct moral superiority to most other members of the international community. However irritating this may have been to others, there was a peculiar suitability in India's adopting the role of international moral teacher. The politics of saintliness have always been a powerful part of the Indian social tradition. The holy man was reverenced in every village. In Mahatma Gandhi the genuine saint and the consummate politician co-existed without friction or strain. Only in India could such a figure command so irresistible a force; only in India could the gospel of non-violence sweep all before it. Hence Gandhi's death at the hands of an assassin became an apotheosis, turning a historical personage into an unchallengeable and supremely significant myth. And it seems entirely appropriate some forty years after Gandhi's death that another authentic saint, Mother Theresa, an Albanian by birth and a Christian, should live her life and gather her influence in India.

When we consider the skill, continuity and effectiveness of the management of Indian foreign policy, there is at least one large exception to this generalization. In 1962 the Chinese suddenly attacked the Indians on their north-eastern frontier. The Chinese withdrew of their own accord after delivering their brutal but salutary warning: salutary in that it revealed how unprepared and inadequate Indian defences were for this kind of warfare. The shock of the humiliation was the more severe in that Nehru and his Minister of Defence, the left-inclined Krishna Menon, laboured under the illusion that such a war was unthinkable since they were united in a bond of socialist brotherhood, formally enshrined in the five principles of friendship negotiated in 1955. Nehru, the founding Prime Minister and, with Gandhi, one of the fathers of the country, was a brilliant and persuasive politician, less ferocious than his formidable daughter and successor, Indira Gandhi, and more committed to an ethical, Fabian kind of socialism, not dissimilar from that practised in Britain by Attlee and Gaitskell. Like many of his generation in Britain and India, he was also deeply influenced by, and often an uncritical admirer of, Russia. His policies in government, in consequence, laid great emphasis on extending the public sector, on developing heavy industry, on the production of capital goods, and on capturing 'the commanding heights of the economy'. The means to this end were, of course, to be planning and intervention.

'The failure', writes Judith Brown, 'of the country's original economic strategy in terms both of production and redistribution of resources was due to a complex combination of influences – including faulty planning (in particular too great an emphasis on heavy industry and insufficient on consumer goods and agriculture), under-used and badly managed public enterprises, diversion of vital government funds into defence expenditure as relations with Pakistan worsened, unpredictable supplies of foreign aid, and in 1965–66 a catastrophic drought and two bad harvests.'[13]

Part of this 'failure' – if indeed failure is the right word for a situation only to be expected in a country with India's physical resources, population, problems and history and one not by any means unknown in other countries, whether developed or not, which had the same political philosophy and economic approach – is what I must call the decrease in available space. This must seem a paradoxical oddity given India's physical vastness and geographical variety but it is, all the same, central to the predicament of life in India.

India is the second most populous country in the world, having something like fifteen per cent of the world's population but less than two and a half per cent of its resources. The population, in spite of every effort and more than eleven million vasectomies, continues to grow as medical science cuts the killing diseases and prolongs life and the new types of pest-resistant grain help to feed the people. There is, therefore, immense pressure on all available productive land, which itself has always been the key to power and riches in India, and the land itself naturally varies enormously in productive capacity from the rich fertility of the Punjab to the meagre misery of Bihar and Orissa. A fifth of country people own no land at all, while a quarter own more than three-quarters of the land. Rights over land were for many hundreds of years of the cloudiest and most undefined kind. For most peasants they were little more than the customary right to work the land and pay taxes on it to the *mansabdars* and the *zemmidars*, who themselves in Mughal times were given control over the land – but not necessarily the right to dispose of it – by the ruler himself as a personal benefaction. Property rights in the Western sense have been defined only very slowly and spasmodically. A fairer distribution of and among those who need it to live is as yet far from being accomplished, as any reforms like this which so affect the fabric of society have, in India, to take account of the extraordinary weight of historical tradition and social custom as well as of the tissue of intricate caste and personal relationships. Moreover there still continues to be an increasing fragmentation of holdings among the peasants because of inheritance, and an ever-increasing number of rural workers are without land of their own at all. In such a context the moneylender, always so prominent in India, becomes even more central and menacing a figure.

But however cramped for space the farmer may be, his position in comparison with that of the city dweller is positively roomy. The most extreme example of this particular kind of urban plight – as indeed of every other – is Calcutta. It has been most graphically described by Ved Mehta in *The New Yorker* of 21 March 1970 in a passage quoted by Karl de Schweinitz Jr, in *The Rise and Fall of British India*:

> Although parts of New York and parts of Tokyo have a population density comparable to parts of the Calcutta Metropolitan District, it, unlike the two other metropolises, has few buildings more than three stories high, and most of its people are housed in one- or two-storey structures. Few of the houses are *pukka* structures. Rather most are *kutcha* made of bamboo, mud or unbaked bricks. Except for the palatial quarters of the rich, most houses, *pukka* and *kutcha*, have no inside plumbing and the *pukka* structures are often in disrepair. Many of these structures were originally intended only as temporary shelters for migrant workers, but they now house big families. Even so, a large number of people must sleep in and around the dockyards, in factories, in offices, in shops, on construction sites, in railway stations, in hallways and on stairways of buildings. More than half the Calcutta Metropolitan District is taken up by streams or the marshland that is unreclaimable for reasons of cost or technology; the demands on the remaining land are so intense that several hundred thousand people sleep out on the pavements and tens of thousands of people now live, as a matter of course, on low, undrained, disease-infested land bordering the salt-marshes. All available public or private land is occupied by colonies of squatters. There is no place – not even the border of Calcutta's refuse dump – that is left unoccupied.

To the Western reader this will seem monstrous and intolerable. But such is the enigma of India, and so resilient, patient and tough are Indians that they can snatch comfort even from conditions like these. How vividly this is illustrated by V. S. Naipaul's story, *One Out of Many*, in which a servant from Bombay is taken by his diplomatic master to Washington. (V. S. Naipaul's documentary account of India may be harsh and unjust, but his Indian-based fiction is not only comic and touching but also deeply discerning.) In Bombay the servant, Santosh, had been to Western eyes little more than a slave although neither he nor his master saw himself as such. He had a position, he was a member of society, he had his comforts, even his privileges:

> I was so happy in Bombay. I was respected, I had a
> certain position. I worked for an important man. The
> highest in the land came to our bachelor chambers and
> enjoyed my food and showered compliments on me. I also
> had my friends. We met in the evening on the pavement
> below the gallery of our chambers. Some of us, like the
> tailor's bearer and myself, were domestics who lived in the
> street. The others were people who came to that bit of
> pavement to sleep. Respectable people: we didn't
> encourage riff-raff.

What the passage also testifies to is a certain inner calm, a tranquillity of self-possession which is the product of a developed civilization and the dignity of having a defined and recognized place in a coherent society. Even the beggars in India have their status and the assurance that goes with it. They may have had atrocities committed against them to enable them to qualify as mendicants but they do not feel obliged to be effusive in their thanks. Indeed they sometimes convey an impression of moral superiority to the charitable to whom they have given the opportunity to indulge a generous impulse and to garner merit. This sensitivity, this quality of personality, is matured in the making of one of the great civilizations which has its own metaphysics and morality, its own presuppositions and values, its own idiom and purposes. We are so apt to be agitated by India's Third World problems – its poverty, its population, the intermittent violence of its politics – that we forget the weight, the complexity and the beauty of its civilization.

After these individual, different, but by no means wholly unrepresentative reactions or impressions, both positive and negative, I want to conclude this section with a number of more general and summarising observations. India was from the first a prominent item in British consciousness, as it is now surely in that of the world at large. In the eighteenth century the focus of this awareness was the East India Company.

It was as 'the jewel in the crown' of the Empire that India figured so vividly for the next hundred years in the mind, imagination and - as the democratic spirit grew and spread - social conscience of the British. The Company had by no means wholly neglected its duty to its Indian subjects, since such they were, to contribute to the physical substructure of the country. But the conception of trusteeship, first articulated by Burke in 1788 during the trial of Warren Hastings, brought, after the transformation of the Company into the Raj, a clearer and firmer sense of the obligations owed by the ruler to the ruled. India during the Raj was seen in the context of British geo-political interests - but not exclusively so, and not always to the disadvantage of India. The history of England during this period, as Asa Briggs explained in *The Age of Improvement*, (1959) has to be related not only to that of the English-speaking peoples but to those of the tropics and the antipodes and most particularly to that of India.

India posed problems as absorbing as those of Ireland, and different 'schools' of Englishmen as well as great individuals tested their theories and tried out their ideas on Indian soil. Whigs, Utilitarians, Evangelicals, even men of the Manchester school were drawn or driven to concern themselves with Indian as with English questions, with the balance sheet of commitment and responsibility, with the serious issues of freedom, authority, plan and force, above all with questions of 'scale' which did not always arise in the development of 'improvement' in England itself. 'We are all of us', exclaimed one member of Parliament later in the century 'members for India.'[14]

The problems of freedom, responsibility and authority occupied the minds not only of British Parliamentarians but also of British admin-istrators in India and - as the nineteenth century closed and the twentieth opened - of more and more Indians too. I have already referred to the analogy drawn by Nirad C. Chaudhuri between the fate of the Aryan invaders of India - also people of a temperate climate moving into a tropical one - and that of their British successors. Chau-dhuri, criticized in India for an excessive Anglophilia, has a particularly sharp summary of the defects of character and conduct among the British living in a cruel climate amid the gathering hostility of a people ruled by aliens and harassed by the strain of playing the imperial role - defects which led to an atrocity like the massacre of unarmed Indians by the British troops of General Dyer at Jallianwalla Bagh in Amritsar in 1919 when more than three hundred were killed and a thousand were injured. These defects, says Chaudhuri in *The Continent of Circe*, were: 'race pride and sense of superiority; segregation of the conflicting elements; aggressive self-defence; suppression and unconscious ill-treatment of the indigenous population; unwillingness to share culture and continued mental strain' (p. 130).

But of course the problems of freedom, authority and responsibility occupied an even larger place in the consciousness of the ruled if not in that of those described by Lord Curzon as 'the syots and the peasants whose life is not one of political aspiration, but of mute penury and toil' – at least that part of the population that had received a Western education. At one time, then, we see in the development of this educated class in India the rise and spread of the Congress Party, the beginning of the decline of British economic pre-eminence and the weakening among the British in Britain of the imperialist drive. It was the Congress Party that came in the course of time to articulate these convictions and perceptions. Founded in 1885 as the Indian National Congress, not as a political party but, as Judith M. Brown declares in *Modern India*, (p. 175) as 'a loose confederation of local men interested in the distribution, use, and abuse of public power', it had little in the way of a formal constitution – a fluidity which kept it responsive to the development of politics in India – and it was dominated by Hindus, Brahmins and lawyers and supported by a minority of landowners and businessmen. There were Muslims in Congress but they were few and their reluctance to join Congress turned into active suspicion and led to the foundation of the Muslim League in 1906 out of a variety of smaller and more local Muslim groups. It was an arrangement that institutionalized the differences between Muslim and Hindu and prepared for ultimate partition.

This 'loose confederation' began by attempting to represent and to improve the lot of all Indians, Hindu and Muslim. But while the Muslims under Jinnah increasingly saw their interests in a separate party and in a separate country, the Indian National Congress developed into a powerful Hindu Socialist party to which the Raj was compelled to hand over the government of non-Muslim India. The good fortune both of Congress and of India was that it came at a time when other leaders were less committed and less effective, under the influence of Gandhi, who combined personal sanctity with a profound sense of the Hindu and Jain religious tradition and overwhelming charismatic power. Gandhi was born into a modest middle-class family in 1869. After a gawky and unimpressive youth he was sent to Britain by his family to train as a barrister where he was noted for little apart from his speeches in favour of vegetarianism. He was no more successful in Bombay on his return to India, and he took a contract

:o work for a year in South Africa. In fact he stayed in South Africa for twenty-one years and became the principal representative of Indians, both Muslim and Hindu. He was recognized as a great social reformer and honoured as such by the British Raj itself. It was in South Africa that he developed his theory and practice of Satyagratha, non-violence, and with it a weapon perfectly fitted to the Indian tradition and exactly suited to defeat the British, already uncertain in their consciences about their presence in India. He had grown to despair in South Africa of the materialism of Western society and his vision for India was of a tradition devoted to spiritual values and a way of life symbolized by the spinning wheel. Whether this vision was ever fully accepted by any but his most devoted disciples is open to question, but it remained as a potent and persuasive ideal. Gandhi was not in the ordinary sense a politician. He had not the touch or the political sense of his brilliant follower, Nehru, or of Nehru's formidable daughter, Indira Gandhi. Sometimes his non-violent campaigns had to be called off because of the very ferocity of the violence they provoked. But he was a politician in a more important, Coleridgean sense. He saw that politics was a form of moral activity, and morality is not just an occasional quality of humanity; nor is it simply the attribute of maturity. It is the ground of thought, and it both supplies the energy and regulates the direction of action.

Gandhi was above all in the Indian tradition of the good, the wise, the ascetic man. He was – more than Nehru, more than anyone – the father of his country. He is also proof of the extraordinary resources of the civilization which produced him. But Gandhi transcends both nationality and civilization. He is part of the forces of life and light in the world.

References

1. *The Legacy of India*, ed. G. T. Garratt (Oxford, 1937), pp. 150–51.

2. *Modern India: The Origins of an Asian Democracy* (London, 1985), p. 23.

3. *The British Impact on India* (London, 1952), p. 240.

4. *A Cultural History of India*, p. 294.

5. *Modern India*, p. 28.

6. *A Concise History of Indian Art*, p. 131.

7. *The Legacy of India*, p. 251.

8. *The Art of India and Pakistan* (London, 1950), p. 14.

9. *An Experience of India* (London, 1966), p. 16.
10. Quoted in *The British Impact on India*, p. 51.
11. *Ibid.*, p. 56.
12. *Ibid.*, p. 57.
13. *Modern India*, p. 373.
14. *The Age of Improvement* (London, 1959), pp. 6–7.

Chapter 2

Prose: Sages and Autobiographers

Indians were writing effectively in English even before Macaulay's Minute and before Lord William Bentinck, the large-minded Governor General, endorsed it in 1835 as government policy. Under the influence of these two the object of the British government came to be the promotion of European literature and science among the native inhabitants. The aim reflects the reforming zeal and the extravagant self-assurance of the utilitarian philosophers Bentham and Mill, which, through Bentinck and his appointees, was to have a direct and pervasive influence on the intellectual and social life of India during the middle decades of the nineteenth century. Bentinck himself was wholly under the influence of Bentham. 'I shall govern in name, but it will be you who govern in fact,' he wrote to Bentham. It was an influence reinforced from another direction by that of the Evangelical revival which brought enthusiasm and, through the members of the Clapham Sect, considerable political influence to the moral reform – as they saw it – of India and to the abolition of slavery and *suttee*, which would be effected above all, they thought, by a strong missionary movement. The third force which fitted neatly into these two influences and played upon the Indian scene with comparable effect was the conviction about the beneficent consequences of free trade in a market economy – a conviction held without any strain or unconscious hypocrisy, such was the spirit of the times, by members of a society founded squarely on the principle of monopoly.

Opening India to the currents of Western thought and science was something the British imposed on Indians for what they took to be, with complete assurance, their own good. But there were also Indians, of whom Ram Mohan Roy was one of the most distinguished, who welcomed this policy from more disinterested motives. He was born in 1772 of an old Brahmin family in Calcutta. He had an Indian version of the education of John Stuart Mill, a figure he resembles in other ways. He was taught Persian at home, Arabic at Patna, and Sanskrit at Benares. He investigated Buddhism in Tibet, and in a cooler, more critical way than many other, and later, students. He had a successful career in the service of the East India Company, becoming Dewar or principal officer in the collection of revenues. He was consulted while in England during later life – he died in Bristol in 1833 – by many in the Parliamentary discussions on the East India Company's charter, and advised the Board of Control on the state of India. He was therefore an experienced man of affairs, as well as a thinker, critic and theologian. He could be said to be a founder of the study of comparative religion, and certainly was one of the earliest to write on the subject in English. Ram Mohan Roy was a large-minded, independent and gifted writer and journalist who introduced a sharper bite into the languid Indian intellectual scene and offered to his successors a prose that was a model of clarity, energy and point. He inaugurated that tradition in which Indians have found a peculiar intimacy with the English language, making it a natural second voice for the Indian mind and sensibility.

Ram Mohan Roy's vigorous English, which balanced Victorian fluency with a quality of eighteenth-century measure and formality, used an extensive vocabulary, a slightly abstract diction, and long, poised, supple sentences. It carried with it some of the certainties as well as the structure of the contemporary sermon and admirably fitted his double intention, which was first to reform Hindu religious thought and practice by introducing into it a stricter Protestant ethic, and second to associate with a profound loyalty to the Hindu spirit – there was no touch of 'cultural cringe' in Ram Mohan Roy's temperament – a more open attitude to Western thought, particularly scientific thought. He argued, therefore, with energy and determination, for women's rights, for religious toleration, for the freedom of the Press, for the radical improvement of the conditions of peasants, and for science, education and democracy in the manner of the best of the disinterested and liberal Victorians.

A new edition of The English Works of Ram Mohan Roy, first published in 1902, appeared in 1982. It gives us a sense of the range of this energetic defender of the public good and of rational conduct, as he unselfconsciously and with the utmost sincerity saw himself. He addressed the world on a large variety of topics, from the modern encroachments on the rights of females to the precepts of Jesus, and from the burning of widows alive to the English education. I say 'addressed' because in spite of the formality of his writing and the remains of the eighteenth-century influence, the ear is aware that the speaking voice is never very far away. No doubt this is why so much of his work is cast in the form of direct speech to a specific audience as addresses, letters, memorials, appeals, petitions, dialogues and questions and answers. Here is a passage from an autobiographical sketch

written in answer to a request from a correspondent, a Mr Gordon of
Calcutta.

When about the age of sixteen, I composed a manuscript
calling in question the validity of the idolatrous system of
the Hindoos. This, together with my known sentiments
on that subject, having produced a coolness between me
and my immediate kindred, I proceeded on my travels,
and passed through different countries, chiefly within, but
some beyond, the bounds of Hindoustan, with a feeling of
great aversion to the establishment of the British power in
India. When I had reached the age of twenty, my father
recalled me, and restored me to his favour; after which I
first saw and began to associate with Europeans and soon
after made myself tolerably acquainted with their laws and
form of Government. Finding them generally more
intelligent, more steady and moderate in their conduct, I
gave up my prejudice against them, and became inclined
in their favour, feeling persuaded that their rule, though a
foreign yoke, would lead more speedily and surely to the
amelioration of the native inhabitants; and I engaged the
confidence of several of them even in their public capacity
by continual controversies with the Brahmins on the
subject of their idolatry and superstition, and my
interference with their custom of burning widows, and
other pernicious practices, revived and increased their
animosity against me; and through their influence with my
family, my father was again obliged to withdraw his
countenance openly, though his limited pecuniary support
was still continued to me.[1]

I mentioned above the closeness of the speaking voice to Mohan
Roy's writing in spite of the influence upon it of Augustan correctness.
An even more important connection was the closeness of his life and
work. These were most emphatically all of a piece throughout. Even the
occasional note I have quoted touches upon many of the chief themes
of Mohan Roy's life and work. The ground he took in his controversies was not that of opposition to Brahminism but to a perversion
of it; and the idolatry he fiercely opposed was, he claimed, contrary to
the principles of Brahminism and to the teachings of the sacred books.
He took the same attitude to the monstrous practice of burning
widows. There is something extremely attractive about Ram Mohan
Roy, who combined rational principles with a strong practical side.
Attacking specific abuses and promoting particular causes, as Mohan

Roy always did, was, given the contemporary bias towards the nebulous and grandiloquent, an exceptional virtue.

There was a clutch of intelligent, industrious reformers and teachers – none of them writers in a serious, artistic sense – who followed in the line begun by Mohan Roy. Two examples are a Parsee, Behramji Malabari (1853–1912), and a western Indian, Nagesh Wishwanath Pai (1860–1920). Both were also poets in a bloodless, late Romantic manner. The first continued Ram Mohan Roy's efforts to reconcile East and West, and to correct the abuses of women's rights; the second in *Stray Sketches in Chakmakpore* (1894) showed welcome touches of observation and humour, rare in an age of genteel abstraction and gestures towards the ineffable. But more important than anything these writers, or others like them, did themselves was the part they played in establishing English as the language in which the intellectual life and public debate came to be conducted – an immense contribution towards opening the Indian mind to the modern world, one which was necessary in a civilization of so many major and minor indigenous languages, and one which was not damaging to national pride since none of these writers wished in any radical way to desert and destroy fundamental Indian tradition.

I have referred to Ram Mohan Roy as the first, and by no means the least, of the Indian sages to write in English. Another and grander was Swami Vivekananda (1862–1902), a man of profound spiritual force, powerful intellect, great learning and Franciscan spirituality. According to the editor of his Collected Works there were three influences which contributed to form Vivekananda's personality and thought. The first was his education both in Sanskrit and English, the first admitting him to the most profound insights of Hindu religious thought, the second equipping him with the gift of logical analysis and its contemporary language. The second was his years as a disciple of the mystic Ramakrishna Paramahamsa who lived and taught in the temple garden at Dashimeshwar. He was a guru who could neither read nor write yet seemed the embodiment of the truths in the sacred books, and was so brimming with instructive goodness and grace as to appear to many who knew him as an avatar of the divine. Third was the period Vivekananda spent as a mendicant preacher wandering the length and breadth of India, learning from all, teaching to all, and living with all. The Shastras, the guru and the nation helped to compose this highly individual genius, of whom, says C. D. Narasimhaiah, 'no single individual before Gandhi and Nehru . . . did more to de-hypnotize a complacent, slumbering people'.[2]

Vivekananda detested abstractions and his analysis and evocation of the ancient Indian spiritual tradition, which he wished both to recover and revivify, are made with the utmost precision and concreteness. He resisted an undignified and philistine submission to Western, pragmatic thought, just as he had little sympathy with an indulgent nostalgia for the past. He was a moralist, not just a moral philosopher; a thinker, not just a theorist; a speculative critic, not just a man of erudition. His intelligence had an active inclusive character; it had also an attractively sardonic sharpness. The Hindu man drinks religiously, sleeps religiously, walks religiously, marries religiously and robs religiously: this is the abrasive part of his message.

Religion is the note struck insistently by Vivekananda in his various commentaries on the Vedas and in his accounts of Indian psychology and history. He saw it both in its sublime and homely aspects as the chief creative influence on, and the distinguishing mark of, Indian civilization. 'To the other nations of the world, religion is one among the many occupations of life. There is politics, there are the enjoyments of social life, there is all that wealth can buy or power can bring, there is all that the senses can enjoy; and among all these various occupations of life, and all this searching after something which can give yet a little more whetting to the cloyed senses – among all these, there is perhaps a little bit of religion. But here in India, religion is the one and the only occupation of life.[3]

Vivekananda could be cutting about the trivialities of what passed for traditional religious discussion among Hindus – such questions as, 'Should I eat with the right hand or the left hand?' Or 'Should I eat this or that?' – and he could dismiss ritual as the kindergarten of religion, but he stood strongly for what was ancient and orthodox. This made his stand on, for example, women's rights – and particularly the position of widows – seem at least to the foreigner to be enigmatic or even hedging, and certainly less robustly liberal than Ram Mohan Roy's.

There is a broad distinction to be made between the work of Vivekananda composed as commentaries on the sacred texts and close accounts of the spiritual life and his other work meant for persuasion and propaganda, often for foreign audiences. The first category had an immediacy, spontaneity and simplicity and a relaxed buoyant tone which could be effective and affecting. It shows an exceptionally gifted mind grappling with real questions of life, destiny and conduct. The other category, the writings and sermons of a missionary and hortatory kind, like the address to the so-called Parliament of Religions at Chicago in 1893, seem, in contrast, sentimental, histrionic and self-conscious and one has the impression of a series of rather feverish encyclicals delivered with pomp and ceremony *urbi et orbi*. Here is an illustration written for the Hindus in Madras in 1894 as a reply to their address of welcome and congratulation to Vivekananda on his success

in the United States. It displays the less attractive qualities of Vivekananda which the missionary role was apt to evoke.

> Shall India die? Then from the world all spirituality will be
> extinct; all moral perfection will be extinct; all ideality will
> be extinct; and in its place will reign the duality of lust
> and luxury as the male and female deities, with money as
> its priest; fraud, force and competition its ceremonies, and
> the human soul its sacrifice. . . . Is it not curious that,
> whilst under the terrific onset of modern scientific
> research, all the old forts of Western dogmatic religion are
> crumbling into dust . . . whilst Western theology is at its
> wit's end to accommodate itself to the ever-rising tide of
> aggressive modern thought; whilst in all other sacred
> books the texts have been stretched to their utmost tension
> . . . and the majority of them have been stored away in
> lumber rooms . . . the religions which have drunk the
> water of life at that fountain of light, the Vedas –
> Hinduism and Buddhism – alone are reviving?[4]

Embedded in such writing, of which there is a great deal in Vivekananda, are certain convictions. One is that the genius of India is
essentially religious and that the character of the civilization, the
psychology of the people, and the nature of the society have all been
shaped by that fact. Another is that religion is identified with spirituality so that if an activity is not religious, art, say, or the intellectual
life, then it is not spiritual but is relegated to the world of materialism.
And thirdly there is Vivekananda's profound belief that this Indian
spirituality is to be contrasted with Western materialism, out of which
came his lively concern with India's spiritual mission to the West. The
assurance of spiritual superiority and the attendant missionary impulse
existed in all the influential Indian thinkers of Vivekananda's time – in
Tagore and Aurobindo as much as in Vivekananda himself. It was
present too in the early Congress Party as well as later in the policy
premises of the Government of India, particularly in Nehru's cabinets
and most markedly in his leadership of the non-aligned nations and in
his relations with Britain. In a humbler and more familiar guise this
certainty that Indian civilization is animated by a spirituality far superior to the materialistic civilization of the European nations is seen
among the young of the West who seek in India some profound spiritual experience or the teaching of some saintly illuminated guru.

This phenomenon has been studied most closely by Dr Ursula King
who notes incidentally that there is no word either for religion or spirituality in any of the Indian languages. 'There is only *dharma*, referring

to the complex interdependence of the universal, social and individual order.' Dr King sees the idea of the essential spirituality of Indian civilization as part of the Hindu Renaissance, a reinterpretation of Hinduism based, in fact, on the work of British orientalists. It included historical rediscovery, linguistic modernization and social and religious reformation.

> This Hindu apologetic was, by and large carried out in the
> English language; it was a defence of Hinduism and its
> value vis-à-vis the West and a self-defence against the
> incisive criticism of missionaries and civil servants. Based
> on the orientalists' rediscovery of a glorious past, new
> images were created by Hindus to convey the message of
> a revived and strengthened Hinduism full of vitality.
> Linked to the image of a golden age in the past, as
> opposed to the situation of decline in the present, there
> evolved the notion of the greatness of Indian spirituality in
> contrast to the shortcomings of Western materialism;
> consequent upon this emerged the belief in India's spiritual
> mission to the West.[5]

I have dilated on this subject because it is of some historical importance, playing a modest and sometimes a distorting part in India's relations with Britain, and because Vivekananda was one, possibly the chief, of those who put the idea into circulation. But it would be quite wrong to leave the reader with the impression that this constituted Vivekananda's principal claim to attention. Far from it. He was above all a religious writer of outstanding merit. In his missionary work he may have been flamboyant but he was invariably sincere. At his best he has the intuitiveness, the intensity, and the bare immediacy of the true mystic. Some of the most attractive as well as the most comprehensible of his writings are those on Buddhism where he exhibits not only discernment and appreciation but that marvellous open-minded hospitality so characteristically Indian.

> To many the path becomes easier if they believe in God.
> But the life of Buddha shows that even a man who does
> not believe in God, has no metaphysics, belongs to no
> sect, does not go to any church or temple, and is a
> confessed materialist, even he can attain to the highest. We
> have no right to judge him. I wish I had one infinitesimal
> part of Buddha's heart. Buddha may or may not have
> believed in God; that does not matter to me. He reached
> the same state of perfection to which others come by

Bhakti – love of God, Yoga or Jnana. Perfection does not
come from belief or faith. Talk does not count for
anything. Parrots can do that. Perfection comes through
the disinterested performance of action.[6]

The modern English reader with his sharply diminished appetite for
the ineffable is not best placed to view with the sympathy it deserves
such work as Vivekananda's in which morals, politics, history,
theology, metaphysics flow in and out of one another, blurring the
distinctions he has been brought up to expect and giving off a dated,
hortatory air. If this is true of one's response to Vivekananda, it is still
more so of one's response to the English prose works of the great
Bengali poet Rabindranath Tagore (1861–1941), perhaps a greater
mind and a more formidable scholar, if not so fine an artist, who after
St Paul's and King's College, Cambridge, returned to India to become
a university teacher at Baroda and a journalist and politician in Calcutta
before retiring from the world – in the classical Indian tradition – to
live for many years as an oracular hermit in Pondicherry. Both Tagore
and Aurobindo (1872–1950) took the Vivekananda line about the
essential spirituality of India and the essential materialism of Europe.
Both, in spite of occasional disclaimers, equated spirituality with
Hinduism and both saw the Indian tradition as the essence of Asia
itself, thereby obliterating the richness and variety of the rest of Asia.
But while it is not surprising that the content of the thought of two
serious and scholarly men in a given period should be strikingly
similar, there is an interesting difference in its character. Aurobindo
was a thoroughly Westernized Indian who, on his return to India, fell
upon a revived Hinduism with the appetite of a convert, and there was
always in his version and application of Hinduism an uncritical and
lyrical enthusiasm as well as, it may be said, an undue degree of
abstraction. The titles of some of his essays published in the journal
Arya between 1914 and 1921 convey the tone: 'The Life Divine', 'The
Synthesis of Yoga', 'Tenets of the Veda', 'The Ideal of Human Unity',
'The Human Cycle', 'The Future Poetry'. It is one which is peculiarly
mystical and evasive, showing colossal energy, moral earnestness,
general benevolence and a sense of the vastness and continuity of
human experience. But it also seems to be deficient in the self-
propelling life of genuine literature. Tagore, on the other hand, for all
the intense emotion of his life as a great Bengali poet – or possibly,
one reflects, because of it – possessed in his prose writings a more
cautious, concrete and conservative temperament. In the latter part of
his career, in his 1930 Hibbert Lectures, *The Religion of Man*, for
example, he took a slightly cooler attitude towards India's supremacy
as a source of spiritual value and showed a touch of impatience with

India's reputation for indiscriminate tolerance, going so far as to recommend 'a wholesome spirit of intolerance . . . characteristic of creative religion'.[7]

Another who accepted the Vivekananda–Tagore–Aurobindo anti-thesis – spiritual India versus materialist Europe – was Sarvepalli Radhakrishnan (1888–1975) the eminent historian and philosopher of religion. His was perhaps a more qualified version of the theory – he criticized, for example, the contention of those Indians who believe that true spirituality has never appeared anywhere in the world but on the sacred soil of India. Supposing, however, one asks: What, apart from their common belief and the practical result of their work in confirming the English language as a medium of Indian intellectual life, makes these different men members of one party?' Dr Ursula King, whose valuable paper I have already made use of, offers an interesting and novel answer. It has to do with the motive which energized their work and left a glow of satisfaction with its consequences.

> A contrast with the West had to be sought in order to compensate for both Western political and economic dominance, and to fight Western contempt for India's material retardation. In this situation, to affirm, vindicate, and glorify the superiority of 'Indian spirituality' was the Hindu reformers' and proto-nationalists' particular way of opposing the West's own technological and organizational superiority: 'spiritual triumph' was set over 'material domination'; 'spirituality' could 'conquer' even more than 'materialism' had done.[8]

If there is a warrant for this view – and I believe there is, although it may be more oblique and less explicit than the passage I have quoted suggests – then Dr King's words lead us on neatly and logically to the architect and the builder of Indian independence, the two great men to whom I now turn.

I intend in the next section to concentrate on the autobiographies of Gandhi (1927) and Nehru (1936). Their political writings, though many, various and significant, hardly belong to the world of literature. But an autobiography, like that of Gandhi, gives us the Indian version of an art which establishes not only the character of an individual but also the nature of the society out of which he grew. Gandhi's auto-biography was written during his imprisonment at Yerauda and later in South Africa, and was published in two volumes: 1927 and 1929. It was written in Gujarati and the translation into English by Mahinder Desai was supervised, revised and corrected by Gandhi, and we are assured by him and his fellow workers that it gives a faithful account of the events of his life as well as a true expression of his character and, we may add, of his genius.

As one follows the bare, painfully honest and deeply engaging narrative certain things impress one vividly and at once. The first is the dense, sharply outlined, packed detail of the material, a tonic contrast to the flights of Vivekananda and Aurobindo. For example, while he was still a boy of sixteen at school his wife – he had been married as a child – was expecting a baby. His father had fallen seriously ill with a fistula and Gandhi, with his mother and an old servant, shared the nursing. He describes his part precisely, and it meant a full share in the most exacting of human duties.

> I had the duties of a nurse which mainly consisted in
> dressing the wound, giving my father his medicine, and
> compounding drugs whenever they had to be made up at
> home. Every night I massaged his legs and retired only
> when he asked me to do so or after he had fallen asleep. I
> had to do this service. I do not remember ever having
> neglected it. All the time at my disposal, after the
> performance of the daily duties, was divided between
> school and attending on my father. I would only go for an
> evening walk either when he permitted me or when he
> was feeling well.[9]

Gandhi's devotion to his father was blended of duty and love, motives which in his character were not at odds. Indeed they completed and reinforced one another since they were even in his earliest days the expression of a whole and unified personality. This is a personal quality to be seen in the Indian artists, writers and saints, a calm assurance of personality derived from the radical certainties and stabilities of an ancient and comprehensive civilization.

The psychological paradox in Gandhi's character which makes a strange qualification to what I have just said is revealed in the paragraph following the one I have just quoted. Here it is.

> This was also the time when my wife was expecting a
> baby – a circumstance which, as I can see today, meant a
> double shame for me. For one thing I did not restrain
> myself, as I should have done, whilst I was yet a student.
> And secondly, this carnal lust got the better of what I
> regarded as my duty to study, and of what was even a
> greater duty, my devotion to my parents, Shravama
> having been my ideal since childhood. Every night whilst
> my hands were busy massaging my father's legs, my mind

was hovering about the bedroom – and that too at a time
when religion, medical science and commonsense alike
forbade sexual intercourse. I was always glad to be
relieved from my duty, and went straight to the bedroom
after doing obeisance to my father.[10]

We observe that motives of love and duty are clouded with guilt.
In other societies – the Puritan, the Jansenist – such feelings would be
diffused throughout the personality, dividing and fracturing it. In
Gandhi, the product of a history and a society based on absolutely
assured and accepted premises, the sexual guilt is specific and localized.
It seems to have been part of his moral struggle for much of his life,
but so robust was his spiritual constitution that this particular
morbidity did him no deep or permanent damage.

On a purely personal level, Gandhi was disablingly shy and embar-
rassingly tongue-tied. It was odd, then, that he should choose to study
for the bar, which he did on the advice of family connections. His
family belonged to the Bania caste who were originally grocers, but
for three generations had been of the administrative and functionary
class who had modest possessions but useful connections. He went to
England with the help of a generous but hard-pressed brother, but
against the express wishes of his caste who, in fact, expelled him for
going abroad, an act regarded as a grave sin. His experiences in
England were on the whole agreeable. At this time he was generally
in favour of the British Empire and the British system. He even
dressed in a top-hat and frock coat and sang the National Anthem.

There were some friendly attempts to convert him to meat-eating
but these served only to reinforce his vegetarianism. There were, too,
occasions when his sexual scruples were agitated but his peremptory
conscience dealt decisively with them. His return to India was followed
by complete failure in his barrister's career and he was persuaded to
take up some representative legal work in South Africa. It was here
that he found himself in the midst of the brutality of the surly Boers,
the object of the ugliest and most blatant discrimination and of
manifold injustices, legal, social and economic. The inhumanity of the
conditions, particularly of the indentured Indian labour, obliterated
Gandhi's temperamental shyness and maladroitness and released his
astonishing creative energies. Nursing, he once commented, for which
he had an aptitude became a passion, and nursing was the model for
his social action, the exemplar of his tender, tireless, sensitive work
with which he helped thousands of his brothers. He founded a newspaper, a trade union, a branch of the Indian National Congress, and
ran these organisations efficiently, economically and successfully. He
could do so because the strength of his will, the humanity of his feel-

ings and the clarity of his sense of justice were founded upon reason: '. . . morality is the basis of things,' he wrote, 'and truth is the substance of all morality.' The utter reasonableness of Gandhi's stance was extraordinary in a country where irrationality ruled and where, for example, a booking clerk could sell an Indian a first-class railway ticket before his journey only for him to be thrown off the train by an angry guard halfway, as indeed happened to Gandhi himself. He became an irresistible influence among his compatriots and a national and international figure.

The incessant travelling, organizing, speaking, writing and collecting consumed energy and time like firewood. Let me give a single example of this part of Gandhi's life. It has the further advantage of having a wonderfully authentic Indian tang. It also hints at Gandhi's inhuman or angelic patience, not to speak of a childlike simplicity which seems quite unaware of the fine mute comedy in the scene, of a sort that R. K. Narayan could have made much.

> On one occasion during this tour the situation was rather
> difficult. We expected our host to contribute £6, but he
> refused to give anything more than £3. If we had accepted
> that amount from him, others would have followed suit,
> and our collections would have been spoiled. It was a late
> hour of the night, and we were all hungry. But how
> could we dine without having first obtained the amount
> we were bent on getting. All persuasion was useless. The
> host seemed to be adamant. Other merchants in the town
> reasoned with him, and we all sat up throughout the
> night, he as well as we determined not to budge one inch.
> Most of my co-workers were burning with rage, but they
> contained themselves. At last, when day was already
> breaking, the host yielded, paid down £6 and feasted us.[11]

In Gandhi's eyes events and their consequences, men and their relationships, were in South Africa dependent upon 'the sweet will of the police', one of the few memorable ironic phrases in his autobiography. This was an offence against reason and morality and the product of a deeply corrupted society. It was to be corrected by non-violence (*ahisma*) by the unity of all Indians, by the abolition of untouchability and the practice of *swadeshi*. 'The practice of *swadeshi*', writes Judith M. Brown, 'would signify self-limitation of wants and simplicity of life-style, simultaneously eroding one of the benefits of India to Britain and thereby weakening the imperial commitment to the existing form of raj.'[12] This last political flick to a noble moral gesture is characteristically Gandhian. It was with such a programme that Gandhi returned to India when he left South Africa for good. He came primarily as a moral and social reformer, as I have indicated in my reference in Chapter One. Political freedom was to be a by-product of the greater aim. It is impossible to exaggerate the originality and radicalism of Gandhi as these qualities appear so unobtrusively out of the hurly-burly of his life of committees, meetings, negotiations and crises. He put reason above revelation, thereby earning the hatred of the rigidly orthodox. He took what his mind approved from the Hindu tradition and dispensed with more.

I should like to conclude this note on Gandhi's modest, spare but unforgettable autobiography by alluding to another work of R. K. Narayan in which he appears as a minor character, *Waiting for the Mahatma* (1955). It gives us an impression of Gandhi and a certain truth about him which no amount of social or historical reporting can do. It is a picture drawn without a touch of sentimentality or pretentiousness. Gandhi represents in his dry and thoroughly human way absolute simplicity, total integrity, complete disinterestedness. His genius is made to appear as one of utter honesty and unqualified ordinariness. He was one in whom maturity ripened into wisdom, commonsense into a clairvoyant perception of reality, and ordinary kindness into a rare and sensitive responsiveness. The racial and spiritual wisdom which is usually in Narayan's novels implicity in the fable itself is, in *Waiting for the Mahatma*, concentrated in the figure of Gandhi. Gandhi is both a real, warm, ordinary person and a god who, as Lawrence said, knows what the realities are and never fails in that knowledge.

The autobiographies of Gandhi and Nehru were both written in gaol; both men read for the Bar in London; both became leaders of the Congress Party and established India as a great independent nation. But it would be hard to exaggerate the difference between the middle-class functionary's awkward son and the Kashmiri Brahmin son of a successful barrister living on an ever-increasing income – as Nehru puts it – whose education was at Harrow and Trinity. At Cambridge Nehru veered uneasily between an aestheticism derived from Oscar Wilde and Walter Pater and the scientific humanism of Bertrand Russell. He entered politics from the top, belonging to a class with an almost divine right to rule, something which his descendants also seem to be endowed with. He had the vaguely socialist ideas of many of his class and period both in India and in Britain. It was the arousal of his patriotic instincts which gave point and direction to his life and turned him to politics. In India the humiliations of a subject people imbued politics with moral passion and turned Nehru from aristocratic indolence into a dedicated politician. For this it appears he was superbly equipped. The mind that had seemed so ordinary in both the academic and the legal world showed itself to be brilliant in politics, discerning and subtle and capable of both the synoptic view and of analytic acumen. He was particularly sharp in his delineation of Indian politics, its structure, background and personnel.

> My politics were those of my class, the bourgeoisie. Indeed all vocal politics then (and to a great extent even now) were those of the middle classes, and Moderate and Extremist alike represented them and in different keys sought their betterment. The Moderate represented especially the handful of the upper middle class who had on the whole prospered under British rule and wanted no sudden changes which might endanger their present position and interests. They had close relations with the British Government and the big landlord class. The Extremist represented also the lower ranks of the middle class. The industrial workers, their number swollen up by the war, were only locally organised in some places and had little influence. The peasantry were a blind, poverty-stricken, suffering mass, resigned to their miserable fate and sat upon and exploited by all who came in contact with them – the Government, landlords, money lenders, petty officials, police, lawyers, priests.[13]

This passion for the poor, and especially for the peasants, remained with Nehru all his life. His well-bred manner and cultivated expression, so different from Gandhi's sharp unaccommodating voice, had the politician's knack of nodding in several directions at once while keeping to a few well-defined opposition targets – capitalists, moderates, liberals, the middle-class. The feeling with which he speaks of the peasants and of unacknowledged agricultural India was sincere and generous and was the positive motive animating his socialism, which was of the British type of Attlee and Bevin, a begetter of State capitalism and economic intervention. This was very different from the Gandhi view of government, for whom the less of it, the better.

He had little or no religious feeling but this strangely enough did not affect either his devotion to Gandhi, the religious reformer, or his relations with the people of a profoundly religious country. His own popularity in the long years of his power did not suffer the surges of for and against that his daughter's was to do. Instead of religion, he offered the people what he himself was firmly committed to, a secular religion of high-minded ethics and Fabian progress. This was to serve him well in his own country. The blend of admiration and selective oblivion with which he speaks of Marxism and Soviet Russia in his autobiography, reminiscent of some of the more lyrical writings of the

Webbs, abated with age and responsibility but was never wholly
excised from the psychology of this complex, warm-hearted, most
distinguished man.

The fact that the Indian writers in this book worked in English is
a large though implicit recognition of the influence of British civilization in India, even when this was something they wished to reject
or overthrow. But none evinces a more conscious and detailed recognition of the British connection than Nirad C. Chaudhuri. I have
spoken in the first chapter of *The Continent of Circe* (1965) where Chaudhuri appears as a social analyst evolving a theory of Indian
development which provided him with a causal explanation of the failures of Indian society. He displays there, too, the structure and
qualities of a personality which is confidently positive to the point of
arrogance and crackingly irascible to the point of bloody-mindedness.
Not, as his work reveals, that he has not a good deal to be irascible
and bloody-minded about. In *A Passage to England* (1960) we see Chaudhuri as a writer with a gift for registering fresh and exact impressions
of what he observes about him, and also as one capable of some highly
subjective analysis of the British Welfare State. It is a graceful, unusual
travel book but slight by the standards of *The Autobiography of an
Unknown Indian* (1951). Its main attraction lies in its being an Indian
version of the sensibility of recognition seen most enchantingly in the
autobiographical studies of Henry James, by which something known
in literature is now known in life; by which, in fact, life verifies literature and corroborates imagination. If we add to the sharp eye of *A
Passage to England* and the intellectual audacity of *The Continent of Circe*
an intense and unabashed fascination with and appreciation of himself,
we can see that gifts which might not qualify him to be an impartially
objective critic of national life might well help to make him an auto-
biographer of a rare kind.

Which indeed they do. *The Autobiography of an Unknown Indian* is
one of the finest examples of this genre to appear in English in this
century, and the most significant, single discursive work to be generated by the love and hate of Indian–British relationships. I have spoken
of Chaudhuri's fascination with himself in *The Continent of Circe*.
Naturally, the same thing appears in *The Autobiography* but, paradoxically, in a much more disciplined way. Here Chaudhuri sees himself
as an object in a landscape or as an impulse in a more inclusive and
controlling rhythm, and the whole presentation of the self is impressively tranquil and objective. Chaudhuri was born in 1897, and the
book which begins in the early nineteen hundreds takes him to the end
of his university career, its substance being the treatment of his childhood and youth. It is written in a masculine, confident English of long,

balanced sentences, which combine a degree of formality with considerable ease and lissomness, and its only oddity is a curiously Celtic use of continuous tenses. It is an idiom which is distinctly late-Victorian in flavour, with all the positive strength and assurance of that, and it is wholly consistent with the period and sensibility of the writer.

The Autobiography is organized round a conception of place, which is shown as the great means by which embodied history is brought to bear upon growth. The significance of place in Chaudhuri's life is the principle of composition in *The Autobiography*, and its development through the sequence of places – Kishorganj his country birthplace, Banagram his ancestral village, Kalikutch his mother's village, Shillong the Assam hill station, an imagined England and a more than actual Calcutta – is handled with imaginative tact which makes the book a genuine composition obeying an inward initiative, except for the final part where it comes to an end in a huddled and clumsily inappropriate conclusion in a long theoretical essay on the course of Indian history.

The life of the places in which Chaudhuri lived is revived with a kind of creative thoroughness. There is, to begin with, the fully pictured actuality of the town, the villages, the hill station, the city of Calcutta – everything in their physical presence from the quality of the dust and the shape of the trees, to the design of the houses, the material of the roof, the layout of the neighbourhood, the character of the rivers and the configuration of the land; next, displayed with lucidity and warmth, there is the intense, enfolding family life with its routine, stresses and rituals; and then the complications of the social world outside the family with its severely functional divisions and its absolutely arranged organization; and all of these are supported and surrounded by a massive fund of anthropological and historical learning and penetrated by sensitively intelligent sociological speculation. This intricate treatment gives the reader a double insight. He has a sense of the young Chaudhuri's life picking its way through a variety of densely detailed locations and assuming definition and individuality as it goes; and he catches, too, glimpses that steady into a vision of an extraordinary society, which combines something from the Victorian past of our own history, a high-minded, ethically serious, self-improving middle class with another ancient and mysterious universe.

Each of the places Chaudhuri lived in has a particular meaning in his development – not meaning in the sense of anything emblematic or mystical but, more straightforwardly, meaning as a special and precise twist in the shaping of his character. The town of Kishorganj, which came into existence as a municipal township in the eighteen-sixties, was the constant in the family existence. Life there was solidly

based, plain, industrious, but also on occasion exciting, when en-
livened by feasts, fairs, gypsies and the attractions of the river and the
rains, or perilous during the season of cholera, when a workman
would pass along the road swinging a censer full of sulphur. The
family house stood on a plot of two acres and was composed of an
intricate collection of buildings around an inner courtyard. It was
furnished with beds and chests, baskets, books and trunks. The
simplicity of furniture and the complexity of structure of the house
corresponded to the life lived in it. There were innumerable traditions
and customs, a whole complex of habits, rituals and disciplines but at
the same time great simplicity and directness of feeling. The father was
a liberal 'protestant' Hindu, monotheist and enlightened and mainly
concerned with educating his children in a rational way of life and
encouraging them in what were thought of as the English qualities of
energy and self-reliance. It was a calm, regular life for the elders
absorbed in their profession and for the children occupied in learning.
Colour and movement broke into it only at rhythmic intervals. There
was a remarkable feeling of equality among the citizens but, of course,
the idea of citizenship was a restricted one, excluding the workers and
peasants and indeed government officials and wealthy landowners. It
was a town ruled by some hundred families. There were few old
people in the population of the citizens and a large number of children.
Profession and education were two serious concerns of these people
and they all worked unremittingly at them. The children were in touch
through their father and his clients (as well as being vice-chairman of
the municipality he was a lawyer with a wholly criminal practice) with
the world of human violence. Murder, robbery, rape, arson were
common events in the town and outside it. But these things were
balanced by two other forces. Around them there seemed to be an
immutable sphere of justice and order presided over by an organization
the ordinary people still called the 'company' and the educated the
'government'; and underneath they felt the unquestioned foundations
of religion and morality, 'things in which everyone believed and things
to which in the last resort everybody returned'.

Life in Kishorganj made for a rational habit of mind. It offered
stability but, largely because of the influence of an admirable, level-
headed father, it also encouraged moral and intellectual independence.
Parental connections led back to the villages, the ancestral village of
Banagram and the mother's village of Kalikutch – 'so self-effacing in
bamboo and cane greenery'. Here the children's experience fed a rich
emotional life. The rhythms of the country, the feeling for blood and
family, the living Bengali tradition of drama and folk-poetry, the
intimate connection of family life and art deepened and refined the

children's feelings. *The Autobiography* presents, through the minutely detailed round of daily life, a portrait of a highly civilized society, in which drama, poetry, religion and ordinary life were intimately united.

> We always had these plays at the time of religious festivals and weddings, and at times also for their own sake. The repertory, though large, was almost exclusively drawn from either of the great epics, the *Ramayana* or the *Mahabharata*, and the stories were thus familiar to the audience. From this followed that the watching of the plays was even for young people like us not a passive gulping down of a story but an appraisal, in the light of a critical code which was never crude, of points of composition and acting, and, at times, even of doctrine.[14]

At the same time this is not an idyll of lyrical nostalgia. Chaudhuri makes very clear the claustrophobic atmosphere, the suspicions and distrusts and the envies and meannesses which this patrician society was capable of, particularly for women. His mother felt imprisoned in it and she was sure that her own health – she was subject to some pathological, mental condition – was ruined by her sojourn in Banagram. His father felt that to live permanently in the way the gentry did in the villages would be to live without work and without purpose. He had the deepest possible conviction of the sanctity of the present and the future and he hated the spirit of Byzantinism that he saw expressed in this society.

Shillong, the paradisal Assam hill station, with its pure, cool air and pine trees, where the children visited an uncle who collected orchids, makes a natural bridge to another place which exercised a profound influence on Chaudhuri's nature – England – for it was in Shillong that the amazed children first saw the English in the flesh, men and women and doll-like babies. England had been a living presence in Chaudhuri's imagination from his early days, partly because of his father's care that he should learn English and the good sense of the teaching methods he adopted to this end, partly through the books and pictures in the house, and partly through the poems he read and the history he studied. Nor could any educated person escape the influence of England that came through the political administrative system imposed on India by the British, an influence that was recognized and supported (even if it was rejected on patriotic grounds) by great names of Hindu and Bengali thought like Michael Dutt, Bankim Chandra Chatterji, Tagore, Rammohun Roy. Chaudhuri's feeling for England was a more explicitly conscious attraction than any English boy could have had, but it was added to a personality which had the strongest natural affinity for English civilization. He saw it vaguely at first, and more precisely as he grew older, as a necessary penetration of the East by the West in one of its most beautiful and worthwhile forms. It was of course England and the English civilization, it should be stressed, which influenced Chaudhuri, not the English in India. He was the last person alive to be impressed by colonial insolence. If one asks why Chaudhuri should have had this extraordinary understanding of and sympathy with English civilization, the answer seems to be that he saw in it an essential corrective to certain Indian qualities. He was fascinated by the vitality and pragmatism of the English character, by the genius for the concrete shown in English art, by the English capacity to give form and solidity to its insight, and by the English gift evident at every point and in all its production for the differentiated and particular.

Chaudhuri, himself a man with a relish for the specific, loved the quality of concreteness in English civilization. And it was the absence of this in Indian civilization to which he gave a measured philosophic expression towards the end of *The Autobiography*.

> I think there is even in the highest and most characteristic
> teaching of Hinduism (apart from the layer on layer of
> infinitely varied primitiveness which constitutes its buried
> foundation), something impelling a Hindu towards the
> unmerged in preference to the emergent, and towards the
> general in preference to the particular. According to some
> of the noblest teaching of Hinduism, the manifested
> universe is an illusion, the ultimate reality attributeless,
> and man's supreme happiness lies in putting an end to the
> cycle of births and deaths, or, in other words, in
> eliminating precisely those particular forms possessing
> sensible attributes which confer qualities and values on
> reality, and clothe it with an attractiveness for us. With
> such a philosophical background it is not surprising that a
> Hindu should tend to ignore distinctions. To me,
> however, Hinduism appears to be swimming against the
> current. Although its penchant for the undifferentiated and
> attributeless is undoubtedly due to its anxiety to bite on
> the rock of truth and reality lying underneath the flux of
> changes, I would still say that in actual fact it is retrograde
> and out of sympathy with reality. For I believe in change
> and hold all reality to be a process, a process which is
> justifying itself, as well as making itself more significant,
> by becoming more particular and differentiated and by
> endowing itself with ever more new values.[15]

Kishorganj, Banagram, Kalikutch, Shillong and the implied presence of England, together with the vast and terrible city of Calcutta, which I shall come to in a moment – these, with one exception, complete the pattern of influences which inaugurated Chaudhuri's fundamental sensibility and fixed the scale and organization of his interests. The exception is his parents. The Chaudhuri family was a real family in the Western sense and not, as was common form in Bengal, a joint family. It enjoyed its own forceful identity and not merely the passive existence of a cell in an amorphous clan. Chaudhuri's father and mother asserted their parental authority and responsibility against their relatives so that their children were brought up by them and not by a set of surrogates in some vague, impersonal community crèche, a system which eliminates the influence of mother and father by abolishing parental exclusiveness, and one which, in Chaudhuri's view, Plato would certainly not have recommended so strongly had he seen the results it produced in Bengal. The father was physically robust, conscientious in his work in court and afterwards in business, liberal, intelligent, disinterested, concerned to develop the initiative and the independence of his children, and a solicitous nurse of his wife during her bouts of melancholy madness. The mother was ferociously honest and emotionally grasping, at once intensely self-centred and cool and objective towards the children, and deeply afflicted by her mental disease. Chaudhuri shows himself to have the courage and the ethical and intellectual values of his father and the honesty and the impassioned egocentricity of his mother. The life of the family in the places he lived in as a child was the source of everything positive and committed in Chaudhuri's nature. Calcutta, when he came to it as a student and undergraduate, opened to him the possibilities of detachment. The context of his childhood was one into which he fitted naturally and happily; that of the next part of his life one in which he was to feel himself at more and more painful odds with his environment.

> Kishorganj, Banagram and Kalikutch are interwoven with
> my being; so is the England of my imagination; they
> formed and shaped me; but when once torn up from my
> natural habitat I became liberated from the habitat
> altogether; my environment and I began to fall apart; and
> in the end the environment became wholly external, a
> thing to feel, observe and measure, and a thing to act and
> react on, but never to absorb or be absorbed in.[16]

His treatment of Calcutta, where he was to spend thirty years – although *The Autobiography* takes him only to the beginning of his career – is as full and as positively thick with information as ever. His inquisitive, analytical eye turns upon everything from architecture to social relationships, from the method of garbage disposal to nationalist politics, from his own intellectual history to the current taste in furniture. But the tone is increasingly less cordial, the attitude more antagonistic. Place in his early life focused the paradisal Indian light; Calcutta was a prism breaking it into its component and colder parts. He was, of course, a failure in a worldly sense. He was a brilliant undergraduate but he collapsed during his graduate studies, and the academic life that would surely have been his natural habitat was shut off from him. Perhaps it needed a near lifetime of failure and poverty to prepare him for writing this book, because behind it burn not simply events but a life and a character. He shows himself bitterly forging a will capable of resisting an overwhelming environment. The powerful intellect is the servant of the will and the theoretical speculation is the necessary instrument for making the action of the will rational and defensible. Sometimes he suggests – not altogether mischievously – that the troubles of India are caused by an exclusive diet of carbohydrate sprinkled with chilli, or by a belief, as he puts it, in a pantheon of gods as corrupt as the Indian administration. But at the centre of his work is an attempt to account for the destruction of a spirit originally strong by an appalling external world. He fiercely cherishes what most people would find intolerable, the identity of the alien, but that again he makes coherent – at least for himself – by a theory which involves making half the population of India foreigners in their own country.

If I say that in the end the theories do not count, this is not to dismiss an intellectual framework raised on the basis of great learning and experience; nor is it to reject the force and relevance of Chaudhuri's criticism of Indian society – although I believe that one would really need to be an Indian to be able, and to have the right, to judge this question. But it is to claim for *The Autobiography* a different existence and significance – literary rather than philosophical or sociological. Its achievement rests less on the correspondence of its theory with actuality and much more on an inward life and coherence. It is not the doctrine propounded but the presence evoked which justifies and supports the book. *The Autobiography* depends on a fully realized rendering of the growth of a character of genuine and singular individuality, by turns arrogant, despairing, nervy, complacent, melancholy, but always faithfully Indian and saltily himself. Through the lucid agency of this convincing self-portrait we see an age-old society, with a powerful disposition towards inertness, in the state of being penetrated by Western concepts of God, nature, personality, nationalism and freedom. The formation of Chaudhuri's character is the means by which we are enabled to observe the transformation of Bengal society, and to watch the fundamental categories of thought and the modes of sensibility altering before a silent onslaught more significant and lasting than the public action of governments or any change imposed on the physical scene of India by the work of administrators and engineers.

The development so exhaustively detailed in *The Autobiography* is not just an evolutionary one in which a Western protestant astringency displaces the warm appeal of an Indian past – although it certainly is that. It is also a more personal and strenuous achievement which involves, on the one hand, hacking out an area of freedom and manoeuvre from a choked jungle of inheritance, and on the other, constructing a fresh identity which would join a questioning Western mind to a temperament laced with Bengali fury. The instruments of demolition and of building, and the elements out of which the new self was to be made, were concepts and principles, usages and styles, which Chaudhuri found, not in the imaginatively cramped local British population or the restricted Anglo-Indian tradition, but in the immensely more inclusive source of the English language and its literature. It was an undertaking which required on the part of Chaudhuri not only intellectual energy and analytical skill, but also courage, will, stamina and a quite unabashed interest in himself. The psychological composition or structure that results is a triumph of self-education and a model of the formative power of language and of its capacity to disturb and rearrange at the depths of the personality. It is also – like *The Autobiography* itself – a monument to the creative clash of two civilizations.

Chaudhuri appears in several places in this book – witness to his indefatigable energy and the range of his gifts – but I shall refer only cursorily to his other books. He has written studies of Robert Clive and Max Muller, subjects naturally close to his own interests, which were well thought of by the appropriate specialists. In 1987 Chaudhuri, born in the year of Queen Victoria's Jubilee, published *Thy Hand Great Anarch*, an immense production of some thousand pages and the second volume of his autobiography, but by now no means that of an unknown Indian. It offers the expected combination of fascination with, and pity for, self, truculent disdain for enemies from Gandhi onwards, paradoxical opinion, erudition and an extraordinarily creative memory. The book covers Chaudhuri's life in India up to 1952, and there are brilliant glimpses of Bengali family life and custom and evocations of Bengali scenery.

Perhaps this long book has not the intensity of insight and description of *The Autobiography of an Unknown Indian*, but there is one opinion, an emphatically singular and to many even an outrageous opinion, which is argued with all the combative passion of Luther. He contends that the worst crime the British committed in India was to desert it and to fail in their mission to bring European civilization in thought, art and science to the sub-continent. Chaudhuri combines with this powerful implicit defence of the nature and purpose of the British Raj the utmost scorn for the British in India, who were incapable of forming human or even humane relationships with Indians, and severe contempt for the ones he has lived among for the last eighteen years as an exile in Britain. The former he detests for their inhumanity, the latter for their illiteracy.

But of course any mind calmer than Chaudhuri's would be bound to acknowledge that by history and purpose the British Raj had at best only an indirect connection with European civilization, and at worst a barely existent one. It was primarily a commercial, economic, political and geo-political organization. When the British left India it was partly because of the *zeitgeist* – partly because they wanted to and partly because they had to. And what the British bequeathed on their departure besides certain practical achievements like roads and railways, the beginnings of a competent civil service and a highly trained army were many political, judicial and educational ideas based on the British model but capable of being adapted to an Indian way of life. The most basic, and the one most in accord with Chaudhuri's lofty vision of Britain's betrayed responsibility, was the English language itself or at least its use among the educated classes for the most significant administrative and intellectual purposes. Indians had thereby an entrance into the world of Western thought, science and technology. The British may deserve some credit for the start of this process – although their motives may not have been of the purest – but the principal credit belongs to the Indians themselves who energetically developed and spread the habit of English usage often, as has been noticed elsewhere, when it required considerable courage to do so.

I move now to a work slighter in content and function than Chaudhuri's autobiographical volumes: the modest, entrancingly readable memoirs of India's most eminent contemporary novelist R. K. Narayan. (I shall deal with his fiction at some length later in this book.) To omit *My Days* (1974) would be to neglect observations of Indian life, glancing and ironic as they may be, missing from grander and more formal accounts, as, for example, the simmering hostility of orthodox Hindus to Christianity which erupted in Vellala Street in Madras outside the three temples of Ganesha, the elephant-faced God, Krishna and Ponni Amnan, the goddess who guarded the frontier at a time when Madras was a village, when the tactless Lutheran missionary harangued the people to disown their gods.

R. K. Narayan has produced a sizeable body of work – more than a dozen novels and collections of short stories – which makes him one of the most respected novelists now writing in the British Commonwealth. His devoted readers are spread across the world from New York to Moscow, and Malgudi is as familiar to them as their own suburbs. His writing is a distinctive blend of Western technique and Eastern material, and he has succeeded in a remarkable way in making an Indian sensibility at home in English art. He was born in 1907 in Madras to a Brahmin family. His earliest memory is of himself sitting half buried in the sand, with a peacock and a monkey for company (*My Days*, p. 3).

> All day long, I sat buried in sand piled in a corner of our garden, raising castles and mountain-ranges, unaware of the fierce Madras sun overhead. I had a peacock and a monkey for company. The monkey was chained to a post on top of which a little cabin was available for his shelter, but he preferred to sit on the roof of his home, hanging down his tail. He responded to the name Rama by baring his teeth, and kept a wary eye on the peacock, which was perpetually engaged in scratching the mud and looking for edible insects. I cannot say exactly when they came into my life, but they seemed to have been always there with me. . . . The peacock was not fully grown yet, but he bore his three-foot tail haughtily, and enjoyed the freedom of the house, pecking away every ant that had the ill luck to come within the range of his vision. . . . When a shower of water descended, the peacock fanned out its tail, parading its colours. At this moment, one could hear Rama rattle his chain, since he always felt uneasy when the peacock preened itself thus, and demonstrated his protest by clanking his chain and tumbling around on the roof of his cabin. . . . Quite a variety of persons had to pass in and out of our home all day, having business with my grandmother – mendicants, vegetable vendors, the tailor and goldsmith – and if anyone stepped in without warning the were viciously chased by the peacock.

Tamil was the language spoken at home, and when the family moved to Mysore, Narayan learned English from one of those ferocious and eccentric schoolmasters who flourish in his fiction. His higher education was at Maharaja's College, which is now part of the University of Mysore, and he makes it clear that he had no gifts as a scholar, and indeed some pronounced deficiencies in that line. His first book, *Swami and Friends*, was published in 1935 with the help of Graham Greene, and he has continued to produce regularly ever since.

My Days is a set of autobiographical sketches. It lacks the implacable inclusiveness of the full-scale autobiography as well as its impassioned self-regard. Indeed, in many ways it is very similar to a Narayan novel. It certainly brings home to one how much of his fiction, and not only the strikingly personal *The English Teacher* (1945), is firmly tethered in the detail of his own experience. Narayan's autobiography, like his novels, is regional in that it conveys an intimate sense of a given place – in the novels, Malgudi; in *My Days*, Mysore – but it is not parochial or shuttered. The life in *My Days* is that of Narayan's own class, the Indian middle class, where people are not too well off to be unworried about money or brutalized by the total lack of it. He appears like the hero of one of his novels as sensitive, ardent, modest and wry about himself, and with a hidden resolute will. (How clearly, for example, one sees this in the crisp quality of his businesslike approach to writing and particularly to the economics of it. He has a positively Jamesian sense of the obligation that publishers have to their authors.) In *My Days* we see, as we do in the novels, first the context of the town and the skills and problems of various kinds of work which so fascinate Narayan; within this the subtler circle of the family; and then at the centre a figure posing modestly but with an inward conviction, Narayan himself, another Narayan hero. He has been formed by the immense weight of the inherited tradition of India in balance with a positive but subdued individuality. Narayan's novels are comedies of sadness, and the quiet disciplined life unfolded in *My Days* is both suffused with a pure and unaffected melancholy and also lighted with the glint of mockery of both self and others.

As in the novels, there is a fundamental perception enlivening and organizing the experience of Narayan's life. Although one is conscious of the overwhelming background of the Indian past, of the great crowd dead and alive moving in the mind and along the highways, of the intense and even smothering life of the family, one becomes increasingly aware of what Narayan wrote in *The English Teacher*: 'A profound and unmitigated loneliness is the only truth of life.' In this lightly buoyant, delicately developed account of his life, his childhood, his family, his work, and the tragedy of the loss of his wife, the artist who created and populated Malgudi, working in the same easy, limpid English and with the same tolerant and attentive attitude to life, brings to bear on his own nature the gift for moral analysis, the marvellous comic talent, and the eye for human queerness that distinguished the novels. The naïveté of being human, the subject of Narayan's art, is what this account of his own life convincingly testifies.

I once heard students in Madras bitterly attack Narayan for his exclusive concern with the middle class; a treachery, they thought, to the pullulating poor and the dominantly agricultural character of the country. (But Narayan, as he himself said, writes about the Indian middle class because he is a member of it and it is the only class he understands.) And I have heard readers in England comment about the necessary limitations of perception which this must imply. It is true that Narayan works by focusing his attention sharply, and that part of his strength is never to ignore his instinct for limitation. But he has the serious writer's gift for achieving representativeness by concentration. And so the Mysore of his personal life, the Malgudi of his novelist's life, becomes an intense and brilliant image of India itself. Whatever happens in India happens in Malgudi, and whatever happens in Malgudi happens everywhere. This indeed is the impression *My Days* finally makes upon one: that for all the charm and authenticity of its Indian colouring it speaks of a substantial and common human nature; and in particular it shows Narayan's fascination with the complex association of sincerity and self-deception in human life. How nimbly, how deftly, but with what forgiving kindness Narayan unravels this universal riddle of mankind, or the version of it lodged in the breast of an eighty-two-year-old Indian novelist.

How he came to be that is revealed casually, obliquely, in this engaging, ripplingly humorous production. We come to have so clear a sense of his individuality because the gifts that make his fiction so fresh and humane are present here: in the first place the ability to communicate the representational surface of things, a creative accuracy of notation; in the second, considerable deftness in the analysis of motives; and then here and there, tactfully, cogently, a succinct and restrained poetry of reference when significant points of action or time are related to the ancient Indian myths. Perhaps the monkey with which his life began was Hanuman, the monkey god of wisdom and benevolence, while the peacock pecking away at every ant that came within range of his vision is the image of his alert, undeceived and mocking eye.

I want to conclude this chapter by turning to a writer nimbler and more accessible than some of the heavyweight moralists with which I have had perforce to be concerned. I mean Ved Mehta (b. 1934) the journalist – journalist, that is, in the good sense of the abused term. He is a sharp observer and cogent commentator – all the more remarkable in that he has been blind since a childhood attack of meningitis. He left home in Lahore before the age of five to be trained in a blind school, a gloomy building of sooty stone, directed by a Christian Indian with Western ideas of education. He continued his education at another blind school in the United States and then at Oxford and Harvard. He is a person of extraordinary gifts who has had the courage and will, in spite of a shattering disability, to make the most of them.

At the age of twenty-six he became as staff writer for *The New Yorker* and the clarity and wit of its house stye has influenced his own. His work falls into two categories. One is autobiographical, and so far consists of four separate volumes, *Daddyji, Mamaji, Vedi* and *The Ledge Between the Streams*. The other category is documentary and journalstic, and includes *John is Easy to Please, Fly and the Fly-Bottle, Face to Face* and *Walking the Indian Streets*. Perhaps I can make a comment on each kind.

Ved Mehta's autobiographical works show how the life of the extended Indian family provides the richest sort of material to the chronicler. Its size, complexity and ritual and its combination of formality and intimacy provide the substance and suggest the form most appropriate to it, the discipline of the documentary mode. The detachment that this requires fits Mehta's personality as a writer. It is served by a powerful memory and an extraordinary power of inference: at least it seems so to a person with sight. From his other senses, from his intelligence and imagination and from his ceaselessly interrogated informants he draws the most accurate sort of knowledge of what is occurring around him.

Here is a passage from the most recent of the family volumes, covering the years between 1940 and 1949 which ends with Ved on his way to study in America. It communicates the true flavour of a significant Indian occasion, a marriage in the family and a sense of the restless curiosity of the inquisitive child.

> I ran around the house like a top, touching everything, greeting everyone, trying to find out what was happening. In the back part of the inner courtyard, where the confectioners were stoking makeshift fires, pouring dough for *puris*, stirring something in vats, I breathed lungfulls to savour the cooking. In the centre of the courtyard, I paced round the *vedi* – four banana trunks firmly set in the ground under a canopy and forming a biggish square. I helped bring branches and twigs with lots of leaves between them, to form arches and, on the arches, fruits, flowers, balloons, and strings of lights. I barged into Mamaji's bedroom and was chased out, because Sister Pom was being dressed there. . . . I went upstairs and downstairs into the garden and out to the gate, feeling the strings of lights on walls and bushes, eaves and pillars, to see if the bulbs were warm. . . . The whole house was restless and hot. . . . 'What's happening? What's happening?' I asked. . . . I collared my younger cousin Ravi. 'What's happening?'[17]

It was after this wedding that Ved Mehta was taken with the party to Lahore Railway Station to say goodbye to his sister and her husband. His father abruptly let go of his hand. He could neither step forward for fear of the gap between track and train nor back because of the handcarts clattering behind. 'I remembered the frightening train that had taken me far, far away and deposited me in a strange city, in a strange school among terrifying strangers, and remembered how, no matter how much I cried and begged, there had been no way to get back home.'[18]

Ved Mehta's existence in the orphanage for the blind, where they spoke Marathi, the language of Bombay, which he did not understand, is the subject of the most moving of his family chronicles. It is the most moving but also unemotional in that the feeling is fully justified by the situation and wholly absorbed in its details. The school consisted of some forty blind and partially sighted boys and girls, all of them except Ved from the poorest in the city. The Headmaster, the very decent and progressive Mr Ras Mohun, could hardly believe that such a boy with such normal looking eyes and such an open cheerful expression was intended for his school. Ved's father had decided that he did not want for his son the fate of the blind he had so often seen in his service as a public-health officer – men and women living like wounded animals. Above all he wanted independence for his son. His son had an intuitive understanding of his intention and at no time did he question the decision or bear his father a grudge because of it. He seems to have had an absolute conviction of his family's love in circumstances which, to many, would have made it incredible.

The child's fidelity to this belief is all the more astonishing in that he was translated from a secure and significant place in an affectionate household to a universe divided between blind and powerless children and sighted, incomprehensible and potent adults.

> Some of us who were totally blind had been sighted once,
> but we could no longer remember what that was like. We
> thought of sighted people as awesome and powerful,
> always able to take a discarded shoe to one who wasn't
> sighted. For when we thought of being sighted we could
> think of ourselves only as the Sighted Master . . . we
> would dream of growing up and becoming the Sighted
> Master – living in the boys' dormitory, snoring away,
> catching boys doing naughty things, beating them with a
> discarded shoe – even as we would automatically
> straighten ourselves at the very mention of the Sighted
> Master.[19]

If the personal and family chronicles represent the Indian side of Ved Mehta's nature, the work for *The New Yorker* speaks for the American side. It was the United States that enabled him to use his great gifts to live the independent, dignified life his strong-minded and far-sighted father wanted for him. He became an American citizen in 1975. The American essays, although they are by no means all about American subjects, have an unusual lightness, a freedom from the weight of inherited assumption carried by the Indian writings. Instead they display a youthful freshness and sparkle, an expectant, sunlit consciousness. And they are, at least in one particular, reminiscent of the Henry James's memoirs, *A Small Boy and Others, Notes of a Son and Brother* and *The Middle Years* in the astonishing retentiveness of mind that is shown. What Ved Mehta's mind, like James's laid hold of, it kept. 'The truth', James said 'is much less in the wealth of my experience than in the tenacity of my impressions; the fact that I have lost nothing of what I saw.'[20]

Of Ved Mehta we can say in admiration that he lost nothing of what he did not see. These pieces – the substance of most of them is an interview or interviews – fairly bristle with visual detail. It is difficult to account for what is almost an intuitive quality of the writing. The writer refers at one point to 'the accoucheurs of accuracy' too numerous to acknowledge, and these I suppose must be responsible for the information which made these details possible. But however the material is come by, it is worked on by so vigorous and shaping a literary intelligence that we are made vividly aware of both its uniqueness and its representativeness. In one collection of *The New Yorker* pieces, Ved Mehta quotes as an inscription a question and answer from Wittgenstein's *Philosophical Investigations*: 'What is your aim in philosophy? To show the fly the way out of the fly-bottle.' If we ask a similar question of Mehta the answer might be: 'To show the movements of the fly, the shape of the bottle and the subtle tint of the glass which imprisons it.'

Ved Mehta spent some years in universities. He remained fascinated by academic life, its nature, conduct, manners and peculiarities; the best of *The New Yorker* pieces have to do with academic experience. His habit is to light on some critical issue, controversy or innovation in a humanity with which he is at home – philosophy, theology or history, for instance – and to give a lucid, competent and impartial account of it, and then to take the enquiry back from the subject to those engaged in it, thus supplying a context filled with figures from past and present, and incidentally, humanizing the most remotely abstract of intellectual activities. Ved Mehta's attitude is that of the interested, innocent enquirer, occasionally bemused, often wondering.

But blended with his attitude is a modest subtext of exposure, mild, diffident but in its way devastating.

For example, in *A Battle Against the Bewitchment of our Intelligence* he starts with Gilbert Ryle's refusal to publish a review in *Mind* of Ernest Gellner's book *Words and Things*, a polemic against linguistic philosophy on the ground that Gellner's work was abusive and made imputations of disingenuousness. The violent controversy which this seemingly obscure rejection set off provided Ved Mehta with all the energy, drama and *dramatis personae* he needed for a concentrated and perceptive investigation of an influential side of British intellectual life. In *Argument Without End* he chooses Trevor-Roper's onslaught on Arnold Toynbee's *A Study of History* to open a clear and closely-packed analysis of contemporary British historical writing. It is an essay crammed with brilliant cameos of the great characters of the *genre*. 'Namier attributed the causes of men's actions, like Marx, to something besides their professed motives; like Freud, to subterranean springs; and like Darwin, to something beyond the mind and its ideas.'[21]

These studies are most densely particularized but certain larger findings are nevertheless slowly and gently distilled. On the moral side we see how the highest intellectual endeavours can be accompanied by, indeed often seem peculiarly susceptible to arrogance, malice and self-deceit; on the intellectual side we find how ordinary the most brilliant are in the presence of a self-evident genius like Wittgenstein; and on the practical and social side we observe what talent, what devotion and labour can be put by a self-appointed intellectual aristocracy to what trivial ends. This was the gravamen of Bertrand Russell's charge – 'I don't like Oxford philosophers. Don't like them. They have made trivial something very great.'[22] It is illustrated by Ved Mehta like this.

> 'What is truth?' Oxford philosophers are liable to say. . . .
> 'Look at all the different ways the word true is used in
> ordinary speech.' They refuse to look into the uses of
> words in extraordinary speech, like poetry, because
> English philosophy has been dominated since Hume by a
> prosaic contempt for the imagination. 'When you have
> considered all the ways "true" is used in ordinary speech,'
> they say, 'you have understood the concept of Truth.'[23]

Ved Mehta is the contemporary voice of a long line of Indian prose writers in English stretching back for two hundred years. It is fitting, therefore, that the complex tradition of the Indian family which sustains part of his writing should be balanced by different, modern analysis couched in an attractive 'New Yorker' idiom. With the exception of the first version of his book *Walking the Indian Streets*, a giggling, adolescent production, he has kept a high and even standard. In all his work he has made the traditional view exciting and engaging. He has made the most of experience limited by handicap. Indeed he has made blindness itself a means of insight.

References

1. *The English Works of Raja Ram Mohan Roy*, ed. Jogandra Chander Ghose (Delhi, 1982), p. 224.

2. *The Swan and the Eagle* (Simla, 1969), p. 58.

3. *Lectures from Colombo to Almora* (Calcutta, 1956), pp. 6–7.

4. *Selections from Swami Vivekananda* (Calcutta, 1970), p. 419.

5. King, Ursula, *Social Action*, 1978, Vol. 28, pp. 62–63.

6. *The Complete Works of Swami Vivekananda* (Calcutta, 1955), Vol. IV, pp. 136–37.

7. *A Tagore Reader* (New York, 1961), p. 104.

8. *Social Action*, Vol. 28, pp. 84–85.

9. Gandhi, M. K., The Story of my Experiments with Truth *An Autobiography* (Ahmadabad, 1927), p. 21.

10. *Ibid.*, p. 21.

11. *Ibid.*, p. 109.

12. *Modern India: The Origins of an Asian Democracy* (London, 1985), p. 207.

13. Nehru, J., *An Autobiography* (London, 1936), p. 48.

14. *The Autobiography of an Unknown Indian*, p. 60.

15. *Ibid.*, p. 439.

16. *Ibid.*, pp. 257–58.

17. *The Ledge Between the Streams* (London, 1984), pp. 272–75.

18. *Ibid.*, p. 280.

19. *Vedi* (New York, 1982), p. 197.

20. James, Henry, *Autobiography*, ed. Dupée, F. W. (London, 1956), p. 60.

21. *Fly and the Fly-Bottle* (London, 1963), p. 172.

22. *Ibid.*, p. 41.

23. *Ibid.*, p. 86.

Chapter 3
Fiction: The Founding Fathers – Mulk Raj Anand, Raja Rao and R. K. Narayan

In the nineteen-thirties a number of Indian novelists began to write in English – genuine novelists, that is, for whom the art of fiction was an end in itself and not just a means for communicating other kinds of truth. Fifty years later it is clear that this was a form peculiarly suited to the Indian sensibility and one to which Indian writers have made a distinct and significant contribution. In this chapter I shall deal with three writers who are distinguished not only for their own work but as the inaugurators of the form itself since it was they who defined the area in which the Indian novel in English was to operate, drew the first models of its characters and themes and elaborated its particular logic. Each used his own version of an English freed from the foggy taste of Britain and transferred to a wholly new setting of brilliant light and brutal heat.

The three are Mulk Raj Anand (b. 1905), Raja Rao (b. 1909) and R. K. Narayan (b. 1907). Mulk Raj Anand's first novels, containing some of his best work, appeared between 1935 and 1940: *Untouchable* (1935), *Coolie* (1936), *Two Leaves and a Bud* (1937), *The Village* (1939) and *Across the Black Waters* (1941); he had, in fact, written a considerable amount before this; for example, a study of Persian painting and a book about curries! Rao has written only three novels – *Kanthapura* (1938), *The Serpent and the Rope* (1960) and *The Cat and Shakespeare* (1963) – as well as a volume of short stories (1947); R. K. Narayan's first novel *Swami and Friends* came out in 1935 and he has published steadily ever since.

Mulk Raj Anand was born in Peshawar in 1905. He was educated at Punjoot University and University College London, with a final year at Trinity College, Cambridge. In her essay 'Mulk Raj Anand and the Thirties Movement in England'[1] Gillian Packham writes: 'Mulk Raj Anand was not the typically well-heeled young Indian sent to complete his education in London. His love of study and his poor relationship with his father had led him to escape his father's *petit bourgeois* conditions. With the encouragement and the material support of the poet Iqbal, his college principal and his mother, he arrived in London in

1924, a poor student forced to earn his living by working in Indian restaurants. . . .' He completed a doctoral thesis on 'Bertrand Russell and the English Empiricists' in 1928 and he lived in England for twenty-one years. As Gillian Packham's perceptive essay demonstrates, Mulk Raj Anand became an essentially thirties man in thought and sensibility, politically committed to Marxism if not to Soviet Communism, involved with the Unity Theatre and the left-wing literary movement of the period. He even wrote plays in which, says Gillian Packham, 'two characters would talk out an issue for five hours, regardless of time or act divisions'.[2] Mulk Raj Anand regarded himself as a rational humanist rather than a Marxist but his ideas on art – he is clearly not a thinker, let alone an original one – are almost comically reminiscent of the Left Book Club at its most ingenuously youthful. 'All art is propaganda. The art of Ajanta is propaganda for Buddhism. The art of Ellora is propaganda for Hinduism. The art of the Western novel is propaganda for humanity against the bourgeoisie. Gorky as a humanist dared to speak of man, man's condition, not to say how awful it is, but he also suggested what man could be. And thus he did propaganda for man.'[3]

But however derivative Anand's thought may have been his feeling was genuine and his own and his experience of the poor in India and in Britain gave him every warrant for it. His fiction is, of course, exclusively concerned with India. He is passionately involved with the villages, the ferocious poverty, the cruelties of caste, the wrongs of women, and with orphans, the untouchables and urban labourers. He writes in an angry reformist way, like a less humorous Dickens and a more emotional Wells of the personal sufferings induced by economic injustices. It is really economics he is writing about, even when the subject is caste. His sharp well-organized early novel *Untouchable* was very highly thought of by E. M. Forster. It is a fascinating combination of hard material, intense, specific theme and throbbing Shelleyan manner. The action, occupying a single day, is precipitated by a great 'catastrophe', an accidental touching in the morning. Everything that follows is affected by it, even the innocent and vividly realized hockey match. Of the three solutions hinted at to the problem of the untouchable – Christ, Gandhi and main drainage – it is the last which is most favoured by Anand. He is a committed artist, and what he is committed to is indicated by Bashu's mockery in *Untouchable*: 'greater efficiency, better salesmanship, more mass-production, standardization, dictatorship of the sweepers, marxian materialism and all that.' 'Yes, yes,' is the reply, 'all that, but no catch-words and cheap phrases, the change will be organic and not mechanical' (p. 175).

Organic standardization, unmechanical mass-production, advertisement without catch-words – how clearly this kind of thing confirms

Mulk Raj Anand's deficiencies as a thinker and the capacity of his Marxist enthusiasms to glide gaily across the most deeply entrenched differences. This, together with his furious indignation, unself-critical ideology and habit of undue explicitness, make him a writer whose work has to be severely sieved. Like other writers impelled by social motives, however worthy, whose attitude to life is all too patently dominated by theory, he has the habit of preaching at the reader and trapping him into sharing his unexamined motives. But when his imagination burns, and the dross of propaganda is consumed, as in *Untouchable, Coolie* and *The Big Heart* (1945), there is no doubt that he is a novelist of considerable power.

Even politics – that is, even politics as abstract, rigid and doctrinal as this – can be humanized by the ingathering and melting capacity of the Indian mind. It is something working right through *Coolie* where Anand shows himself to be one of the first of Indian writers to look on the savagely neglected, despised and maltreated Indian labourer with an angry lack of resignation. The novel combines an acid indignation at the condition of the poor with a Dickensian vivacity in physical registration and a delicate sense of the psychology of Munoo, the waif-hero, in particular of the rhythms of his growth from child to adolescent. Munoo's victim role brings home to one the passive quality of the Indian poor in what Anand shows to be a markedly static and hierarchical society, just as the immense distances from Simla to Bombay, covered in the boy's enforced journeys, convey in a way quite new in Indian fiction the continental vastness and variety of India.

In a perceptive note on Anand's fiction, Anna Rutherford writes: 'Anand's characters invariably fall into three classes: the victims who are usually the protagonists; the oppressors, those who oppose change and progress; and the good men. Under the last category fall the social workers, the labour leaders, all those who believe in progress and can see how modern science can improve the lot of the sufferers and help bring about the equality of all men.'[4] While this shrewd observation is an accurate account of some of the more Marxist protest fiction, it is hardly adequate for the novels, like *Across the Black Waters* or *The Private Life of an Indian Prince* (1953), in which there is a subtler distribution of forces and a more complicated division of sympathies. *Across the Black Waters* is the middle part of a trilogy published between 1940 and 1942, the other volumes being *The Village* and *The Gourd and the Sickle*, in which the peasant boy Lal Singh is taken from his North Indian village and a life stifled by suffocating layers of custom and religion into the ferocity of the Great War in Europe and then back to India and a new political stance. Anand, whose father was a soldier, shows himself to have a fine apolitical understanding of the soldier's life, and its instantaneous transitions from excessive boredom to

extreme danger. He conveys, too, without any sense of superiority the
soldiers' muzzy bafflement and anger at the politics and honours of
war. *The Big Heart*, on the other hand, answers more closely in structure to Anna Rutherford's analysis. The theme of this distinctly
Dickensian novel is stated in the first sentence.

> In the centre of Amritsar is Kucha Billimaran, a colony of
> traditional coppersmiths called Ihuthiars, now uprooted
> and on the brink of starvation due to the advent of the
> factory and the consequent loss of their traditional
> occupation.

The contrast of the two worlds, vividly delineated, is a splendid
vehicle for Anand's largeness and generosity, qualities which soften the
rigidity of the formal structure pointed to by Anna Rutherford and
certainly prevent any sense of imposition or distortion. The ideological
and organizational friction between money and craft is the more
intense because it is ultimately located in one individual, Ananta. He
feels the attractions of both kinds of life. On the one hand, he has an
artist's fulfilment in the craft of working the intractable metal with a
skill honed over generations. On the other, he appreciates what indus-
trialization could do for the half-starved coppersmiths. Moreover,
Ananta suffers not only the oppression of the capitalists but also the
moral prejudice of the poor because of the widow he lives with. The
inward friction which frays Ananta is related to that which Anand
himself suffers as an artist, the tension between art and ideology, which
he has managed to assuage in only a handful of his novels.

One of this group is certainly *The Private Life of an Indian Prince*
published in 1953 and revised in 1970. At first glance the material of
this novel would make it a ripe subject for the Marxist side of Mulk
Raj Anand: a depraved and neurotic monarch, a corrupt court, an
impoverished and mutinous people, and a tense and critical period of
Indian history. In fact, in spite of the very occasional radical *longeur*,
the novel is refreshingly free from politics of the oppressive, ideological kind. Anand shows a powerful empathy for the morbid and
suffering character of the maharajah. Indeed there is evidence that trau-
matic events in Anand's own life, the break-up of a marriage, the loss
to another of the woman for whom his marriage had ended, informed
his sense of Victor's personality and his feelings for his predicament
to such a degree indeed that the author seems both possessed by and
possessed of the prince's character. Such self-projection makes all the
more necessary the device of the candid confidant, the Maharajah's
personal London-trained physician, Dr Shankar, which Anand uses,
deftly and economically, to ensure balance, distance and control. In

most of his fiction Anand shows very much a nineteenth-century conception of the novel, seeing it as an organization based on a double foundation of character and circumstance: a character which has to be clearly defined and then developed, largely through the causality of other forces, social circumstances and influences, usually of a harshly oppressive sort. This is a pattern which is present in *The Private Life of an Indian Prince* but less insistently so than usual. The Rajput tradition of autocracy, the family tradition of self-indulgence, his profligate education and his promiscuous upbringing, the servility of advisers, the overwhelming influence of the Prince's prostitute mistress – much of the vicious disorder of the character of Vicky is attributed to these and other external influences. But the relationship between the Prince and Dr Shankar makes it possible to concentrate on the self-created chaos of the Prince's personality, so that he is seen to be much more than the echo of his past and the mere effect of the influence of others. It is the autotelic quality of the Prince's mental and moral ruin which finally stamps itself on the reader's mind in spite of the elaborate delineation of external influences, conditions and causes which form the substance of the many conversations between him and Dr Shankar. It is this which pulls him towards the status of tragic hero and away from that of pathetic victim. In the end he finishes, I suppose, somewhere between the two, but closer to hero than victim. The rhythm of his progress towards utter mental collapse is defined with precision and informed conviction, as indeed is the whole personality of the dissolute, stricken protagonist.

Anand also has his share of the Victorian gift for creating a gallery of minor figures, each of which has its particular flicker of life. The women, for example, are remarkably well done: the illiterate prostitute mistress, Ganga Dasi, with whom the Prince is hopelessly infatuated, who exists solely on the plane of instinct and animal cunning and whose musky presence can almost be smelt; the virtuous and neglected Maharani, the wife who has given Victor a son and who travels from Sham Pur to Poona to care for her husband in the insane asylum; the young shop assistant June whom Victor seduces in London: each of these has an individual life of her own, plays a significant part in Victor's downfall and in the design of the novel. The same is true of the men, particularly of the political figures whether of the lightweight provincial kind or the more powerful national sort of politician. There is an especially strong, even menacing portrait of Jardar Patel.

The most interesting and the most complex character in the novel is Dr Shankar. The Prince for all his neuroses, extravagance and moral insensibility is after all a straightforward, uncomplicated figure. Dr Shankar is the narrator, the focuser of the reader's attention, the surrogate conscience of the Prince, and his interpreter and analyst.

Above all he is the moral man whose every act or judgement is made against the presence, or at least the possibility of a moral standard. The novel is not, in consequence, simply the documented case-history of a collapsing mind, but the dramatized conflict of a human and tragic kind, conducted implicitly through Dr Shankar's scrupulous effort to refine his own moral sense and explicitly in his relationship with the Prince, where he struggles continually to nourish a moral sense in one who proves finally incapable of supporting it. Dr Shankar's moral sense may be derived from limited sources, from progress, science, humanism of a commonsensical kind, but it is a worthy one and fitted for its purpose in the novel, which is to provide another, moral dimension in an aimless world of privilege and cruelty.

I have referred more than once to Victorian characteristics in Anand's work. The reader should imagine an Indian writer of Anand's type and period as stepping instantaneously from a Victorian ethos, from Victorian style, prose and feeling into the leftish, progressive world of the thirties. But Anand did not thereby shed all his Victorian habits and manners. One which persists is his extraordinary Victorian fluency of communication, which has in it something both Victorian and Russian (Anand was influenced by Russian novelists). E. M. Forster was a critic of the purest taste and the most candid expression, and in arguing in the Preface to the novel, not altogether convincingly, that the conclusion of *Coolie* was really integral with the story in spite of 'being too voluble and sophisticated in comparison with the clear observation which has preceded it', made this essential point in the one word 'voluble'. Creation appears to be no agonizing struggle for Anand and communication is something he engages in with an unstrained and vivid enthusiasm and much of the facility of a nineteenth-century Russian novelist.

Mulk Raj Anand does not have the profound commonsense of Narayan which enhances both actuality and myth, the fact and the poetry of life. He does not have that sense of the metaphysical nature of man we find in Raja Rao. But he has a deep feeling for the deprived, a grasp of the social structure of his society and the clearest vision of its injustices and malformations. When his imagination burns and the propagandist is forgotten, he is a novelist of considerable power.

Raja Rao is an Indian and a novelist; but these generalities apart, he is as a novelist as different from Mulk Raj Anand as it is possible to be.

It would be hard to conceive of two writers more different from one another than Mulk Raj Anand and Raja Rao: the former a man of the future committed to science and Marxist humanism who sees the past as a brutal drag on progress and enlightenment; the latter with a profound sense of the richness and creativity of the past, metaphysical, poetic, traditional. And yet there is more than one significant similarity. In his first novel *Kanthapura* (1938) Raja Rao remarks in the introduction – which was written, he tells us, at the instance of his publishers – on those very qualities of volubility and pace I referred to as characterizing Anand's manner. 'The tempo of Indian life must be infused into one English expression. . . . We, in India, think quickly, we talk quickly, and when we move we move quickly. There must be something in the sun of India that makes us rush and tumble and run on.' Anand met this requirement, as M. K. Naik shows in his acute and patient study of the short stories,[5] with a whole battery of devices. Indian locutions, idioms and images are rendered directly into English. Even the Indian vernacular is translated immediately into English. Anand's English, says Naik, shows its Indian origin in its 'oriental opulence, its passion for adjectives, its tendency to use more words than are absolutely necessary and its fast, galloping tempo'. As one would expect of a temperament like Raja Rao's, his method of realizing an Indian sensibility in the English language is subtler than Mulk Raj Anand's. His technique is much less extractable from the text, and is more incorporated into the body of the fable. His writing is closer to speech, and he is able to use the rhythms of speech – and particularly the intimate, sharing rhythm of folk speech – to indicate character, feeling and a vast tissue of assumptions and beliefs. It is a method which works beautifully in a story like *Kanthapura* concerned with the intensity of village life, with its physical immediacy, its traditional swaddling, and its religious murmurations.

Here is a characteristic passage from early on in the novel.

> The day dawned over the Ghats, the day rose over the
> Blue Mountain, and churning through the grey, rapt
> valleys, swirled up and swam across the whole air. The
> day rose into the air and with it rose the dust of morning,
> and the carts began to creak round the bulging rocks and
> the coppery peaks, and the sun fell into the river and
> pierced it to the pebbles, while the carts rolled on and on,
> fair carts of the Kanthapura fair – fair carts that came from
> Maddur and Tippur and Santas and Kuppur, with chillies
> and coconuts, rice and rogi cloth, tamarind, butter and oil,
> bangles and kumkum, little pictures of Rama and Krishna
> and Sarkara and Mahatma, little dolls for the youngest,
> little kites for the elder, and little chess pieces for the old –
> carts rolled by the Sampur Knoll and down into the valley
> of the Tippur stream, then rose again and ground round
> the Kenchamma Hill, and going straight into the temple

grove, one by one, with tolling bells and muffled bells,
with horn-protectors in copper and back-protectors in lace,
they all stood there in one moment of fitful peace:
'Salutations to Thee, Kenchamma, Goddess Supreme', –
and then the yokes began to shake and the bells began to
shiver and move, and when the yoke touched the earth,
men came out one by one, travellers that had paid a four-
anna bit or an eight-anna bit to sleep upon pungent
tamarind and suffocating chillies, travellers who would
take the Pappur carts to go to the Pappur mountains, the
Sanpur carts to go to the Sanpur mountains, and some too
that would tramp down the passes into the villages by the
sea, or hurry on to Kanthapura as our Moorthy did this
summer morning, Moorthy with a bundle of Khadi on his
back and a bundle of books in his arms. (pp. 54–55).

Even in this passage, which is descriptive and introductory, one
finds the love of intimate chat and endless gossip, while the repetitive
incantatory rhythm induces a sense of age-old oft-told tales. The hard
facts about geography, about the place, the carts and their cargoes, the
animals, the travellers and the price of their journey and the salutations
to the reigning goddess are communicated obliquely as bits of information casually imparted to a confidant. And the whole passage is
sustained by a rippling rhythm, with hardly a formal stop, adjusted
neatly to the breathing of the speaker. Most significantly the whole
passage concludes with Moorthy observed as he hurries towards
Kanthapura 'with a bundle of Khadi on his back and a bundle of books
in his arms'. The khadi is the cotton Gandhi wished each Indian, but
above all each peasant, to spin every day in the fight for economic
independence; the books represent Gandhi's gospel of pure truth.
'Truth must you tell,' he says, 'for Truth is God, and verily it is the
only God I know.' And he says too, 'spin every day. Spin and weave
for our Mother is in tattered weeds and a poor mother needs clothes
to cover her sores' (p. 16).

The combination of folk speech, which can be both sly and broad,
insinuating and direct, with the vigorous tradition of Indian story-
telling going back two thousand years to the Ramanyana with all the
resonance and subtlety this implies, allows the novelist suppleness and
variety in rendering the response of the villagers to what is the quick
and the theme of *Kanthapura*, the transfiguration of the village by the
influence of Gandhi. Such a complex of resources is needed to render
the life of the South Indian village, which is a more complicated structure than the mere collection of simple farm labourers foreigners have
taken it to be. C. D. Narasimhaiah reminds us of this truth in his book

on the novelist. In this village there is a Brahmin Quarter, a Pariah Quarter, a Potters' Quarter, a Weavers' Quarter and an Indra (workers') Quarter. There is a busy economic life and differences in status and possessions. There is an intense social and religious life with festivals – the Rama festival, the Krishna festival, the Ganesha festival – gladly and devoutly observed and the goddess Kenchamma joyously celebrated. Outside this village, and a warning to the villagers of what might befall them without their village and its close-knit society, stands the Skeffington Coffee Estate which had lured armies of starving coolies to work there as serfs for the Red-man, 'a four-anna bit for a man hand' and 'a two-anna bit for a woman hand'. And the place positively bristles with characters: from Renge Gouda, the village head – 'if Renge Gouda says No you can eat the bitter bean leaves and lie by the city gates, licked by the curs' – to waterfall Verhamma who moved day and night against Rengamma because she was jealous of her house; from the cunning Bhetta walking the streets in a loin cloth and assiduously adding to his property, to Concubine Chinna who stayed on in the village when the others left 'to lift her leg to her new customers'; from Postmaster Suryamarayana, who had a two-storeyed house, to Corner-House Moorthy, 'who had gone through life like a noble cow, quiet, generous, serene, deferent and brahmanic, a very prince, I tell you' (p. 6).

But while Moorthy, who has had a Pauline conversion to Gandhiism, lives so vividly in the minds of the Kanthapurians, he makes a fainter impression on the reader. He is young, unformed and without weight. It may be that this quality enables him not to be an obstruction between the village and Gandhi himself, and that he is designed to be no more than a minor and local projection of the Mahatma. Certainly he conveys with conviction the author's essential belief that the Gandhian revolution, while it has political and social aims and consequences – independence from Britain and equality among Indians – is above all a religious conversion requiring a fundamental realignment of values and a reforming of human nature. This is not only in keeping with the Indian tradition where religious and social reform were always intimately connected, but is also exactly fitted to the assumptions and expectations of a spontaneously religious community. It is natural therefore for the humorous and weathered grandmother who tells the story to make racy connections between the events of the fiction and ancient Indian myths. The one becomes translucent to the other. Gandhi is the God as well as the politician marching to the salt-pans, Moorthy the God's manifestation as well as the non-violent frantic young leader. Bhatto the policeman is the whole negation and evil of life. The novel is dense with the actualities of village existence and brilliant with an implicit, unforced spirituality.

E. M. Forster thought *Kanthapura* the best Indian novel written in English, and this is one of his many judgements for which a case could still be argued. Later critics have assigned this equivocal laurel to Raja Rao's second novel, *The Serpent and the Rope*, published in 1960. Although Raja Rao is by no means a prolific writer this elaborate work gives no impression at all of any constricted or meagre talent. On the contrary it strikes the reader with its flowing abundance and endless intricacy. The action or, perhaps, since external events do not have a high status in the novel, I should say the scene swerves from India to France to Britain and takes in a large number of authentic, sharply realized characters, French, Indian and Russian. In essence the novel is a philosophical meditation on the nature of existence in which the drama lies in the activity of meditation and not in the action, plot or progression we are used to in a European novel. For Raja Rao, experience naturally falls into a series of antinomies – life and death, being and becoming, knowing and unknowing – and the inner debate about the nature of existence is seen as the tension between appearance and reality, figured as the serpent and the rope. The examination of this central question of human life is done through the intense diagnosis of its hero Rama, Southern Indian, Brahmin, intellectually brilliant, spiritually sensitive and tubercular. His relationship with his French wife Madeleine, their disintegrating marriage and the subtle nexus with his mother-in-law (Little Mother) are beautifully realized but the novel's primary concern is with laying bare Rama's individuality and his predicament. 'His choice is between the serpent – unreality masquerading as reality, seductive because it is apparently verifiable – and the rope – reality hidden because man sees through the serpent's eyes.'[6]

The defect of this remarkable novel, which at the very least extends our concept of what the novel can be, is that Coleridgean fault of unstoppable fluency. Raja Rao does go on and on, and being intellectually lively and curious he thrusts upon us scholarly information and innumerable reflections on masses of subjects; Asian, European, religious, historical and mystical. Presumably the point is to show both the range of Rama's consciousness and the absolute relevance of the appearance–reality distinction, but even the most attentive and appreciative reader can find his concentration drooping.

The Serpent and the Rope is a rich and complex creation. Its defects are a tendency to slip too easily into formlessness or into the ineffable. There are also attempts, which fail, to employ Sanskrit rhythms in English. And if there is sometimes too tenuous a connection between the novel's highest flights and the humble details of ordinary existence, it is still clearly the work of a writer of exemplary integrity and of an artist with a pure and impressive talent. A fine and delicate vehicle for that talent is *The Cat and Shakespeare* (1965) which is much freer from the somewhat inhuman unattachment of *The Serpent and the Rope*. It is a *novella* of 117 pages marked by a patterned complexity and a subdued sardonic poetry.

The basic concern animating the fable is not much different from that in *The Serpent and the Rope*. It shows itself here as a scrutiny of being and individuality and, in particular, as the active contemplation of the ways in which appearance and reality approach one another, jostle, mimic and supplant one another, as they do in the narrator's relationships with his wife-like mistress and his money-driven business-woman wife. The reader is invited 'to weep on every page, not for what he sees but for what he sees he sees'. But not simply to weep because the questioning tone – which is mild on the part of the story-teller Ramakrishna Pai, and is caustically comic on that of his neighbour and fellow Ration Office clerk, Govindar Nan – opens the door to both simple gaiety and philosophical, or more precisely epistemological wit. And one notes also that while the questioning note in the narrator's tale is puzzled and plaintive, the interrogation of existence and its enigmas by Govindar Nan implies more positively that there may well be answers to these problems hidden in the traditional wisdom of the Hindus, and even that he quite possibly possesses the key to it.

In this story Raja Rao shows a gift for design less evident in the more diffuse and sometimes theoretical *The Serpent and the Rope*, and conspicuously absent in one of his final works, *Comrade Kirilov* (1976), which presents in rather essay-type form the opposing attractions of cerebral Soviet Marxism and historical Brahminical wisdom in the mind of a South Indian Brahmin, though without ever making a living union out of the two elements. But in *The Cat and Shakespeare* both the major themes and the smallest details fit vitally together. There is no separate conceptual cloud hovering over the story; no vague disconnected wash of feeling around its edges. The racial and poetic wisdom which is everywhere implicit, the evidence of Brahminical thought, the profoundly philosophical vision are all absorbed in, and sustained by, the particulars of the fable. The characters, Ramakrishna Pai, Govindar Nan, Horaham, John, Saroja and Shantha are both psychologically convincing and lucid and effective symbols; each is in Henry James's terms, 'a strikingly figured symbol' because each is also 'a thoroughly pictured creature'. And this is also true in its degree of the other details of the story, the Ration Office, the Ration Books, the cat, the rats, the work. They are also symbols which work, symbols with bite. Moreover the innumerable literary and philosophical hints and suggestions, the analogies, the muted quotations, the remote, insinuated connections which echo and re-echo throughout are used with that musical propriety, wholly different from merely explicit or pedagogic pointing, which is the infallible evidence of an authentic art.

It seems fitting to end these remarks on a genuinely 'difficult' writer with his own modest and concise account of his work.

> Starting from the humanitarian and romantic aspect of man in *Kanthapura* and *The Cow and the Barricades* [his early volume of short stories] – both deeply influenced by Mahatma Gandhi's philosophy of non-violence – I soon came to the metaphysical novel, *The Serpent and the Rope* and *The Cat and Shakespeare*, based on the Vedantic conceptions of illusion and reality. My main interest increasingly is in showing the complexity of the human condition (that is, the reality of man is beyond his person), and in showing the symbolic construct of one human expression. All words are hierarchic symbols, almost mathematical in precision, on and of the unknown.[7]

R. K. Narayan is the author of a substantial body of fiction, some dozen or more novels, all of them remarkably even in the quality of their achievement. The world established in these novels (although 'established' is too harsh a term for the delicate skill in implication everywhere evident) impresses the reader with its coherence, its personal stamp and idiom. The action is centred in the small town of Malgudi in Mysore – small by Indian standards, that is – and although the physical geography is never dealt with as a set piece but allowed to reveal itself beneath and between the events, one comes to have a strong feeling for the place's identity. The detail suggests, surely and economically, the special flavour of Malgudi, a blend of oriental and pre-1914 British, like an Edwardian mixture of sweet mangoes and malt vinegar: a wedding with its horoscopes and gold-edged, elegantly printed invitation cards; tiny shops with the shopkeeper hunched on the counter selling plantains, betel leaves, snuff and English biscuits; the casuarina and the Post Office Savings Bank; the brass pots and the volumes of Milton and Carlyle; the shaved head and ochre robes of the *sanyasi* and Messrs Binns' catalogue of cricket bats. Especially is this true of the details of public life, of the shabby swarming streets and the stifling by-lanes, the cobbles of Market Road and the sands on Sarayu bank, the banyan tree outside the central Co-operative Land Mortgage Bank (built in 1914), the glare of Kitson lamps and the open drain down Vinayah Mudali Street. Even the names strengthen this double quality: Nallappa's Grove and Albert College, Mill Street and the Bombay Ananda Bhavan (a restaurant), Kabir Street and Lawley Extension, the Mempi Hills and the Board

School; while Malgudi Station is both Euston and the East and the Krishna Medical Hall both ancient and modern medicine.

But although these novels convey so full and intimate a sense of place, they are not in any limiting way regional. They send out long, sensitive feelers to the villages where the inhabitants are 'innocent and unsophisticated in most matters excepting their factions and fights', and to the cities where they are 'so mechanical and impersonal'. They concern themselves too with such varied spheres of interest as business, education, journalism, film-making, money-lending. One must not, of course, exaggerate this matter of the scope of reference. Narayan does work by focusing his attention sharply. Part of his strength is never to ignore his instinct for limitation. But he has the serious artist's gift for achieving representativeness by concentration. His preoccupation is with the middle class, a relatively small part of an agricultural civilization and the most conscious and anxious part of the population. Its members are neither too well off not to know the rub of financial worry nor too indigent to be brutalized by want and hunger. They may take their religion more easily than the passionately credulous poor, but even in those with a tendency towards modernity one is always aware under the educated speech of the profound murmur of older voices, of 'Lakshmi, the Goddess of Wealth, the spouse of God Vishnu, who was the Protector of Creatures'.

Narayan chooses for his heroes – modest, un-selfconfident heroes, it is true – members of the middle class who are psychologically more active, and in whom consciousness is more vivid and harrowing. They have some room for independent, critical existence; but there is always a tension between this and that deep source of power, the family where the women rather than the old represent 'Custom and Reason' and know 'what is and what is not proper'. The family, indeed, is the immediate context in which the novelist's sensibility operates, and his novels are remarkable for the subtlety and conviction with which family relationships are treated – those of son and parents, and brother and brother in The Bachelor of Arts (1937); of husband and wife, and father and daughter in The English Teacher (1945); of father and son in The Financial Expert (1952), of grandmother and grandson in Waiting for the Mahatma (1955).

It is against the presence of the town, finely and freshly evoked, and amid a net of family relationships, each thread of which is finely and clearly elaborated, that Narayan's heroes engage in their characteristic struggles. The conditions of the struggle vary from novel to novel, the stress is highly particularized, the protagonist may be a student, a teacher, a financial expert, a fighter for emancipation. One still discerns beneath the diversity a common pattern, or predicament. What is so attractive about it is the charm and authenticity of its Indian colouring;

what makes it immediately recognizable is that it seems to belong to a substantial human nature. The primary aim of all these characters is to achieve, in the words of Chandran in *The Bachelor of Arts*, 'a life freed from distracting illusions and hysterics' (p. 132). (The 'distracting illusions' are in the Indian tradition; the freedom from 'hysterics' is the cool qualification introduced by Narayan. The complete phrase suggests the subdued association of seriousness and comedy which distinguishes the tone of these novels.) At first the intention is obscure, buried under the habits of ordinary life, personal responsibilities and – since this is India – a heavy, inherited burden. The novels plot the rise of this intention into awareness, its recognition in a crisis of consciousness, and then its resolution, or resolutions, since there are more often than not several mistaken or frustrated efforts at a resolution.

This theme – it does not seem extravagant to call it the aspiration towards spiritual maturity – is sustained throughout Narayan's work. Clearly it is one with its own special dangers. How easily it could slide into formlessness or puff itself into grandiosity. It is a remarkable achievement – given such a theme and an Indian setting – that Narayan's work is singularly free of pretentiousness. A cool sympathy, a highly developed sense of human discrepancy, a rare feeling for the importance and the density of *objects* – these check any straining after undue significance or any tendency to lapse into a search for large truths about life. In particular each stage of the impulse towards maturity is defined with meticulous accuracy in minutely specified circumstances, so that the reader is left not with a vague scheme of some dialectical progress but the conviction of an individual living his chequered, stumbling life. Let me give an illustration of this. Here is an example of one of these young men – it is Krishna and it occurs on the first page of *The English Teacher* – at the beginning of his development when what I have called the impulse or aspiration is still too dim to be recognized and when it simply produces vague feelings of dissatisfaction and irritable moods of brooding and analysis. 'The urge had been upon me for some days past to take myself in hand. What was wrong with me? I couldn't say, some sort of vague disaffection, a self-rebellion I might call it. The feeling again and again came upon me that as I was nearing thirty I should cease to live like a cow (perhaps, a cow, with justice, might feel hurt at the comparison), eating, working in a manner of speaking, walking, talking, etc. – all done to perfection, I was sure, but always leaving behind a sense of something missing.'

The same mild hopelessness, the same domestic accidie, is to be seen in Srinivas in *Mr. Sampath* (1949), a man so bogged down in indecision that 'the question of a career seemed to him as embarrassing as a physiological detail'. 'Agriculture, apprenticeship in a bank, teaching, law – he gave everything a trial once, but with every passing month he felt the excruciating pain of losing time. The passage of time depressed him. The ruthlessness with which it flowed on – a swift and continuous movement; his own feeling of letting it go helplessly, of engaging all his hours in a trivial round of actions, at home and outside.' It is present in the lighter, less formed character of Chandran in *The Bachelor of Arts*: 'Chandran emerged from the Professor's room with his head bowed in thought. He felt a slight distaste for himself as a secretary. He felt that he was on the verge of losing his personality' (p. 30). Even in *The Guide* (1958), Narayan's most complex novel, where the lines of development and of narrative are folded in subtler convolutions, one comes across this feeling of being lost in a pointless, endless routine, although here it is expressed in the nervier, more sophisticated manner proper to this 'advanced' character. 'But I was becoming nervous and sensitive and full of anxieties in various ways. Suppose, suppose – suppose? What? I myself could not specify. I was becoming fear-ridden. I couldn't even sort out my worries properly. I was in a jumble' (p. 102).

The issue from this malaise comes about through some critical event which precipitates a crisis of consciousness and a new effort of will. In *The English Teacher* the event is the illness and death of Krishna's wife, but more often it is a meeting or series of meetings. The meetings may be disconcerting or terrifying, bewildering or exalting. In *The Financial Expert*, Margayya, perhaps Narayan's most brilliant single comic creation, gradually realizes his desire for a life 'freed from illusions' (but for him this means ironically a life dedicated to the cult of money – not money which with gross simplicity is spent across the counter of a shop but money as a beautiful living force) in a series of encounters: first with Arul Doss, the dignified peon of the Co-operative Bank who shows up Margayya's utter insignificance, then with the strangely impressive priest in the seedy temple who rehearses him in rituals for propitiating the Goddess of Wealth, then with Dr Pal, 'journalist, correspondent and author', whose 'sociological' work, *Bed Life* (later changed to *Domestic Harmony*), combining the Kama Sutra with Havelock Ellis, eventually makes Margayya's fortune, and finally Mr Lal, the large, astute, but fundamentally uncomprehending businessman. The effect of these meetings, the effect of Sriram's exalting meeting with Gandhi in *Waiting for the Mahatma* or Chandran's baffling meeting with the middle-aged rake in Madras in *The Bachelor of Arts*, is to wake the character from 'an age-old somnolence', from what he now sees to have been his illusory and hysterical past and to determine him wholly in favour of a completely new life.

If the analysis of the subject's struggle to extricate himself from the habitual, dreamy automatism of his past – and in a country like India where the influence of the given is so powerful, the severity of the effort required must be arduous and intense – if this shows Narayan's gift for serious moral analysis, then the various solutions adopted by his *personae* in the search for another, more conscious life, exhibit his remarkable comic talent. (Not of course that the fiction offers a neatly logical division just like this. The serious and the comic flow in and out of one another throughout in an intricate, inseparable alliance.) Tracts of human experience are looked at with an affectionately ridiculing eye, and with that kind of humour in which the jokes are also a species of moral insight. Such treatment brings out the note of the bizarre, of human queerness, in the activities of many sorts of people: businessmen, printers, teachers, holy men, press agents, moneylenders. At our most commonplace we are all exotic if scrutinized by a fresh eye. The range is impressive but it has to be said that it follows naturally on Narayan's reading of the key experience at the heart of his novels. Since it was a meeting, the intervention of human difference, human otherness, into the hero's narcissistic world which first shattered it for him, he feels in response that he has to break out of his solipsistic circle into a novel, even a deliberately alien, field of action. To evoke so much variety with such casual, convincing authority and to make it also organic and functional testify to a notable and original talent.

Sometimes these solutions end in a moment of illumination like Krishna's vision of his dead wife in *The English Teacher* – 'a moment for which one feels grateful to Life and Death' (p. 184) – or in a total reversal like Margayya's bankruptcy, or even for Raju in *The Guide* in death. Often they show a character now more solid yet also more conscious, more finished, yet more sensitive, accepting, though with misgivings and backslidings, the responsibilities of ordinary life. Always they conclude on a note of acceptance. The following lines towards the end of *Waiting for the Mahatma* convey the feeling, although it is usually quieter and more implicit than this. 'For the first time these many months and years he had a free and happy mind, a mind without friction and sorrow of any kind. No hankering for a future or regret for a past. This was the first time in his life that he was completely at peace with himself, satisfied profoundly with existence itself. The very fact that one was breathing, feeling and seeing seemed sufficient matter for satisfaction now' (p. 237). 'Accepting' indeed, is the word which best defines the attitude, not just here but Narayan's attitude generally in the face of his experience. 'Welcome' would be too shrill and hearty, 'resignation' too passive and submissive. In any case his attitude is too nimble with irony for one or the other. And that irony, it should be noted, is an irony of recognition, not an irony of correction.

Perhaps irony is too sharp a word for the calm scrutiny turned on these ardent young men and earnest old ones. Irony has a social reference and the characters in these novels seem to be tested against something deeper than conscious, formulated standards. And irony is in place in the presence of corruption; but all these people, even the seedy, the stupid and the vain, retain a core of essential innocence. The naïveté of being human: that is the daring subject of this decidedly self-effacing writer.

For Narayan is not a pushing or intrusive novelist. He has no anxiety to be tugging at our sleeve or to be giving us a knowing look. He has no message, no doctrine. The half-baked is not an item in his diet. The acceptance of life, which his art expresses, has no doubt a root in the national condition. One feels that a more than individual sensibility – more than simply personal categories and feelings – is operating under the surface. But his acceptance, a kind of piety towards existence, is not simply an inherited temperament with its corresponding technique of passive reflection. It is something that has to be worked towards, grown up to, gradually matured. Nor is it – as I mean to imply by calling it 'piety' – in any way rapt or mystical but altogether homely and human. It includes delight in the expressive variety of life, cognisance of its absurdities, mockery at its pretensions and acknowledgement of its difficulties. And like other kinds of piety and other sorts of tradition, it tends to focus itself in objects. Objects become hallowed with more than their own nature and invested with singular and lasting importance. This appreciation of the weight, the form, the value of *things* is both a feature of the temperament sustained throughout these novels and a device of the art employed in their construction. It pins down and solidifies the lightness and fluency of a manner that might otherwise be too evasive, too 'spiritual'. The effect of Krishna's clock, of his father's 'steel pen with a fat green wooden handle' and his ink made up by hand in a careful, yearly ceremony, or of Sriram's teak and canvas chair, is to help to enclose the souls of these people in flesh, pitted, worn and ordinary flesh. Here is an example of this particularizing power of objects at work, a passage from *Mr. Sampath* which gives a new meaning to the words 'an object of sentimental value'.

> He prayed for a moment before a small image of Nataraja which his grandmother had given him when he was a boy. This was one of the possessions he had valued most for years. It seemed to be a refuge from the oppression of time. It was of sandal wood, which had deepened a darker shade with years, just four inches high. The carving represented Nataraja with one foot raised and one foot pressing down a demon, his four arms outstretched, with

his hair flying, the eyes rapt in contemplation, an
exquisitely poised figure. His grandmother had given it to
him on his eighth birthday. She had got it from her
father, who discovered it in a packet of saffron they had
bought from the shop on a certain day. It had never left
Srinivas since that birthday. It was on his own table at
home, or in the hostel, wherever he might be. It had
become part of him, the little image. He often sat before
it, contemplated its proportions and addressed it thus: 'Oh,
God, you are trampling a demon under your foot, and
you show us a rhythm, though you appear to be still.
May a ray of that light illuminate my mind.' He silently
addressed it thus. He never started his day without
spending a few minutes before this image. (p. 19)

The permanence of objects makes them a protection against the
oppression of time. Clearly the direct reference here is to the Indian
scene, to the hard agricultural tradition, the vast distances, the ruthless
climate, the terrible poverty. But it seems to me to have as well, like
so much in Narayan's writing, a measure of the wider validity that
belongs to genuine works of art – the universal imprisoned but visible
in the particular. In utterly different conditions, where nobody's grandmother could have handed down an image of Nataraja discovered by
her father in a packet of saffron, we are probably like Srinivas and
'grasp the symbol but vaguely'. And yet as we contemplate its proportions we are not, I think, deceived in detecting through the appearances
of stillness and strangeness a rhythm, the common and extraordinary
rhythm of life.

Narayan's novels belong to a difficult *genre*, the serious comedy.
Success in it calls for a sensibility preserved from ambivalence or frac-
ture, an unusual unity in the point of view as well as a social tradition
in which the comic and the sad are not sharply marked off one from
the other. It requires too a certain equanimity, an evenness of temperament and manner, to hold back both the exaggeration of farce and the
one-sidedness of sentimentality.

The Man-Eater of Malgudi (1962), and *The Sweet Vendor* (1967) show
Narayan at the pitch of his powers, and I should like now to look more
closely at these. In each he shows that peculiar discernment of the
novelist which can fix the authentic individuality of a character and
simultaneously establish it solidly in a social world. We see this clearly
at the beginning of *The Man-Eater of Malgudi*. Nataraj runs a modest
printing press in Market Road and lives at home with his wife and little
son, the traditional extended family in which they would normally
have lived having broken up in litigation and ill-tempered squabbles.

The wife keeps a well-stocked pantry, the kitchen fire aglow, and continues the traditions of the old home, while the young Babu goes to Albert Mission School and is adequately supplied with toys, books and sweets, as is the wife with silk saris glittering with lace for special occasions, and plenty of others, bought for no particular reason, at other times. For all this, Nataraj is grateful to the goddess Laxmi and has a framed picture of her poised on a lotus on the wall in the little room in front of his press in Market Road. His small establishment is next door to the prosperous Star Press which has a large staff and an original Heidelberg printing press, with groaning double cylinders. Nataraj, particularly when customers are present, is apt to shout for his foreman, his compositor, his office boy, or his binder, but in fact all he has in the way of staff is the respectable old man Mr Sastri, 'an orthodox-minded semi-scholar', who helps him to set up the type, print the forms, sew the sheets, and carry them away for ruling or binding. Nataraj is vague about the exact line between his establishment and the Star Press and importunate customers are sometimes passed through to the grander establishment to view the machinery: 'I was so free with the next-door establishment that no one knew whether I owned it or whether the Star owned me' (p. 5).

Nataraj uses the small room in front of his press as a club for his friends, so that the poet and the journalist who were his constant companions could endlessly rehearse events in the town and analyse the state of the nation. Indeed, anyone who found his feet aching as he passed down Market Road was welcome to visit Nataraj's parlour. Even the sanitary inspector, a parched and dehydrated man given to gulping down glasses of water in one mouthful, drops in for a rest and a chat when his limbs ache from too much supervision of the Market Road:

> I had furnished my parlour with a high-backed chair made
> of teak-wood in the style of Queen Anne, or so the
> auctioneer claimed who had sold it to my grandfather, a
> roll-top desk supported on bow-legs with ivy-vines carved
> on them, and four other seats of varying heights and
> shapes, resurrected from our family lumber room. (p. 1)

Character is action, and action is plot, and it is by means of the action of his character that Narayan summons up the world in which he lives. Nataraj is a nervy, friendly, unambitious man who could not explain himself to sordid and calculating people. He, his family, his friends, the district, the unfolding tissue of history, and the delicate film of relations among them, are established by means of a patient accumulation of detail, each point of which, whether common or not, is seen with freshness and organized with subtlety. On his way to the river to bathe in the morning before light, Nataraj has his established, well-defined encounters with the milkman, the old asthmatic at the end of the street, the watchman at the Taluk office, with his cousin who hated him for staying in the ancestral home, with the lawyer, Mr Adjournment (so called because of his skill in prolonging cases), and with the garrulous old septuagenarian who owned a dozen houses in the locality. Everything in this universe is concrete, manifold, multiplying backwards and forwards, so that the reader has a sense of life reported with infinite patience and completeness. The society is formal, but the relations are quick and spontaneous. Narayan has perfect pitch in his sense of human relationships. This is exactly what people say and do, this is precisely how they behave, we are persuaded simply by what we are shown, without explanation, analysis or theory. As Henry James said about Balzac, 'If he was a knowing psychologist he was so by grace; he was just and true without apparatus and without effort.'[8] Into this world composed of shades and subtleties of relationships, of tradition, of feeling, of ancient hallowed objects transmitted to the generations, of modes of conduct and habits of thought which are both realistic and homely, there suddenly intrudes the abstract and brutal will of 'H. Vasu, M.A., Taxidermist', as he is described on his card:

> Now an unusual thing happened. The curtain stirred, an
> edge of it lifted, and the monosyllabic poet's head peeped
> through. An extraordinary situation must have arisen to
> make him do that. His eyes bulged. 'Someone to see you,'
> he whispered.
> 'Who? What does he want?'
> 'I don't know.'
> The whispered conversation was becoming a strain. I
> shook my head, winked and grimaced to the poet that I
> was not available. The poet, ever a dense fellow, did not
> understand but blinked on unintelligently. The head
> suddenly vanished, and a moment later a new head
> appeared in its place – a tanned face, large powerful eyes
> under thick eyebrows, a large forehead and a chock of
> unkept hair, like a black halo. (pp. 12–13)

The reader will be struck by the concreteness of this passage, by the sharp sensory observation upon which it is based, by the simplicity of the line and the focusing upon significant points of action in the incident. The effect of these and of the extreme clarity of language brings home to one both the nervy, over-responsive psychology of

Nataraj and the unclogged, custom-free directness of Vasu. The symbol of the denying curtain means nothing to him. He is one who is the embodiment of will, who affronts the assumptions and despises the values Nataraj and his friends live by. His words and actions violate accepted manners and every tradition implicit in them. The phrase 'a black halo' with which the passage concludes, a submerged paradox, hints that Vasu may constiute a more obscure, profound threat to the system by which Nataraj and his neighbours live. It is a hint taken out of another sensitive place in the novel, even the phrase itself is repeated, and it gives a more general and religious significance to the tale of the taxidermist-hunter who goes from stuffing dead animals to killing live ones. Vasu is not only the present as opposed to the past, he is also a darker influence opposed to light and grace. Nataraj and his friends express a style of life and habit of sensibility sanctioned by the experience of generations. A complex, a practised exercise of memory makes them persons who are the product of history, but Vasu, in some ways like Patrick White's Voss in the novel of that name, is one in whom the will is unqualified by the past. It is a form of abstract causality, it simply and absolutely initiates action. Vasu is maddened by any whiff of what is established or unquestioned, because that would signify an external or impersonal discipline threatening his absolute status. Vasu disrupts arrangements, as for example when he leaves Nataraj high and dry after whipping him away into the forest in a jeep, or summoning Nataraj as a wrack-renting landlord after being given, or taking, free lodging; he excludes himself from the world of familiar intercourse, as when he rejects the friendship proffered by Nataraj and his friends or even the acquaintance of Nataraj's boy, Babu. He has a nihilistic and menacing air which becomes, in the Indian context, a force not negotiable on human terms.

The crisis of consciousness which extricates Nataraj from the protection of his daily routine, and from the deeper, impersonal passivity of his Indian past, is precipitated by the presence of the violent taxidermist-hunter, Vasu, who is not only a character, but an oppressive and disruptive force. He not only takes advantage of Nataraj, but shows him a motiveless enmity which leaves Nataraj, who cannot tolerate strain or hostility, distraught. Nataraj was not constructed to sustain enmity.

> I could never be a successful enemy to anyone. Any
> enmity worried me night and day. As a schoolboy I
> persistently shadowed around the one person with whom I
> was supposed to be on terms of hate and hostility. I felt
> acutely uneasy as long as our enmity lasted. (p. 93)

The opposition between the two is figured in their different relationships to animal life. Nataraj has been brought up in a house where he was taught never to kill, where even flies had to be swatted when the elders were not looking. His grand-uncle would give him a coin every morning to buy sugar for the ants, and kept an eye on him to see that he put it around the house. This uncle taught him that he must let the crows and sparrows share his food, and allow the squirrels and mice to deplete the granary in the house. But now his establishment had been turned into a charnel house. Whenever Vasu returned his jeep was loaded with bloody objects. He killed the establishment cat in order to do some research on the smaller feline species. He upset the neighbours with the stench of drying leather. A petition of complaint was got up by the neighbours and presented to the municipal authority complaining about his tanning of hides, the bad odours, and the carrion birds hovering above the terrace. 'One part of my mind admired my neighbours for caring so much for sanitation; the rest of it was seized with cold despair.' He kept a wooden chest filled with eyes, round ones, small ones, red ones, and black circles. As Vasu himself says:

'The first thing one does after killing an animal is to take out its eyes, for that's the first part to rot, and then one gives it new eyes like an optician. I hope you appreciate now what an amount of labour goes into the making of these things. We have constantly to be rivalling Nature at her own game. Posture, look, the total personality, everything has to be created.' This man had set himself as a rival to Nature and was carrying on a relentless fight. (p. 64)

Vasu is terrifying because he cancels out, by brutally refusing to acknowledge their existence, the values implicit in the life which Nataraj and his friends live.

In the contrast between Nataraj and Vasu, in the more and more frantic and frightened efforts of Nataraj to oppose Vasu, we see how Narayan writes within a settled scheme. The mode of belief, the pattern of life, the method of thinking and feeling, the historical inheritance and the characteristic reaction to the social and physical environment – all these recur in his novels. They are the conditions of the civilization Narayan seeks to embody and interpret. It is true, too, that the central predicament of the characters reappears in novel after novel, but the solution adopted by his protagonists, the particular escape from the precise predicament and the conditions in which it takes place – these are different from novel to novel, and show themselves to be capable of endless treatment since they are the constituents of a human experience which is inexhaustible in its content and significance.

The deeply serious idea which sustains *The Man-Eater of Malgudi*, namely the opposition between influences fostering life and those hostile to it, the quarrel between the god Vishnu and the *rakshasa*, is filtered through some of the lightest and yet most solidly established comedy in Narayan. It is comedy which is the issue of character, action and plot. Let me take just two examples. The first is a bus journey Nataraj has to take after being deserted by Vasu, who had dragged him away from work for some supposed emergency, at a café on the crossroads near the jungle. He has no money, but he insinuates himself into the favour of the proprietor whose private interest is the local temple which he has rebuilt with his own money. He is just about to celebrate the consecration of the temple on a grand scale with a procession led by an elephant, in which the goddess will be accompanied with pipes and music. Nataraj undertakes to print a thousand notices for him so that a big crowd will turn up on the day. The proprietor agrees to wait for payment for the buns and glasses of tea with which Nataraj keeps himself going, and uses his influence with the conductor of the bus to take Nataraj into town and wait for payment. The bus itself boasts a high signboard, 'Mempi Bus Transport Corporation', although everybody knew it was a vehicle picked up from a war-surplus dump. The conductor treats his passengers like erring pupils, warning them solemnly against being late. He is a car fanatic, and Nataraj obligingly invents a car he does not have, a fifty-one, four-door Morris, the possession of which the conductor regards as a guarantee of honesty and good sense:

> He had now developed a wholesome respect for me as a
> member of the automobile fraternity. He was prepared to
> overlook my unbuttoned shirt and dishevelled appearance
> and ticketless condition; I wished I had some more jargon
> to impress him further, but I had to manage as best I
> could with whatever rang in my memory as a result of the
> printing I had done for Ramu of Ramu's Service Station,
> who sometimes dropped in to talk of the state of the
> nation in the motoring world. (p. 50)

The first part of the journey of the packed and swaying bus proceeds with discipline and at a respectable pace because, as the conductor explains, 'The Circle is expected':

The word 'Circle' in these circumstances indicated the inspector of police for this circle, whose seat at the front was always reserved. If another passenger occupied it, it was a matter of social courtesy to vacate it or at least move up closer to the driver and leave enough space at the end of the seat for the Circle. Once, long, long ago, a planter returning to his estate created a lot of unpleasantness by refusing to make way for the Circle, with the result that the Circle was obliged to travel in one of the ordinary seats inside the bus, with the rabble, and at the next stop he impounded the whole bus with the passengers for overcrowding. (p. 51)

The Circle turns up, a swarthy man in a khaki uniform carrying his bicycle, which the constable loads on to the bus. When the stage at which the Circle disembarks is reached, the journey assumes a different aspect. The bus is driven recklessly, stops every ten minutes to pick up any wayside passengers, and pursues passengers in the remotest hamlets to ferret out possible custom. Thus, a three-hour jeep ride in the morning becomes an eight-hour return in the evening.

Nataraj's meeting with Mr Adjournment, the lawyer, is the second example. It takes place after Nataraj has received a summons from the rent collector accusing him of neglecting the premises and over-charging Vasu, who has not, of course, ever paid a penny rent:

> . . . even the sound of his footstep seemed to me aggressively tenant-like, strengthened by the laws of the rent-control court. He pretended that I did not exist. He seemed to arrive and depart with a swagger as if to say, 'You may have an adjournment now but the noose is being made ready for you'. (p. 92)

Nataraj has a shattering fear of courts and lawyers. First of all he hides the summons away giving himself a sense of reprieve. In the end he has to visit the lawyers. The lawyer when he meets him is panic-stricken, thinking that he has been cornered by Nataraj to extract the money he owes him for printing the invitations to his daughter's marriage. But reassured on this point he perks up and assumes a brusque and grand authority. His office is perched on top of a ware-house full of bales of cotton. Any litigant who is interviewed here is likely to get asthma, at least a cold, and Nataraj's eyes are streaming with hayfever by the time he gets to the office, a positively Dickensian place:

Our lawyer's chamber was right on the landing, which
had been converted into a room, with one table, one
chair, and one bureau full of law-books. His clients had to
stand before him and talk. The table was covered with
dusty paper bundles, old copies of law reports, a dry ink-
well, an abandoned pen, and his black alpaca coat, going
moss-green with age, hung by a nail on the wall. Down
below, the cotton-fluffers kept up a rhythmic beating. He
had a very tiny window with wooden bars behind him,
and through it one saw the coconut tree by a
neighbouring house, a kitchen chimney smoking, and a
number of sloping roof-tiles, smoky and dusty, with
pieces of tinsel thrown away by someone gleaming in the
bright sun. (p. 79)

The relationships between the two are now turned around. Nataraj is
the client seeking a favour, the lawyer the lordly dispenser of one.
Most of the time is spent discussing how Nataraj will pay the lawyer's
fee. It is essential, the lawyer insists again and again, that accounts be
kept separately, and that what he owes Nataraj must lead a wholly
separate existence from what Nataraj owes him: which must, of
course, be paid at once.

Some of the best of the spry and mellow comedy of *The Man-Eater
of Malgudi* depends on Nataraj's increasingly frantic efforts at rendering
the oppressive presence of Vasu at least tolerable. On the face of it he
is working purely in the field of action to circumvent Vasu's persecution of the animals and the harassment of himself:

He brought in more and more dead creatures; there was
no space for him in his room or on the terrace. Every
inch of space must have been cluttered with packing-
boards and nails and skins and moulds. The narrow
staircase, at which I could peep from my machine, was
getting filled up with his merchandise, which had now
reached the last step – he had left just enough margin for
himself to move up and down. He had become very busy
these days, arriving, departing, hauling up or hauling
down packing-cases, doing everything single-handed. I had
no idea where his market was. In other days I could have
asked him, but now we were bitter enemies. I admired
him for his capacity for work, for all the dreadful things
he was able to accomplish single-handed. If I had been on
speaking terms, I'd have congratulated him unreservedly
on his success as a taxidermist – his master Suleiman must

really have been as great as he described him. He had
given his star pupil expert training in all branches of his
work. Short of creating the animals, he did everything.
(pp. 92–93)

But anything Nataraj can think of is hopelessly inadequate to effect the
deeper reconciliation that his nature and indeed the character of the
community call for. Nataraj cannot convert Vasu into a friend, while
he finds open hostility insupportable. He cannot be reconciled with
Vasu because this means reconciling two different and hostile orders
of reality. Or, as the pious foreman Sastri puts it, Vasu satisfies all the
definitions of a *rakshasa*, and to deal with such a one needs the marks-
manship of the hunter, the wit of a pundit, and the guile of a harlot.
Sastri defines a *rakshasa* as:

> . . . a demoniac creature who possessed enormous
> strength, strange powers, and genius, but recognized no
> sort of restraints of man or God. He said, 'Every *rakshasa*
> gets swollen with his ego. He thinks he is invincible,
> beyond every law. But sooner or later something or other
> will destroy him.' (pp. 95–96)

Both his friends and the community at large flinch from the effort
to enfold in an acceptable embrace the malevolently unclaspable Vasu.
Men as tough as the police inspector and the game-warden, strong
voices of the community's outraged authority, recoil at Vasu's
combination of ferocity and legal know-how. All his friends can do
is to copy the poet and develop 'the art of surviving Vasu's presence'.
The problem is to assimilate a wholly alien force, and neither Nataraj
himself nor his immediate circle, nor the community, whether in the
town or the village, is capable of solving the problem. As a result they
all feel to some degree what becomes almost unbearable in Nataraj,
the emotion of panic, that special resonance of disordered feeling which
accompanies the disintegration of the premises of thought and action.

The climax of the comedy and the resolution of the problem of an
assimilation come together in Vasu's grotesque death. He has an overwhelming loathing for mosquitoes and he has made himself, over many
years of superhuman strength, with hands trained to batter thick panels
of teak and iron. In crushing a mosquito on his forehead with his own
fist while he waits in the dark to shoot the sacred elephant, he slaugh-
ters himself. The fantasy of this has been carefully prepared for and
it fits without friction the final 'explanation' of Vasu. He becomes
explicable, as well as dead, when it is realized that he is really some-
body for whom 'the black halo of hair' was wholly suitable. The Man-

eater of Malgudi finally takes his place in the community as a *rakshasa*, a demon, the other side of life. All his enormities now fall into place: his absolute rejection of everything Nataraj and his friends live by now makes sense and indeed testifies to the sanity of the assumptions they had begun to doubt; and everyone takes comfort, especially Nataraj, from grasping that even had he not died he could be certainly relied upon to bring about his own destruction. That it was the frailest of animals, the mosquito, which helped him, the exterminator of animals and the eater of men, to his own death, clinches the lightly drawn parable:

> 'He had one virtue, he never hit anyone with his hand, whatever the provocation,' I said, remembering his voice. 'Because,' said Sastri puckishly, 'he had to conserve all that might for his own destruction. Every demon appears in the world with a special boon of indestructibility. Yet the universe has survived all the *rakshasas* that were ever born. Every demon carries within him, unknown to himself, a tiny seed of self-destruction, and goes up in thin air at the most unexpected moment. Otherwise what is to happen to humanity?' (p. 21)

Sastri's remarks; contingent, interrogative, plaintive but not querulous, offering a modest word of hope about the possibilities of human survival, indicate the quality of the quietly complex tone of Narayan's fiction. His novels make no large claims, assert no tremendous faith. Sastri's words indicate pretty well its measure and character. But as Narayan's work has matured, or perhaps simply as he has grown older, the manner in which he expresses his belief in the nature of whatever it is that supports a hope for humanity becomes less diffident. What at the end of *The Guide* is only the most feathery intimation has become in *The Man-Eater of Malgudi*, in spite of the fantasy of its context, a less oblique statement of his belief in the sustaining role of some other influences – the blessings of the gods or just the stubbornness of life itself.

The Man-Eater of Malgudi can be read as the conflict between the insulated personality and the open and vulnerable one. Or it can be taken as a dramatization of the theory of the necessary flaw, the mysterious balance tremblingly sustained in being by fallibility. This germinal idea, although in another of its aspects, appears again in *The Sweet Vendor*. It is also the technique, now marvellously burnished and prompt to serve every turn of the writer's intention, which brings *The Man-Eater of Malgudi* and *The Sweet Vendor* so close together. Each is written in Narayan's even, limpid manner, without purple passage or

et piece. The basic unit of his narrative, if one can use the term, is
he incident, the event happening, which accounts for the impression
f mobility his novels invariably give. Complex action, even if it is
f the most muted kind, goes on all the time. The exploitation of
ncident, a blend of event, action, context, motive, memory, feeling,
ause and effect, is a perfect target for Narayan. The movement
onveys that sense of flux in human life of which he is so conscious,
nd the transparency of surface, characteristic of his writing, draws the
eader's attention down to deeper levels, a middle level of motivation
nd individual psychology and a more profound level of poetic myth
nd instinctive communal awareness. The effect of this method and of
he lucidity of the idiom is to render the reader sensitive to the woven,
n-going unity of human action.

For example, the incident with which *The Sweet Vendor* opens is a
mall excerpt from experience, issuing not only from a single lifetime
ut from generations, and only with difficulty to be separated from
he flow of life; it is itself an emblem and an instance of continuity.
t is also both suggestive about the nature of the theme to be developed
nd illustrative of the ordinary, limited intelligence of the character to
e developed:

> 'Conquer taste, and you will have conquered the self,' said
> Jagan to his listener, who asked, 'Why conquer the self?'
> Jagan said, 'I do not know, but all our sages advise us so.'
>   The listener lost interest in the question; his aim was
> only to stimulate conversation, while he occupied a low
> wooden stool next to Jagan's chair. Jagan sat under the
> framed picture of the goddess Lakshmi hanging on the
> wall, and offered prayers first thing in the day by
> reverently placing a string of jasmine on top of the frame;
> he also lit an incense stick and stuck it in a crevice in the
> wall. The air was charged with the scent of jasmine and
> incense and imperceptibly blended with the fragrance of
> sweetmeats frying in ghee, in the kitchen across the hall.
> (p. 13)

Jagan, a maker and seller of sweets, at fifty-five is slight and balding.
He shaves only at intervals since he regards looking at oneself in the
mirror every day as a detestable European affectation. He is a man
given to saws and apothegms, quotations from the scriptures and
unexamined assumptions. He is frequently racked with the problem
of national improvement in various directions. He has evolved a
number of prim theories about diet, nutrition, and hygiene and has
written these up in a *magnum opus* on Nature Cure and Nature Diet,

which has been waiting to be printed at Nataraj's Truth Press for th
past several years. He is observant of custom, scrupulous about ritua
a disciple of Gandhi, spins the material for his clothes with his ow
hands as the Mahatma prescribed, and, as one would expect, hi
sandals are made from the hide of a cow that has died from sicknes
or old age. He often had to spend time searching the villages for a
animal in this category. At one time (much to the disgust of his wife
he even tanned the leather in his own outhouse. 'I do not like to thin
that a living creature should have its throat cut for the comfort of m
feet. . . .' Wearing his non-violent footwear, as Narayan calls it, an
peering through a pair of narrow, almond-shaped glasses, he perche
on a century-old brassbound chair like a throne, presiding over
universe of kitchen smoke and frying oil and supervising his staff o
cooks and sellers, his eyes unflinchingly fixed on the pages of th
Bhagavad-Gita until he becomes conscious of the slightest break in th
routine of cooking and selling, when he would shout:

> 'Captain! – that little girl in the yellow skirt, ask her what
> she wants. She has been standing there so long!' His shout
> would alert the counter-attendant as well as the watchman
> at the door, an ex-army man in khaki, who had a
> tendency to doze off on his dealwood seat. Or Jagan
> would cry, 'Captain, that beggar should not be seen here
> except on Fridays. This is not a charity home.' (p. 20)

Jagan's character also contains that small flaw making for safety. Int
the largeness of his spiritual ambition, into his Imitation of Gandhi
there is inserted a small measure of mercantile flexibility. This enable
him, when his staff has been paraded and dismissed for the night, to
make up two cash books. One consists of entries in a small private not
book, the other of elaborate entries in a ledger that can be inspected
by anybody:

> In his small notebook he entered only the cash that came
> in after six o'clock, out of the smaller jug. This cash was
> in an independent category; he viewed it as free cash,
> whatever that might mean, a sort of immaculate
> conception, self-generated, arising out of itself and entitled
> to survive without reference to any tax. It was converted
> into crisp currency at the earliest moment, tied into a
> bundle and put away. . . . (p. 20)

Jagan is both a comic and an anguished figure: comic in his innocen
combination of commercial sharpness, fiscal duplicity, vanity, and
genuine reverence for Gandhian spirituality; anguished in his lacerated

elationship with his sullen, brutish son Mali. He doted on this boy,
poiled him, and found him, as he grew up, utterly incomprehensible
- both his motives and his assumptions quite beyond Jagan's grasp.
Mali announces while he is still at college that he cannot study any
more, and leaves to become a writer. Having written nothing, he
eaves for America to take a course in creative writing at Michigan;
he returns with an American-Korean girl-friend whom Jagan believes
to be his wife, with a scheme to be financed by his father to the tune
of 51,000 dollars – and he is not above blackmailing his father about
the immaculately generated cash hidden in the loft. The plan involves
manufacturing story-telling machines, presumably a species of
computerized typewriter:

> The son looked pityingly at him, rose, opened a packing
> case, pushed aside a lot of brown paper and thread and
> lifted out a small object which looked like a radio cabinet
> and placed it on the table. 'I was only waiting for this to
> arrive; yesterday I had to clear it from the railway office.
> What a lot of time is wasted here! I have never seen a
> more wasteful country than this.' Jagan refrained from
> retorting, 'We find it quite adequate for our purpose.'
> Now Mali stood beside the cabinet in the attitude of a
> lecturer; he patted it fondly and said, 'With this machine
> anyone can write a story. Come nearer and you will see it
> working.' Jagan obediently pushed his chair back, rose and
> stood beside his son, who seemed to tower above him. He
> felt proud of him. 'God knows what he eats out of those
> tins; he looks tired, no doubt, but how well grown he is!'
> he reflected as Mali explained, 'You see these four knobs?
> One is for characters, one for plot situation, one for
> climax, and the fourth is built on the basis that a story is
> made up of character, situations, emotion and climax, and
> by the right combination. . . .' He interrupted his oration
> for a moment to pull a drawer out and glance at a
> cyclostyled sheet of paper; he shut the drawer and came
> back to say, 'You can work on it like a typewriter. You
> make up your mind about the number of characters. It
> works on a transistor and ordinary valves. Absolutely
> fool-proof. Ultimately we are going to add a little fixture,
> by which any existing story could be split up into
> components and analysed; the next model will incorporate
> it.' (pp. 82–83)

Jagan is sad too in his solitariness. His wife is dead, his son cannot
stand him, his other relatives look on him as an outcast. 'His elder

brother had once remarked, "How can you expect a good type of son
when you have a father like Jagan?"' The pathetic side of Jagan is, as
we could expect from one who sees human nature as Narayan does,
nicely balanced by his comic gratitude at thus being released from
family obligations:

> Otherwise they would be making constant demands on his
> time and energy, compelling him to spend his time in
> family conclaves, sitting on carpets with a lot of kinsmen
> exchanging banalities while awaiting the call for the feast.
> Thus he had escaped the marriages of his nieces, the
> birthdays of his brother's successive children and several
> funerals. (p. 126)

This contrariety of trait and tone which yet make a unified, substantial character, follows Jagan through to the high point of his life and
of the novel, his decision to retire from the world, to detach himself
from 'a set of repetitions performed for sixty years' in order to spend
the rest of his life helping a mystical stonemason – in private life a hair-
dyer – to carve a pure image of the goddess for others to contemplate.
The goddess herself is described by the sculptor with a lyrical intensity
rare in Narayan:

> She is the light that illumines the Sun himself. She
> combines in her all colours and every kind of radiance,
> symbolized by five heads of different colours. She
> possesses ten hands, each holding a conch, which is the
> origin of sound, a discus, which gives the universe its
> motion, a goad to suppress evil forces, a rope that causes
> bonds, lotus flowers for beauty and symmetry, and a
> kapalam, a begging bowl made of a bleached human skull.
> She combines in Her divinity everything we perceive and
> feel from the bare, dry bone to all beauty in creation.
> (p. 125)

The sculptor explains that his master had constantly meditated on the
form of this goddess, and now that he is dead he himself wishes to
abandon all other work – in this case the cosmetic blackening of elderly
men's heads – to devote his life to the aim. But he needs a helper. It
is at this point that Jagan's decision to join him is made. It is, of course,
a decision in the classical Indian line requiring, as Jagan puts it, that
at some stage in one's life one must uproot oneself from one's accustomed surroundings and disappear so that others can continue in peace:

It would be the most accredited procedure according to
our scriptures – husband and wife must vanish into the
forest at some stage in their lives, leaving the affairs of the
world to younger people. (p. 126)

Jagan's renunciation of the world, then, is of a piece with the Indian
tradition. But he is also pushed into it by his personal circumstances:

Jagan felt so heartily in agreement that he wanted to
explain why he needed an escape – his wife's death, his
son's growth and strange development, how his ancient
home behind the Lawley statue was beginning to resemble
hell on earth – but he held his tongue. (p. 126)

The angularities of Jagan's character persist even into the act of
renunciation. He is aggrieved, for example, that he is not receiving a
grand, crowded send-off as he did when he was gaoled during the Quit
India campaign. He finds the odour of sacrifice abating almost as soon
as he has made his choice. Like a sound businessman he arranges for
his shop to be opened and worries where he should leave his keys.
Being Jagan, his total denial of the things of the world is qualified by
an appealing human blemish. He cannot refrain from taking his cheque
book with him as a comfort in his exile in the spiritual world. This
is decidedly a small flaw making for safety since it enables him to
rescue his son when he is arrested for drunken driving. But, for all this,
for Jagan himself renunciation is a very big decision, too big in some
ways for his surface or immediate personality, which is dry, fussy,
narrow, commercial and self-regarding. What is necessary to make this
Jagan into a world-renouncing Jagan was supplied by the Indian
religious tradition. The warmth, richness and strength of that tradition
are evoked for the reader by Jagan's detailed and tender memories,
tactfully placed in the middle of this quirky and bleak phase of the
novel, in the earliest days of his marriage: the pilgrimage to beg the
god to favour his wife with fertility, and the conception and birth of
Mali. Even a nature as thin as Jagan's, it becomes clear, is able to be
fed from deep and more than personal sources. Part of Narayan's gift
as a novelist of a more inclusive life is the delicacy and firmness with
which such depths are implied in the structure of his characters. The
gift depends partly upon the power and inclusiveness of the Indian
tradition, partly upon Narayan's own profound acceptance of it, and
partly, as far as the reader is concerned, most, on Narayan's beautifully
executed evocation of the actual presence and specification of the
tradition in the life of the town. The suggested halo of significance
follows naturally upon the meticulously defined detail.

Three areas of the life renounced by Jagan are drawn with the crisp-
est line and shade in *The Sweet Vendor*. First the steady encircling
routine of the community of Malgudi, which laps Jagan round with
the certainties of history and the stability of current relationships, and
which, while testing and proving him in a dozen ways, confirms his
identity and value. Then there is his work as the proprietor of an
establishment making and selling sweets. Narayan is much drawn to
the truth of character shown in a person's work in which the stretched
personality submits itself to impersonal ends, and he describes with
precise effective care the style and method, the ritual and satisfaction
of Jagan's work. Then there is the ambiguous and dangerous ground
of his relations with his son, the sullen Westernized Mali, whose
contemptuous explanations to his bewildered father include all the
divisions which so maddeningly separate the two of them, the division
of East and West, of young and old, of child and parent.

This triple structure makes a composition marked by the combined
ease and authority of an artist in full control of his instrument and
material and it supports a world which has a background, a context,
an immediate presence and a nervous individual centre; a world which
impresses the reader with the quality of its completeness.

When Jagan retires from life – 'I am going to watch a goddess come
out of a stone' – he does so almost unromantically. He seems to be
doing so for comparatively external reasons because of the hell which
his son Mali has made of his life at home, or because he can no longer
face the incomprehensibility of conduct beyond his understanding:

> Puzzling over things was enervating. Reading a sense into
> Mali's actions was fatiguing like the attempt to spell out a
> message in a half-familiar script. (p. 182)

But the real reason is more inward. His life, or that part of it, he
realizes is complete. It has achieved whatever shape it is capable of.
Enlightenment means realizing that one has come to the point at which
struggle and all the comedy of friction are irrelevant. It means recog-
nizing and accepting the bitter conclusion I have referred to more than
once, Narayan's bleak belief that loneliness is the only truth of life. It
is a truth which strikes one with force and clarity as one shares in a
life like Jagan's, so warmly surrounded by a community and so totally
involved in work and family. Mobility, shape and the significance of
completeness – these are the values, and they are not only Indian ones,
which animate Narayan's pure, disinterested art. This specifically
Indian value, the necessity of imperfection, is conveyed in the general
substance and tone of this novel, and in particular in one passage which
offers a small and lucid image of Narayan's utter conviction about this

ruth of experience which is, no doubt, his uniquely individual way
of communicating the sense – crisp and unrebellious – of human
imitation. There is a meeting between Jagan and the stone-carver amid
a grove of casuarina trees in a mysterious garden which contains a
pond covered with blue lotus and a small shrine supported by stone
pillars:

> I always remember [says the sculptor to Jagan] the story
> of the dancing figure of Nataraj, which was so perfect that
> it began a cosmic dance and the town itself shook as if an
> earthquake had rocked it, until a small finger on the figure
> was chipped off. We always do it now; no one ever
> notices it, but we always create a small flaw in every
> image; it's for safety. (p. 119)

I feel it would be wrong to end my consideration of the senior
Indian novelists in English, the founding fathers of the *genre*, without
a note on G. V. Desani, a writer of the same generation as Mulk Raj
Anand, Raja Rao and R. K. Narayan and the author of one extraordinary book. He has an unusual background. He was born in Nairobi
in 1909. He was a Reuters correspondent, a lecturer for the British
Ministry of Information during the Second World War, a BBC broad
caster and then for some twenty years the inmate of monasteries in
India, Burma and Japan. From 1960 to 1968 he was a newspaper
columnist in India and since 1969 he has been a Professor of Philosophy
in the University of Texas. The extraordinary book is *All About H.
Hatterr* published in 1948 and revised in 1970. (Desani's other writings
consist of a few short stories and a prose poem in dramatic form, *Hali*
(1950), which most modern readers would find vague, idealistic in a
gaseous way and intolerably rhetorical.) *All About H. Hatterr* is a
turbulent, deflationary, bawling, magnificently irregular account of the
weird self-education of the fantastic H. Hatterr. It is written 'in what
may be termed', says Anthony Burgess in his enthusiastic and cogent
introduction, 'whole language, in which philosophical terms, the
colloquialisms of Calcutta and London, Shakespearian archaisms,
whinings, quack spiels, references to the Hindu pantheon, the jargon
of Indian litigation, and irritability seethe together.'[9] To this catalogue
we should also add as influences Rabelais, Chaucer, Kipling, Wilde,
Joyce, *The Magnet*, and P. G. Wodehouse. This tumult of sound and
semi-sense – in which an organizing principle is associated, frank,
oblique or hidden – is subject, as Anthony Burgess also makes clear,
to the control of an intricate pattern: seven meetings with seven sages
in seven cities; seven lengthy lessons and seven energetic bouts of
learning; seven superbly comic discussions of seven aspects of living

with his friend Benneroji; seven efforts to teach the lesson to others
– it is worthy of a wild-eyed Indian Joyce but one whose humorous
sanity, however disillusioned, is never cynical.

There would seem to be very little in common between G. V.
Desani, the master of the absurd, and Mulk Raj Anand, the novelist
as social reformer, Raja Rao the novelist as metaphysical poet and
R. K. Narayan, the novelist as moral analyst. They would certainly
find his whole manner and approach relentlessly bantering and self-
mocking, and his choice of narrator, an enlightened clown and auto-
didact, the son of a European seaman and an Indian woman from
Malaysia, utterly alien. And yet threading their way through the comic
rhetoric and the welter of quips and literary allusions are themes all
these novelists are concerned with: the nature of individuality, the
development of the person in a society weighed down by inherited
assumptions, the relationship of appearance and reality, the cogency
of the ancient Indian myths, the cyclical swirl of existence. But most
pointedly they all share a debt to the English language and to English
literature and to its power to serve and to express distinguished talent
of such various kinds. Each has his own way of acknowledging this
debt. G. V. Desani's is shown in his delicious account of his arrival
in England.

> All my life I wanted to come: to the Poet-Bard's adored
> Eldorado, to England, the God's own country, the seat of
> Mars, that demi-paradise . . . And now I have arrived.
> The realization made me feel humble, and O. H. M. S.
> post-haste, thank Almighty for same.
> Forgetting all reserve, forsaking all Do-as-Romans-do
> etiquette, and in full view of Liverpool's sardonically
> inclined docker population and the vastly jocose ship's
> sailor-company, I greeted the soil, both in the true English
> and the Eastern fashion.
> I took off my tropical-lid, the sola-topi, in sincere
> salutation, and next, without a waterproof, in my white
> drill shorts, I knelt on the mud-beds of the old country
> the soft depths of its textilopolis County Palatine, aye,
> keeper, luv, the blessed wet earth of Liverpool, Lancs., in
> a thousand salaams. (p. 36)

References

1. *Perspectives on Mulk Raj Anand*, ed. K. K. Sharma (Ghaziabad, 1978), p. 52.
2. Op. cit., p. 54.
3. Op. cit., p. xiv.
4. Commonwealth Literature ed. James Vinson (London) 1979), p. 22
5. *Perspectives on Mulk Raj Anand*, p. 50
6. *British Commonwealth Literature*, ed. David Daiches (London 1971), Vol. I, p. 437.
7. *Contemporary Novelists*, ed. James Vinson (London and Chicago, 1972), p. 1042.
8. *The House of Fiction: Henry James*, eds Leon Edel and Rupert Hart-Davis (London, 1957), p. 94.
9. *All About H. Hatterr* (London, 1970), p .10.

Chapter 4

The Succession: From Khushwant Singh to Salman Rushdie

I begin this chapter on the Indian novelists who succeeded the founding fathers of the form in an unconventional way with Khushwant Singh (born 1915) who is better known as an eminent Sikh historian, editor and journalist rather than a novelist. He has written just a handful of short stories and a couple of novels, *Train to Pakistan* (1956) and *I Shall Not Hear the Nightingale* (1959). I shall adopt a simple chronological order throughout this chapter since there is no convincing pattern of development among these writers discernible to the impartial spectator.

I Shall Not Hear the Nightingale has few of the qualities of the earlier book. It is by turns sentimental and cynical and has little of the springy ongoing impulsion of *Train to Pakistan*. Sher Singh, the well-off son of the Chief Magistrate, is seen at the start with his gang of layabout cronies as shrill and affected. His and their posturing at a time when great events are on the move – the time is 1942 to 1943 – diminishes them and indeed the national re-awakening. This kind of feeble corruption is exhibited throughout, and the novel seems designed to show the writer's disgust with the worst faults of national character which are made to appear even more distasteful as independence is imminent. The novel has a dour, disillusioned and irritable atmosphere.

In all this it contrasts strongly with *Train to Pakistan*, which is a tense, economical novel, thoroughly true to the events and the people in the story. It goes forward in a trim, athletic way and its unemphatic voice makes the horrors it describes all the more telling. The setting is the communal massacres which followed partition in 1947, and we see them through the eyes of the Sikh and Muslim inhabitants of the Punjab village of Mano Majra, who have lived together in peace for generations. Informing everything that happens are the sensibility and the style of living of the Sikhs. All that we need to know about their background is given in a few preparatory sentences.

> The Sikhs, who emerged as a separate religious
> community in the fifteenth and sixteenth centuries with

the intention of bringing the Hindus and Muslims
together, became militantly anti-Muslim after severe
persecution by Muslim rulers. Their faith and way of life
have much in common with their parent communities.
The Sikhs number about five million. . . . They are a
peasant people who won renown as some of the finest
soldiers in the British army.

Unlike the subjective and, it must be said, self-indulgent *I Shall Not
Hear the Nightingale* (itself an appropriately sentimental, self-pitying
title), *Train to Pakistan* impresses with the author's control, calm objectivity and self-effacement. The treatment, in fact, approximates to the
documentary, a most unusual mode among Indian novels. The objectivity, detachment and impartiality of *Train to Pakistan* make the
horrors it describes – a train standing in the station crammed with Sikh
corpses from Pakistan, another packed with Muslims massacred in
India – with all their madness and ferocity all the more convincing,
all the more devastating. There is no merciful mist shrouding these
accurately reported calamities.

In using such terms as objective, impartial, accurate, detached, I do
not at all wish to imply a lack of imaginative power in the author of
Train to Pakistan or to reduce it to the level of competent journalism.
On the contrary, its varied and strongly individualized characters, its
sense of place and ethos, its feeling for the spirit and style of the Sikhs
are the products of resourceful imaginative strength capable of
imparting life to character and drama to plot. Khushwant Singh's
clipped military prose communicates in its direct unadorned way
surprising subtleties of personality and shades of feeling. Mr Hakum
Chand, magistrate and deputy Commissioner, for all his tastes for
skin-lotion, perfumed talc and young girls hired from venal guardians,
his administrative cunning and corrupted conscience, yet surprises us
with an authentic basic human kindness – even a sort of innocence. His
creature, the sub-inspector of police, is a coarser, more whole-hearted
villain, alert to take up any hint from his devious though troubled
master, and quick to carry it out as brutally as possible. Iqbal Singh,
the ardent, ambitious and nervously hygienic party member, who
despised both his obtuse political masters and the stupidly superstitious
peasants – as he sees them – who are incapable of becoming a real
proletariat, is in his ingenuous moral simplicity a natural victim. In
spite of his town-bred sophistication, he is played like a mouse by the
real wielders of power. These contemporary Indian types throw into
vivid contrast the beautifully evoked peasants, the pious temple
attendant, the gentle ineffective Muslim elder, the ordinary folk and
the local criminals, as well as the wild village tough who will turn out

to be a genuine hero. Together they make up a whole world in miniature. It is a world given shape and coherence by the evoked spirit of the Sikh religion, at once austere and ferocious, and the tactfully realized, deeply impressive details of Sikh life and community. It is this last, 'the accumulation of secondary experience' as Henry James calls it, which provides the human context, the base from which we observe the unimaginable horrors for which human kind can be responsible.

The potent effect of *Train to Pakistan* comes from its releasing great forces, negative and destructive forces, within a tightly defined and packed traditional context; its art comes from the intelligent management of these to serve the revelation of what communal man is capable of as much as what the singular individual may on occasion aspire to. Its technique is largely based on the use of statement rather than suggestion of precise, complete statement which carries within it a strong sense of unaffected sincerity and plain truth.

Train to Pakistan is a novel in which the central experience and the essential meaning are firmly contained within a narrative frame. Another kind of novel attempts to make the narration itself an echoing analogue of the meaning and experience which are the substance of the story. A brilliant example of this kind is Raja Rao's *The Serpent and the Rope* (1960). Another is *The Dark Dancer* (1959) by Balachandra Rajan, an academic who has worked in England, India and Canada and who was for a period a senior Indian diplomat at the United Nations. This cultivated and sensitive novel associates the Bloomsbury cult of personal relationships, so exquisitely realized in the best work of E. M. Forster and Virginia Woolf, with an Indian version of Keats's purpose – to school an intelligence and make it a soul. It is a work lit with quick, glinting insight and many kinds of explicit and muted literary reference. It is indeed a distinctly literary and sophisticated novel and an unusual production on the Indian scene. But just as its themes and *personae* seem a degree too remote, too civilized, so its style seems too bookish, too deliberate: as, I think, even the opening paragraph with its too careful arrangement and elaborate figuring shows.

> It was where he was born, but where he was born
> didn't matter. There was nothing in the cracked arid earth
> to suggest that he belonged to it, or in the river, shrunk
> away from the banks, that seemed almost to wrench its
> way through the landscape, startling the brown into green.
> The soil track, ran forward like an act of the will straining
> across the flat baked plain, to the first muddle of houses;
> and then the road forked from it, driving relentlessly
> through the mantle of dust to an end that might have been
> reached from any beginning.

The quotation from Balachandra Rajan is given not only to illustrate a point about *The Dark Dancer* but also to indicate one of the two extremes between which Indian writing in English moves. One is an emphatically formal English literary manner as used by Rajan. The other is a much more markedly Indian English like that employed by Mulk Raj Anand with the headlong pace of its prose rhythm and the abundance of translations and transcriptions from Urdu and Punjabi. In between leaning towards the Indian side are Raja Rao and R. K. Narayan while Anita Desai approaches more closely to the English mode. One oddity is the apparent failure so far, in spite of its influence on English English, of American English to affect the tone and run of Indian English.

Quite another tradition of English writing, non-linguistic and certainly minor, is represented by the novels of Manohar Malgonkar, born in 1913. This is the line of the pacy romantic novel of action stretching from its refined form in John Buchan, to a rougher sort in John Masters. Malgonkar, who writes in a strikingly British idiom, like other writers of this kind admires military virtues, coherent characters performing orthodox roles, narrative gusto, and neat plots, often with a historical background. His career as a senior army officer, a big-game hunter and a gentleman farmer together with a sturdy independence of the spirit of the age has certainly equipped him for this kind of fiction. *The Distant Drum* (1960) is a racy, informed and rather admiring account of the Indian army from an officer's point of view. *A Bend in the Ganges* (1964) is set against the horrors of the partition of India but is much less effective than *Train to Pakistan*. A more personal and altogether more inwardly felt and perceptive novel is *The Princes* (1963) which tells, with a rare sympathy and some of the understanding of E. M. Forster, of the withering away of the Princely States. A wholly different narrative idiom and technique are employed by Bhagani Bhattacharya, born 1906, who was a student in London in the thirties. Both are emphatically Indian in the manner of Mulk Raj Anand, flowing, fervid, susceptible constantly to the author's intervention and clogged with a good deal of plain man's sociology. On the other hand, both *So Many Hungers* (1947) and *He Who Rides the Tiger* (1954), both novels with big subjects – famine and caste – evoke a genuine flow of feeling, even if it is too generalized and apt to swamp character and event.

I turn now to a group of women writers who have brought renewed life and an extended subject matter to the Indian novel in English. They are Attia Hosain, Santha Rama Rau, Ruth Prawer Jhabvala, Anita Desai, Kamala Markandaya and Shashi Deshpande. Attia Hosain has written just one novel and a volume of short stories and Santha Rama Rau mostly attractive travel books. The others are regularly productive professional novelists who have reached a relatively wide reading public and received critical acknowledgement of their achievement.

Attia Hosain's crisp short stories (*Phoenix Fled and Other Stories*, 1953) are indeed short, some of them no more than anecdotes. But even the briefest, offering a single glimpse of life, are vivid and telling manifesting capacities for summoning physical presence in its impact and roundedness and for discriminating between shades of feeling. In the best stories she incorporates both in a naturally evolving narrative. She can point up in a sentence or two as in *Phoenix Fled*, the title story, the plight and the dignity of an aged woman and imply in a sentence or two a background of horror and devastation. Or she can display in *Ramu* quietly and naturally, the strength and integrity of a child's love for an animal, a hound suspected of rabies and shot. The child consecrates himself to saving the dog and when that fails to saving his name, to proving that he was not mad and did not have rabies.

> The man felt a return of his sorrow as he saw the dog lying dead. He would not explain his feelings to a ragged child – why he had to shoot him, what he felt now that there was a doubt in his own mind. His mind found an obvious solution. He took a silver rupee and held it out to Ramu.
> 'Here child if it's money you want.'
> Ramu stared at the silver coin then said angrily, 'I came to tell you Moti was not mad,' and before the car could be started again he was off, a brown shadow running into the dark shadows by the road. (pp. 202–3)

She deals in a way that is neither indignant nor resigned but calm – and yet, for all its calm, devastating – with the fate (one can hardly use a less portentous word) the fate of women reared in an absolutely male-dominated society where they exist as mere appurtenances of husbands, fathers, brothers, sons and masters. Nor does there seem to be any substantial difference between them whether they are the most defenceless and wretched of workers or members of the comfortably-off middle class as we see in the two stories *The Street of the Morn* and *Time is Unredeemable*.

The literary historian K. R. S. Iyengar thinks that the very qualities that gave distinction to her short stories seem to have stood in the way of Attia Hosain's structuring a full-length novel.[1] While this seems to be too severe a stricture I agree that there is some evidence of a falling off in energy and a deficiency in general architectural skill. Neverthe-

less *Sunlight on a Broken Column* published in 1961 seems to be a
complex and impressive novel which keeps a number of themes
smoothly in play. The two principal ones are politics and a woman's
struggle for independence. Laila is an orphan who lives first with one
aunt then with another. All her family is engaged with the independence movement during the thirties. But neither at the university nor
afterwards can the girl give complete adherence to a party or a cause.
Her fundamental aspiration, never sterile but quiet and controlled, is
towards personal independence, something harder in the Muslim
world than any socially sanctioned struggle. The study of Laila is firm,
clear and sympathetic, and the reconstruction of a society in which
purdah flourishes is genuinely deft and completely convincing. The
intense life of the Muslim family produces women of extraordinary
dignity and strength but it also poses with its claustrophobic pressure
an appalling dilemma for a character with a bias towards independence.
Laila evokes in her character and suffering the experience and the pain
of so many in the sub-continent, the subjected women, just as she
makes us understand the astonishing toughness their life can breed in
women.

Something of the urbanity and enthusiasm – an unusual pairing –
of Santha Rama Rau's travel books infuses her novel *Remember the
House* (1956), the story of a young woman's development from
immaturity to a sense of reality. Santha Rama Rau shows herself to
be a new kind of artist on the Indian scene. Born and brought up in
India, she lives in the United States, writes a very English form of
English, travels extensively and draws the subject matter of this novel,
which is wholly freed from any Indian connections, from Japan, the
Phillipines and China. The heroine, Kay, is a notable creation who
joins a child's innocent intensity of will to an unscrupulous finesse in
manoeuvring her way into other people's lives, that of an Arabian
bureaucrat in Japan, an aristocratic old lady in Manila, a former airforce
officer and then the wealthy, enigmatic David Marins in Shanghai.
This pacy, spirited tale is organized on a system of surprises and
reversals. Small, concealed, explosive devices hurl the narrative along.
But more impressive than her technical dexterity is the author's
genuine sympathy for and creative ability to realize the truth of alien
cultures, strange people, the transient world of travel and difference.

The work of Nayantara Sahgal – autobiography, fiction, politics –
is an excellent example of the new kind of subject matter women have
brought into Indian fiction. There is nothing particularly feminine or
even female in what constitutes the material of her work in several
genres, namely politics: except I suppose, that it *was* introduced into
the Indian novel by a woman. Her interest, and therefore the substance
of her novels, is quite different from the revolutionary and social

passion and the Marxist motives of Mulk Raj Anand. Nayantara Sahgal is not a radical except in having a rooted objection to much that occurs in Indian political life. It is the detail, the daily action, the sliding and side-stepping of politicians and the effect of their arrogance and remoteness on ordinary lives that engages her attention. If this composes the content of her novels, their shape and spirit are given by her conviction that politics should be a form of moral activity. She holds the Coleridgean view that the collective is bound by the same moral order as the individual.

'It were absurd to suppose', wrote Coleridge, 'that individuals should be under a law of moral obligation and yet that a million of the same individuals acting collectively or through representatives should be exempt from all law, for morality is no accident of human nature, but its essential characteristic . . . none but a madman will imagine that the essential qualities of anything can be altered by its becoming part of an aggregate, that a grain of corn, for instance should cease to contain flour, as soon as it is part of a peck or bushel.[2]

It is this strong and lucid idea which invigorates Nayantara Sahgal's best novels, *This Time of Morning* (1965), *Storm in Chandigarh* (1969), *Rich Like Us* (1985). Each deals with the development and influence of particular political events: *This Time of Morning* with the final period of Nehru's power and the fall of a minister, *Storm in Chandigarh* with the partition of the Punjab and the tension between Hindu and Sikh, *Rich Like Us* with the Emergency during Mrs Gandhi's ministry. There is something American (Nayantara Sahgal was educated in the United States) in her fascination with political detail as well as in her indignation at the infringement of people's rights. Indeed the novels blend the documentary and the indigenous in a typically American way. Nayantara Sahgal writes with much – too much – fluency sometimes in a merely journalistic way; her characters are generic rather than individual and are deficient in subtlety as her style is in poetry. But one has to admire that moral stance, the grasp of detail, the energy and the accuracy.

Let me quote a single passage from *Rich Like Us* which gives the brisk professional touch, the sharp notation and the moral protest both against the injustice and the bland and careful lack of scrutiny by a more and more political civil service.

It is uncanny what a bare month of censorship can do, exactly the opposite of what I would have expected of a news blackout. I have heard from people who have lived under it all their lives that censorship really does kill and bury curiosity. What you don't have you stop missing after a while. But one month is just long enough for an artificial silence to start exploding. The facts it is trying to conceal shriek out to be noticed. Since June 26th officially all was well, but it was impossible not to be aware of the sullenness building up along New Delhi's heavily policed roads, and news travelled from the old city of rioting when tenements were torn from under slum dwellers and they were packed off out of sight to distant locations. It did not need much imagination to sense the hate and fear inside the vans with iron-barred windows, like the ones used for collecting stray dogs for drowning, that now roamed the streets picking up citizens for vasectomy. I saw one ahead of me one night, the threatening twinkle of its tail light longer lived than its body disappearing into the dark void. We knew there had been hunger strikes and a breakout of political prisoners from Tihar Jail because the government had printed a denial. The ban on more than five people getting together in a public place did not work in the teeming bazaars of the old city but I had seen a group of seven or eight broken up by the police outside a coffee house in Connaught Place and hustled towards a waiting van. One of the young men had flung the policeman's hand off his shoulder and been kicked from behind for his pains. As he was dragged struggling and shouting to the van his glasses had fallen off. With the unmistakable apparatus of modern authoritarianism all about us, if we could be certain of one fact, it was that everything was not all right. Yet my colleagues and I, passing each other on the stairs and in the corridors of the Ministry, with vague smiles and nods, never stopped to ask each other why we were carrying on as though nothing had happened. Industry was an important Ministry and had to show results.

We see in Nayantara Sahgal's dashing journalistic prose a combination of modern American briskness and of British convention – or illusion, in this case that of a devotedly disinterested Civil Service. How different in tone and address is the work of Ruth Prawer Jhabvala now thought by many to be the most distinguished of all Indian women writers. She was born in Germany of Polish parents and came to England in 1939 at the age of twelve. She went to school and university in Britain and married an Indian architect. She lived in Delhi from 1951 to 1975 and now divides her time between India and the United States. She is thus a member of that peculiarly modern category, the emigré or expatriate or international novelist. She writes of her position as a novelist:

> The central fact of all my work . . . is that I am a
> European living permanently in India. I have lived here for
> most of my adult life and have an Indian family. This
> makes me not quite an Indian but it does not leave me
> strictly an outsider either. I feel my position to be at a
> point in space where I have quite a good view of both
> sides but am myself left stranded in the middle. My work
> is an attempt to charter this uncharted territory for myself.
> I write about Europeans in India, sometimes about Indians
> in India, sometimes about both, but always attempting to
> present India to myself in the hope of giving myself some
> kind of foothold.[3]

Her honest avowal tells us much about her work. She does not see India as a case to be explained by history, politics or sociology. Her main concern is never, as she acknowledges in the same statement, with such subjects as the extent of Westernization or the tension between modernity and tradition. She is as free as R. K. Narayan from any defensiveness about life in India, and freer than any British writer on India from guilt, overt or latent, about India's imperial past.

Here then is the opening of *Get Ready for Battle* (1962), a novel – her fifth – in Ruth Jhabvala's mature style. I quote it in extension because length is necessary to appreciate her technique of accumulated touches.

> Everyone knew the party was for someone, but no one
> quite knew for whom. Almost everyone in the room
> could have been useful to Gulzari Lal, so it was difficult to
> pick on anyone in particular. As a matter of fact, it was
> a very insignificant guest indeed – for a municipal
> engineer who had some time in the future to pass some
> rather tricky plans of Gulzari Lal's; he stood around in his
> best suit and was dazzled by the superior company. To
> dazzle him had been exactly Gulzari Lal's purpose, and
> now that it was accomplished he had lost sight of it and
> was enjoying the party for itself. He always enjoyed his
> own parties: he liked being a host and seeing people grow
> satisfied and expansive on his drinks and his food.

And no one in the room was more unmistakably the host than Gulzari Lal. A tall man, festive in white leggings and a long white coat buttoned up to the neck, he stood beaming on his guests and, smiling from beneath his moustache, he urged them with gentle insistence, a glass always in his own hand, to drink more of the whisky which cost him Rs. 65 a bottle. He made the most of whatever conversation there was, which was sometimes difficult for the guests did not, on the whole, have much to say to one another.

However, no one was bored, for almost everyone in the room could be of use to someone else and this was stimulating. There was a Commissioner who was stimulating to a number of fairly high-ranking civil servants, who were in their turn stimulating to a number of middle-ranking civil servants, and so on, down to the municipal engineer for whom the party was made by the presence of the vice-chairman of his Board. An overall stimulus was provided by a Maharaja, an imposing figure who, now that his kingdom and a good deal of his income were gone, was taking an interest in business affairs; he was really of no importance to anyone, but his presence made everyone feel they had got into good company and had come a long way from where they had started.

These being modern times, many people had brought their wives, who sat in a semicircle at one end of the room and sipped pineapple juice. Most of them were strangers to one another, but even those who had met before did not feel easy enough, in these overwhelming social circumstances, to make any kind of conversation. So they only sat, stiff in their best saris and jewellery, and patiently waited for their husbands to say it was time to go home. They accepted their boredom without resentment, for they understood it comprised the social life which, as modern women, it was their duty to take part in. Only one of their number had joined the throng of men at the other end of the room: an English girl who, after desperately trying to engage the ladies around her in lively small-talk and as desperately failing, had used the prerogative of her earlier and more ingrained emancipation to join her father, who was Gulzari Lal's bank manager. The two of them provided the European element which gave a party like this a little spice and variety; they

vaguely realized their special position and tried to live up
to it by being lively and interested. The girl exchanged a
few words with the Maharaja, which thrilled her, and then
she was taken up by Gulzari Lal's son Vishnu, whom she
entertained with her impressions of India while he looked
down at her with much charm and gallantry and
wondered to himself at her flat-chestedness.

Perhaps the best time of all was being had by Kusum,
Gulzari Lal's mistress, who was supervising the preparation
of the dinner. She bullied the servants with exuberance,
from time to time snatching the cooking-spoon from the
cook's hand and giving an energetic stir herself in one of
the vast stainless-steel vessels. (pp. 7–9)

The passage is a preliminary sketch for the novel itself, which is
concerned with the incessant jockeying and management of others for
the sake of status and position among the middle classes in Delhi. It
is a story of the varieties of selfishness played against the strict social
parameters of the Indian world. It is, however, the tone that is the
author's principal instrument. It helps to establish the universe of
the novel, the viewpoint and the degree of seriousness with which the
action at any point is to be taken. There is a note in this tone which
is strikingly European – continental European, that is, not British –
a note of unsurprised, disillusioned but uncynical calm and tolerance
which derives from the long tradition stretching from Montaigne to
Stendhal. This is the sensibility which backs the sharp but forgiving
eye with which Mrs Jhabvala observes middle-class Indian society. Not
that this pervasive tone and limited subject-matter makes for anything
like monotony or narrowness. On the contrary there is within the
given boundaries quite considerable variety.

Even social problems which, as I have indicated, are a secondary
interest appear as part of the matter in Get Ready for Battle. In To Whom
She Will (1956) and The Nature of Passion (1956) she deals with
romantic love and its peculiar difficulties in the Indian setting; in
Esmond in India (1958) she is concerned with the tension between
European sophistication at its most objectionable and a more human
traditional morality; in The Householder (1960) she writes of people at
the poorer end of the middle class who are well acquainted with the
anxieties and frustrations of near poverty. There is a positively
nineteenth-century abundance of character in this tale of the domestic
and professional relations of Ram the young newly-married teacher
and his ridiculous wife, his colleagues and their wives, his amazing
headmaster, Mr Khanna, the swami and the naïve European seeking
spiritual enlightenment. The tea party at Mr Khanna's is a superbly and
naturally comic episode which has suggestions of Dickens himself.

Mrs Jhabvala has collaborated on several occasions with the distinguished film-makers James Ivory and Ishmael Merchant. She has written film scripts based on her play *Shakespeare Wallah* (1965) and on her novel *Heat and Dust* (1975), which takes place in a princely household in the time of the Raj, which was awarded the Booker Prize in 1975 and which Anna Rutherford described as a minor masterpiece both as a novel and a film.

Mrs Jhabvala's prose, always flexible and adaptable, became during this work on film scripts even more expert in concision, elision and implication, as we see particularly in her short stories, which include, incidentally, several tales of 'everyday, urban, suffering India that people in the West didn't know about', as she herself puts it. The stories, packed with fact and detail, show an extraordinary knowledge of different sorts of people and categories of feeling. They are much concerned with the tension between reason and feeling in a traditional European way, in the potency and pointlessness of passion, and in the overwhelming strength of certain kinds of feeling which rule some to the utter bafflement of others. There are also those stories, 'My First Marriage', 'The Widow', 'A Spiritual Call', which tell in a style both free and controlled of the special pathos attaching to the experience of women in a male-dominated world, experience foresworn, experience lost and experience exploited.

Passion is the subject of more than one tale and it is shown positively to flourish on difference, to a degree, in some cases, which is truly bizarre. In 'Passion' a young English woman working for a British cultural organization falls deeply in love with a strange young Indian clerk whom she sees standing in a bus queue holding his small, worn brass tiffin container as she taxies home from work. When he visits her flat for the first time he behaves in a lordly inquisitive way, picking up objects in the room and asking their price, wants to know the girl's salary, drinks alcohol for the first time as though it were lemonade and is sick on her sitting room rug. As a lover he is lordly, condescending, self-centred; the profoundly tyrannical male. He is bitter about the girl's economic advantages, horrified by her lack of respect for her employers, employers being a class deserving of respect even in their absence and however bad they are as employers. He is, of course, a married man with children who rages with fury when the girl uninvited comes to visit his wretched household. The girl is not just willing but eager in a dream of unreality to give up her comfortable life to devote herself to this odd, nervous unattractive creature.

In 'The Man with the Dog' a wealthy Indian grandmother and widow once happily married, devotes her emotions and life to her lodger, a peppery Dutch expatriate of limited means who gives parties in his rooms, for which he pays a nominal rent, to which he might or might not invite his landlady and mistress according to his whim.

She will even part with her beloved children for the sake of this peculiar character with the hairy dog. In 'A Spiritual Call' an intelligent woman, an Oxford graduate, turns herself into the slave of an oily, self-indulgent, hypocritical guru. In 'The Widow' the youngish widow of a rich old man puts her new life of freedom and comfort at risk for the sake of an indifferent, spoilt and shallow school-boy. In 'An Experience of India' the wife of a successful and commonplace journalist becomes without scruple or regret a sort of mendicant prostitute after a love-affair with a village musician in order to be able to devote herself to an even more bizarre passion, a passion for the life of the Indian poor travelling the country with bed and bundle.

Mrs Jhabvala's stories of the sufferings of Indian women have nothing shrill or argumentative about them. They are quiet, factual and powerful, and all the more effective because of their insight into feeling and their assessment of the strength of the will. It is only the women who will go to these absolute lengths for love. In men's emotions prudence, caution, conformity and cowardice play a much more prominent part. Her stories also show the mysterious, impossible fancies separating human beings, men and women, the indigenous and the expatriate. This last obstacle to understanding and sympathy is part of our relationship with all kinds of life outside us, from the intimacies of love to the connections of native and foreigner. And it is, her stories demonstrate again and again, as much a matter of the will, the hard centre of self, as it is of a deficiency of feeling or a lack of understanding. This is how the widow puts it in 'The Man with the Dog':

> Most of the time I don't understand what they are talking about, even when they are speaking in English – which is not always, for sometimes they speak in other languages such as French or German. But I always know, in whatever language they are speaking, when they start saying things about India. Sooner or later they always come to this subject, and then their faces change, they look mean and bitter like people who feel they have been cheated by some shopkeeper and it is too late to return the goods. Now it becomes very difficult for me to keep calm. How I hate to hear them talking in this way, saying that India is dirty and everyone is dishonest; but because they are my guests, they are in my house, I have to keep hold of myself and sit there with my arms folded. I must keep my eyes lowered, so that no one should see how they are blazing with fire. Once they have started on this subject, it always takes them a long time to stop, and the

more they talk the more bitter they become, the
expression on their faces becomes more and more
unpleasant. I suffer, and yet I begin to see that they too
are suffering; all the terrible things they are saying are not
only against India but against themselves too – because
they are here and have nowhere else to go – and against
the fate that has brought them here and left them here, so
far from where they belong and everything they hold
dear.

Anita Desai, born in 1932, is of mixed Indian and German descent.
She went to school and university in Delhi. She is married with four
children. Her earliest work *Cry the Peacock* (1963) and *Voices in the City*
(1965) deal competently with material which, if not conventional, is
orthodox: traditional beliefs and customs enfeebled by modernity and
the effect on three young people of life in a great city. The novels are
more promising than accomplished. Her manifest talent is better seen
in her later work, and I have chosen two novels to comment on which
demonstrate the range of her gifts. *In Custody* (1984) and *Clear Light
of Day* (1980) are more individual, less generalized and conventional
than her earliest fiction. As will be seen *Clear Light of Day* seems to
me the height of her considerable achievement.

In Custody is a novel in which treatment is superior to subject. Not
that treatment is something applied from outside to an already existing
cut and defined subject. Each, as we recognize, influences and modifies
the other. Nevertheless the distinction is invariably and inevitably
made. Anita Desai is a novelist for whom action, plot, development
are determined by character and the subject here is the character of
Deven. Deven is an impoverished, temporary lecturer in Hindi –
although his real interest is Urdu literature – in a private college in an
obscure town some forty miles from Delhi. Deven is one born to be
bullied. He has neither respect nor consideration from colleagues,
students, neighbours. His wife is stupid, disappointed in her roman-
tically silly notions of what marriage would bring. But Deven is not
a virtuous or purely pathetic victim as he treats his wife and child shab-
bily and even spitefully.

Usually he was annoyed by her tacit accusations that
added to the load on his back. To relieve it he would hurl
away dishes that had not been cooked to his liking, howl
uncontrollably if meals were not ready when he wanted
them or the laundry not done or a button missing or their
small son noisy or unwashed. (p. 68)

Anita Desai does not, as an earlier novelist might have done, attribute Deven's condition to the past, to economic oppression or to present sociological conditions. Deven is not seen as a function of other, impersonal influences. It is himself, his character, psychology and action that interest her and that she invests with human value and interest. To do this with such a dreary, feeble spirit as Deven is evidence of a rare gift for creating something completely authentic and true. Even the most limited form of reality has a direct and surprising force. The inner accuracy which enabled Anita Desai to make of the meagre Deven a convincing human character is matched by an accuracy in establishing his context.

It is a gift brilliantly exercised in the evocation of the town of Minpore. It is a place without form or shape, with no centre and not even a river or hill to give it a reason for existing. It had a railway station at one end 'and a bus depot at the other, which gave it an air of being a halting place in a long journey. Minpore seemed constantly agitated by movement and bustle, although it was bustle of an unproductive kind, since nothing was made there but a species of shiny yellow, sugarcane sweets. Minpore had a long past, but no history. Worship may have taken place on a given site for as much as five hundred years but not a soul could say when the temple was built. It might have been thrown up a year ago. There was a Muslim area round the mosque. The rest was Hindu. There were no boundaries or limits but there were differences that were known and observed. If they were not, often processions clashed, then knives flashed, batons flailed and blood ran. Minpore is the image of a thousand small Indian towns, just as the College where Deven lectures is repeated over the whole sub-continent. Lala Ram Lal College combines shabbiness and pretension, a despotic administration, a servile and anxious staff, and none more servile and anxious than the insecure Deven, and students willing to bully and blackmail their teachers for higher exam grades as they do the inept Deven at one point.

What led to this, only the least of the many humiliations heaped upon Deven, a constitutional victim, is what the body of the novel is concerned with. Deven's passion is Urdu poetry and particularly the work of an aged poet, Nud. He is manipulated by a friend from undergraduate days, Murad, who combines literary pretensions with a conman's arts, to tape interviews with the ancient, and it turns out, dissolute wreck of a poet with money tricked from the College by a homosexual colleague. In the course of this increasingly crazy project Deven is gulled, humiliated and tormented by everyone, even by the poet Nud himself, whose art Deven has set out to celebrate in a spirit of disinterested generosity.

Donne once divided a sermon into: the pretext – the preacher's intention; the text – his theme; the context – the past and present setting. Today we should add the subtext – the latent intention and the meaning struggling to be discovered. It is in this last area that Anita Desai's novel, so clear in its definition of theme, so assured in intention and so crisp and delicate in establishing the context, fails through the lack of a necessary complexity, that complexity essential in a novel so firmly based on a single character as *In Custody* is, if there is to be implicit friction, energy and the possibility of development. Poor Deven is too much of one piece throughout to allow the creative impulse room and sustenance.

It has both in the earlier novel *Clear Light of Day*, which I choose to comment on in deliberate contrast with *In Custody*, as it shows Anita Desai's art at its most sensitively effective. *Clear Light of Day* opens with Tara, a diplomat's wife, on holiday in the family home in Delhi, being drawn back into that trance of heat, passivity and family absorption which her managerial husband has taken her from to become in the outer world an organized, energetic modern woman. All the themes, the atmospheres, and the characters that will develop are enclosed as in a womb in this first of the novel's sections. The figure of the womb is an appropriate one because the family is both the substance and the context of the novel. The tensions and pressures are not those commonly present in novels of Indian family life – the burden of a tradition-gripped past, of unsympathetic elders, of male dominance and an oppressive extended family, not to speak of grinding and destructive poverty. Bim and Tara (the girls), and Raja and Baba (the boys), belong to a middle-class, moderately comfortable family living off an insurance firm. The parents, remote and indifferent towards the children, are wrapped up in each other and in their passion for bridge. The mother is diabetic, the father an amateur and casual businessman. They hardly ever see the children except before or after bridge parties. The children live their own lives, the essential interest and love supplied by an imported aunt. As in many families where the children are so close to one another, their unity sustains a marked differentiation of character. Bim is driving, self-reliant and the sturdy support of the others; Tara sensitive and impressionable; Raja imaginative and self-centred; Baba a strange, distant figure, the product of the parents' middle-age and increasingly incapable of engaging with the world outside the family.

The novel begins with Tara's visit to the family home in decaying Old Delhi and ends with her departure with her husband and children. This short span of actual time embraces lifetimes, deaths, growth and disillusion. It can do so because the story unfolds like one of the tales Aunt Mira told the children, her voice murmuring on and on, 'following all the loops and turns of the story as skilfully as water, flowing down its necessary channel'. The analogy of loop and turn, progression forward and turning backward in one clear narrative line exactly fits the structure of the story. Analogy is a principal instrument in the rich poetic style of this novel. It helps to impel the narrative on – the loop both circling and moving forward. It elucidates and illustrates the characters. It suggests atmosphere and defines mood. The house and garden compose an analogy of the family, inward looking, shabby, haunted by relics of past ease and beauty, and holding off, not always successfully, the incursions of the world outside, school, work, the menace of communal disorder.

Or take Aunt Mina, the most beautifully developed of the characters. Married at twelve and a widow while still a virgin, she became a domestic slave to be handed round to whichever part of the clan needed a cheap hand. Now aging, growing dotty and bald, she was brought in to look after the children where she at last was allowed to give and receive affection

> To Tara . . . she was solid as a bed, she smelt of cooking
> and was made of knitting. . . . Quick, heavy and jumpy –
> yet to the children she was as constant as a staff, a tree
> that can be counted on not to pull up its roots and shift in
> the night. . . . She was not soft or scented or sensual. She
> was bony and angular, wrinkled and desiccated – like a
> stick, or an ancient tree to which they adhered. (p. 109)

On the face of it *Clear Light of Day* is a delicate domestic study of the younger members of an interesting but not outstanding middle-class family. They are observed with sympathy and insight and their development is related in a poetic idiom charged with feeling and richly strewn with revealing analogies which make ordinary family life both dramatic and significant. The novel displays a high degree of professional competence and it combines this skill with something more important, a creative idea. The initiating and sustaining conception has to do with the human experience which is both physical and spiritual, of an inner and an outer life. It has its origin in our physical and biological life in which space and distance are felt as they increase and extend to be more and more dangerous. Upon such space and distance society and tradition have imposed rituals of control, of which the most intimate are one's house and its surroundings, like the shabby house and unkempt garden which establish the limits of safety for Bim, Raja, Tara and Baba. Raja and Tara escape – as they see it – or desert as the others see it – the inner family space for an alien external life, Raja absolutely to become a rich Muslim's son-in-law and then as a fake Urdu poet, and Tara to marry a diplomat and to live the strange deracinated diplomatic life. Baba, at the other extreme from Raja, suffers from some genetic defect which makes it impossible for him to leave the nest. He never achieves that degree of autonomy that would enable him to work out a tolerable or even a tentative relationship between inner and outer worlds. The only one of the children who manages a scratchy uneven balance between the two is Bim, the surrogate mother of the handicapped Baba, the effective College lecturer, the chief if strained and worn prop of the family.

Coleridge with his superlative insight locates the tension I have been speaking of deep in the psyche itself, and makes it the impulse of growth and enlargement of self. Speaking specifically of children in the Coleridgean idiom he writes:

> Two things we may learn from little children from three to six years old: 1. That it is a characteristic, an instinct of our human nature to pass out of self – i.e. the image or complex cycle of images . . . which is the perpetual representative of our Individualism, and by all unreflecting minds confounded and identified with it . . . 2. Not to suffer one form to pass into me and become a usurping self.[4]

The rhythm of the movement between the restless search for release from the confinement of the single image of self and the solicitude to keep inviolate the integrity of another self is what we feel pulsing through *Clear Light of Day*. It is a tribute to the strength and finesse of the novelist that we should be able to say of this novel that it is a beautifully realized and completely persuasive version of Coleridge's vision.

Kamala Markandaya is one of the most distinguished of the generation of Indian novelists in English who succeeded the big three, R. K. Narayan, Mulk Raj Anand and Raja Rao. Her work has been notable for an unusual combination of range and intimacy. *Nectar in a Sieve* (1954) is set in a village and examines the hard agricultural life of the Indian peasant; *Some Inner Fury* (1956), which includes a highly-educated young woman and her English lover who are torn apart by the Quit India campaign of the time, has to do with the quarrel between Western and Indian influences, as they are focused in a marriage; *A Silence of Desire* (1960) deals with the middle class, and *A Handful of Rice* (1966) with the city poor; *Possession* (1963) moves from the West End of London to a South Indian village, and is centred on the conflict of Eastern spirituality with Western materialism; *The Coffer Dams* (1969) is a highly contemporary examination of the activities of a British engineering firm which is invited to build a dam in India.

Kamala Markandaya has not the same intimacy and familiarity with all these areas of life, and she has indeed been criticized by Indian critics for a certain lack of inwardness with the life of the Indian poor. Her particular strength lies in the delicate analysis of the relationships of persons, especially when these have a more developed consciousness of their problems and are attempting to grope towards some more independent existence: a fact which relates her to Narayan. She has, too, the genuine novelist's gift for fixing the exact individuality of the character, even if she is less successful at establishing it in a reasonably convincing social context. She has been most successful and at her best, an impressive best, in dealing with the problems of the educated and middle class, and she has a gift for delineating the self-imposed laceration of the dissatisfied.

One of her most achieved and characteristic works is *A Silence of Desire*. It is a subtly precise study of a husband and wife, although the wife has less actuality than the husband, Dandekar, a wrought-up, conscientious, petty government clerk. He is rocked off his age-old balance by his wife's strange absences, excuses and lies. It turns out that she has a growth and is attending a faith healer. The husband is by no means a Westernized person, but he is to some degree secular and modern, and the situation enables the author to reflect on the tensions, the strength, and the inadequacies and aspirations of middle-class Indian life. The book is gentle in tone but sharp in perception, and the mixture of moods, the friction of faith and reason, the quarrels of old and young, are beautifully pointed. There are conventional, perfunctory patches in the novel but Kamala Markandaya shows very high skill in unravelling sympathetically but inflinchingly the structure of the protagonist's motives and the bumbling and stumbling progress of his anxieties.

The Golden Honeycomb (1977), is a historical examination of three generations of princely India, and it has both range and intimacy. The range has to do with the decline both of the princely order, a glittering British surrogate, and with the gradual enfeeblement of British power. The intimacy has to do with an inward and sensitive treatment of the life of a puppet prince in his relations with the contemporary British power, with his Indian civil servants, his lover and family. In earlier novels the balance between range and intimacy was imperfect. Markandaya, able to fix the individuality of a character but less successful at establishing the social context, in this novel keeps the equilibrium of the two poised and sustained. Moreover, she has the added merit of prose of great clarity and point, considerable metaphorical vivacity, and a gift for the nice discrimination of motive. *The Golden Honeycomb* is a novel in the grand manner, large in scope, constructing a world with authoritative ease, with a central figure, a biographical line, a multitude of grasped minor characters, people who are seen from within so that they possess an intrinsic and spontaneous vitality, and from without, so that they are located in time and place in a context of value and feeling. It signals the impressive maturing of an authentic talent.

Shashi Deshpande's *That Long Silence* (1988) is her fourth and most technically accomplished novel. She is the daughter of a distinguished Sanskrit scholar, a married woman with two sons who has worked as a journalist and written books for children. *That Long Silence* is sharply contemporary in matter and manner, being a novel in which a woman is writing a novel about her own oppressed and unsatisfactory life as a form of release-inducing therapy. The book is sprung with tension from start to finish. Jaya is incessantly ravelled by inner conflict, given to copious weeping, constantly analysing her oppressed lot in a male-oriented society. Her relationships with her family, both the immediate one of husband and son and daughter and with the larger surrounding one, are fraught with edginess and anxiety. Her son dislikes her, her daughter seems indifferent, her husband is increasingly distant and disappointed with her. With her mother and brothers her relationship is no more satisfying and she has never forgiven her loved father for dying when she was a child. The complexities of mood, of family feelings clouded with suspicion and lived in stifling intimacy and the sexual and social stresses which compose the substance of the novel are supported by the simplest framework of event. Jaya's husband is suspected of business malpractice and he has withdrawn while an enquiry into his case is pursued. Mohan has admitted to his wife his dubious and probably illegal dealings, actions performed to obtain the luscious perk of a superior apartment in a fashionable district of Bombay from his own unscrupulous chief. Mohan and Jaya have moved back to a seedy flat occupied by them at an earlier, poorer stage of their life. The husband has left to see what his contact can do for him, the children are away with a relative and in this curious retreat Jaya rehearses the life that has brought her to this pass. She can undertake resolutely and independently that introspective analysis which is the feature of her nervy temperament.

It is the combination of the analytical and detached which gives this novel its particular and unusual quality. A turmoil of feeling is conveyed in cool, idiomatic and sensitive prose. And it is served by a memory which is so rich and minutely specific and able to produce not just bright discrete images but rather a flow of naturally related scenes that it is a creative faculty making past life live again in the present, as, for example, when a more energetic focusing of memory reveals that it was not she (as both she and her husband had accepted) who was terrified by the endless tramping of a protesting procession of workers in Bombay but rather Mohan, the husband.

One could align Jaya in more conventional terms with some of

Narayan's young heroes, ardent and sensitive and impatient to throw off the burden of an ancient orthodoxy of ritual and conduct. But while Narayan's young men feel a vague and generalized accidie, Jaya's discontent is fiercer, more personal and deeply sexual. She uses her husband – since, as she says, every relationship evolves its own language – formally to express the orthodoxy she wishes to discard.

> If there was nothing else to reassure me, there was my
> knowledge of Mohan, of the utter strength of his
> convictions: a husband and wife care for each other, live
> with each other until they are dead; parents care for their
> children, and children in turn look after their parents when
> they are needed; marriages never end, they cannot – they
> are a state of being. (p. 127)

As a state of being marriage in Jaya's mind neither corresponded to her experience nor allowed for her aspirations. The romantic longings of adolescence became transformed by tradition, and by its guardians, other, older women, into rigid rules and rituals. Marriage entailed joining their husband's family, or rather becoming a cell in the larger organization, not having a family of one's own. It meant too the disabling feeling of having one's individuality 'wholly blotted out'. Sexual life was only the culmination of the waiting game girls had been taught to practice from childhood. 'The men too – we were married, yet he was a stranger. Intimacy with him had seemed a grotesque indecency.' Sex, of course, in marriage preceded love. Love-making itself was always 'a silent, wordless lovemaking'.

> God, how terrible it was to know a man so well. I could
> time it almost to the second, from the first devious
> wooing to the moment he turned away from me, offering
> me his hunched back. (p. 85)

Jaya and Mohan never spoke to one another of love or sex or their feelings. She found that sex became in the final count something extraneous. It failed to cross the great chasm between women and men. 'They are separated for ever, never more than at the moment of total physical awareness.' In fact the act of sex is the absolute affirmation of one's aloneness and separation.

Jaya suffers by reason of the condition of being a wife in a given society. But she also endures the emotional wounds which are consequent upon being the kind of person she is. For example, she cannot in the world of silence inhabited by women express the anger she feels at the casual violence inflicted on women by drunken and brutal men.

(Women are not allowed to be angry, only neurotic.) She is pulled between her liberal convictions and her traditional instincts: her child, she prays, must be a boy, or fair. She is haunted by an abortion concealed from her husband. When her young son vanishes from home she is crushed by her sense of inadequacy as a mother. She is racked by the fate imposed upon her by her own body: those painful spasms in the middle of each cycle, those massive driving-on-to-madness constricting pains of childhood.

That Long Silence is a novel that is original on the Indian scene in dealing with a woman's feelings with an unusual degree of candour. It will not surprise the reader to find amid so much impassioned and generally persuasive sincerity glimpses of naïveté. There is one comically ingenuous moment when she invokes Marx who, she tells us, held that the relations of man to woman is the most natural of one person to another. 'How wrong you were about this, Mr Marx, prophetically right though you may have been about so much else.' But this kind of ingenuousness is not characteristic of a novel which deals with its very personal material in a fresh, feeling and critically distanced way. The metaphor of silence under which it is organized helps to impose a quiet and cogent discipline: the inner discipline of a self cut off from human communication. Certainly That Long Silence is not a shrill, illustrated 'case' against women's wrongs. It is not even an interruption of that silence but a silent communion with self. There are even in the novel's conclusion, and rather against its logic, hints of life and healing, a suggestion of new beginnings for Jaya and Mohan. But the strongest note that comes from this technically skilful and genuinely felt novel is the voice, human and inconsolable, of sad, wronged women.

Grimus (1975), Salman Rushdie's first novel, uses as an epigraph T. S. Eliot's famous line

Human kind
Cannot bear very much reality.

The purpose of Grimus is to ensure that the reader is not obliged to bear any. Grimus is a mishmash of a novel which applies the manner of the fairy-tale – marvels inconsequentially succeeding one another – to material appropriate to the contemporary and by now conventional taste for the grotesque and mythical, laced with a measure of sexual sophistication and a pinch of science fiction. Modern versions of mythical figures – named with self-conscious and calculated peculiarity – are represented by Vergil Jones, 'a man devoid of friends and with a tongue rather too large for his mouth'; his mistress, the lapsed

Catholic hunchback crone Dolores O'Toole, who stimulated herself
with Church candles; Flapping Eagle, a Red Indian afflicted with the
gift of immortality; Irina and Elfrida, 'two pale exquisite, china
mannequins'; Ignatius Q. Gribb, the town thinker; Count Aleksander
Cherkassov, a handsome perspiring man with two handkerchiefs, one
already sodden, the other catching up. These and similar grotesques
engage in a bizarre dance of life and death in a misty dream world
called Calf Island. The people, like the names, the events and encounters, are carried to irrational and immoderate extremes which only a
very youthful sensibility could enjoy or even envisage. 'Language',
Vergil muses at one point 'makes concepts. Concepts make chains'.
The aim of the novel is to burst through language, concepts and chains
to an anarchic and repetitive universe. What it does burst through to
is the adolescent mysticism with which the novel concludes.

> The man who had been Flapping Eagle and was now part-
> Eagle, part-Grimus, was making love to Media, who had
> been a whore and was now his mainstay, when the Gorf
> Koak, who had transported himself to the peak of Calf
> Mountain, sensed something wrong.
> The mists around the island.
> The mists which circled and shrouded.
> The eternal, unlifting veils.
> The mists were growing thicker. Slowly, slowly, they
> were descending, closing in upon the island upon all sides,
> closer, closer, a dense grey fog now, closing, closing.
> And they were not mists.
> Deprived of its connection with all relative Dimensions,
> the world of Calf Mountain was slowly unmaking itself,
> its molecules and atoms breaking, dissolving, quietly
> vanishing into primal, unmade energy. The raw material
> of being was claiming its own.
> So that, as Flapping Eagle and Media writhed upon
> their bed, the Mountain of Grimus danced the Weakdance
> to the end. (p. 319)

Midnight's Children (1981) dramatizes the beginnings of independent
India in the life of the beak-nosed wildly extravagant Muslim, Saleem
Aziz, who was born on the stroke of the midnight bringing in India's
independence. The novel combines the rush and fluency of Mulk Raj
Anand, the speculative and metaphysical habit of Raja Rao, the shrewd
psychological acumen of R. K. Narayan with the linguistic wildness,
inventiveness and fantasy of G. V. Desani. Its astonishing staple is
composed of elements of magic and fantasy, the grimmest realism

('cripples everywhere, mutilated by loving parents, to ensure them of a lifetime's income from begging'), extravagant farce, multi-mirrored analogy and a potent symbolic structure. All this is indelibly stamped into unity by a powerful personality, which forces both language and fiction to serve a huge purpose, namely the personification of India and the realization of Indian life.

The novelist makes an extraordinarily successful hand at turning into a dense and palpable art the Indian instinct for absorption and inclusiveness. He can do this because he is able to support the mythic and hieratic impulses of his vision with a positively Dickensian sumptuousness of detail. Here is a passage from the middle of the novel in which scent becomes as vital and powerful as Dickens' fog.

Escaping, whenever possible, from a residence in which the acrid fumes of my aunt's made life unbearable, and also from a college filled with other equally dislikeable smells, I mounted my motorized steed and explored the olfactory avenues of my new city. And after we heard of my grandfather's death in Kashmir, I became even more determined to drown the past in the thick, bubbling stew-scent of the present. . . . O dizzying early days before categorization! Formlessly, before I began to shape them, the fragrance poured into me: the mournful decaying fumes of animal faeces in the gardens of the Frere Road museum, the pustular body odours of young men in loose pajamas holding hands in Sadar evenings, the knife-sharpness of expectorated betel-nut and the bitter-sweet commingling of betel and opium: 'rocket-paans' were sniffed out in the hawker-crowded valleys between Elphinstone Street and Victoria Road. Camel smells, car-smells, the gnat-like irritation of motor-rickshaw fumes, the aroma of contraband cigarettes and 'black-money' the competitive effluvia of the city's bus drivers and the simple sweat of their sardine-crowded passengers. (One bus driver in those days, was so incensed at being overtaken by his rival from another company – the nauseating odour of defeat poured from his glands – that he took his bus round to his opponent's house at night, hooted until the poor fellow emerged, and ran him down beneath wheels reeking, like my aunt, of revenge.) Mosques poured over me the itr of devotion; I could smell the orotund emissions of power sent out by flag-waving Army motors; in the very hoardings of the cinemas I could discern the cheap tawdry perfumes of imported spaghetti Westerns and the most violent martial-arts films ever made. I was, for a time, like a drugged person, my head reeling beneath the complexities of smell; but then my overpowering desire for form asserted itself, and I survived. (pp. 316–17)

It is this 'overpowering desire for form', as warranted on the writer's as well as the character's part, that save the novel from anarchy. Life in it sprawls, multiplies incessantly, flows hither and thither but is saved – sometimes it feels at the final instant – from collapse and dissolution by some ultimate appetite for shape. The friction of the two instincts for flow and control, looseness and tightness, generates the astonishing energy of a novel unprecedented in scope and manner in the history of the Indian novel in English.

If the Dickensian strength is weakened, it is by the intervention of a too marked and irritating self-consciousness. This is wholly characteristic of Salman Rushdie's fictional technique. In reading his work we are conscious that he is doing three things at once. First he is telling the story in a straightforward, rather old-fashioned way. Secondly, he is breaking into this narrative line with discussions on his problems and obligations as author in unfolding the narrative. Thirdly, he treats the novel as a species of autobiography, taking every opportunity to link it with phases of his own life. There is no *a priori* reason why he should not for his own artistic purposes complicate his novelist's task in this way. In *Midnight's Children* it is a technique which works for the most part with considerable success. It does not do so, however, either in *Grimus* or *Shame* (1983), as we have seen in one and shall see in the other. Each of Salman Rushdie's novels is initiated by a strong creative idea. Each abounds in vivid and appropriate detail. Between the two, however, there is a gap which should be filled by art. Instead it is occupied by personality.

After the triumph of *Midnight's Children* it is impossible not to feel a pang of disappointment at *Shame*, a novel we are told in the acknowledgements which was 'written with the financial assistance of the Arts Council of Great Britain'. This fable–parable–tale is set at the time of the beginning of Pakistan and goes on to include the division of the country although, as Rushdie says, it could well be set in the fourteenth century or in quite another country.

> The country in this story is not Pakistan, or not quite.
> There are two countries, real and fictional, occupying the same space, or almost the same space. My story, my fictional country exist, like myself, at a slight angle to reality. I have found this off-centring to be necessary, but its value is, of course, open to debate. My view is that I am not writing only about Pakistan. (p. 29)

The fantastic elements in the story are more controlled than in *Grimus*, less than in *Midnight's Children* and less inwardly sympathetic to the theme. The novel is packed with grotesques and eccentrics. It touches on Islamic fundamentalism, political chicanery, British responsibility and guilt, police oppression, military power, 'dangerous talk' even between friends – all this during the development of the theme, namely the practice and malpractice of authority, civil, religious, military, family, in inculcating the appropriate kind of shame.

> Imagine shame as a liquid, let's say a sweet fizzy tooth-rotting drink, stored in a vending machine. Push the right button and a cup plops down under a pissing stream of fluid. How to push the button? Nothing to it. Tell a lie, sleep with a white boy, get born the wrong sex. Out flows the bubbling emotion and you drink your fill.
>
> (p. 122)

But of course, as Rushdie points out, most people do these things and many others like loose-living, disrespect for one's elders, failure to love one's national flag, incorrect voting at elections and so on, and they do them quite shamelessly, leaving their fluid of shame, as he puts it, to be siphoned off by the 'janitors of the unseen'. It is a serious and fascinating theme but it is treated by the author in a disorderly and blatantly self-indulgent way. He constantly pulls up the narrative, a narrative which requires as much inward compulsion as possible, with account of his narrative difficulties, his artistic intentions – even bits of autobiography – with general musings on whatever occurs to him at the moment. It is an ancient, eighteenth-century habit of writing applied to material which in its psychology, politics and aims is wholly of today.

Henry James in the Preface to the *Aspern Papers* when writing about *The Turn of the Screw*, which he calls a fairy-tale, distinguishes in the technique of the novel between, on the one hand, improvisation, the running on and over of invention, and on the other, the stream, 'the channelled impelled narrative'. The latter, he tells us, can be compromised by an unruly fluency of invention. It is a distinction appropriate to apply to the work of Salman Rushdie which is broad, grand in its sweep and extravagantly inventive – a flood, as James puts it – but deficient in stream, impulsion and control. At least the stream is compromised by the flood in *Grimus* and *Shame*. In *Midnight's Children* the two enjoy a more evenly balanced relationship.

When one looks back on the more than fifty years of the Indian novel in English, several distinct impressions remain. The first – again in this context as in others – is the extraordinary plasticity and adaptability of the English language which proved itself capable of expressing the innermost, as well as the strongest and subtlest, feelings of members of a culture immensely remote in history and distance. If the use of the English language was to be attributed in the first place to the presence of the British and the Raj, its persistence, its increasing strength and expanding influence – long after the British had departed and in spite of a natural national hostility and the effort to develop in Hindi a universal national language – owed nothing to the British and everything to the capacities, the resources and the usefulness, national and international, of the English language itself. Again, the English novel in India has its roots in nineteenth-century English literature and, as R. K. Narayan reminds us, in Jane Austen, Kipling and Wodehouse, authors who influenced him. Its beginnings were also affected by French literature and by Marx and the socialist writers of the thirties, as is seen in the work of Raja Rao and Mulk Raj Anand. But as important as the language is the talent of so many practitioners over the last sixty years who have created a body of work of remarkable standard and variety which has engaged at every turn and every level with a civilization of manifold richness and complexity and which has brought into modern consciousness both the Indian experience of changing social structure, permanence and transition, individual struggle, tradition and morality, aspiration, injustice, tragedy and comedy as well as the pattern and detail, both exotic and common-place, of daily living. The language and idiom in which all this has been expressed has, on the whole, been British rather than American, as no doubt would be expected. Nor has the Indian novel in English been much affected by developments in the technique of fiction of the experimental kind. The novelists have rather elected to preserve, or perhaps have naturally felt comfortable in, the ancient Indian tradition of story-telling in which even realistic descriptive narrative has its undertones of poetry and myth.

References

1. *Indian Writing in English* (New Delhi, 1984), p. 4612.
2. *The Friend* Vol. XIII.
3. *Contemporary Novelists*, ed. James Vinson (London and Chicago, 1972), p. 678.
4. *Inquiring Spirit*, ed. K. Coburn (London, 1959), p. 68.

Chapter 5

Poetry: Ezekiel, Parthasarathy, Kolatkar, Ramanujan and Others

The long line of Indian writers in English, stretching from Ram Mohan Roy, the Indian J. S. Mill, to Ved Mehta, *The New Yorker* contributor, have used the Enqlish language with grace and effect. They developed a prose fit for many purposes: theology, philosophy, religion, politics, autobiography, history and criticism. Another smaller group used English for poetry.

Prose, however, is one thing; poetry something else altogether. For one thing it is much harder for readers to accommodate themselves to that limiting period flavour which is so much more apparent in verse than in prose; for another, the special case and intimacy in English which I referred to as existing among Indians show themselves comparatively more rarely in poetry than in prose. Henry Derozio (1809–31) was a pre-Macaulay poet; Kashiprosad Ghose (1809–73) and Michael Madhusudan Dutt (1827–73) post-Macaulay poets. Henry Derozio died young but there is little in what he wrote to suggest the possibility of any substantial achievement. His verse is fluent and vaguely aspiring, without an individual edge, and it recalls the rhythm of an early and listless Byron. His poetry was rather the signal of a young man's intention to be a poet than the exercise of any realized power.

> But man's eternal energies can make
> An atmosphere around him, and so take
> Good out of evil, like the yellow bee
> That sucks from flowers malignant a sweet treasure,
> O Tyrant fate! thus shall I vanquish thee,
> For out of suffering shall I gather pleasure.

Kashiprosad Ghose and Michael Madhusudan Dutt were low-toned versions, the one of Tom Moore, the other of the lesser, romantic Byron. Dutt was a Bengali poet and there was a certain languid sweetness in his fluent English verse. Two sisters, Aru and Toru Dutt

(1854–74 and 1856–77), belonged to the same group. They came of a rich, educated Calcutta family that was converted to Christianity. They travelled extensively and the girls were educated in France and England, even attending the famous Higher Lectures for Women in Cambridge. Both died young of tuberculosis, Toru at the age of 21 in 1877. She made some effective translations of French verse into English and published a novel in French, *Le Journal de Mademoiselle d'Avers* (1879), and an unfinished English novel, *Bianca*, published in the *Bengal Magazine* in the January–April numbers, 1878. Romesh Chunder Dutt (1848–1909), the elder brother of Aurobindo Ghose (1872–1950), wrote a delicate kind of Victorian lyric in *Love Songs and Elegies* (1898).

> By shady soft degrees
> Thicken the leafy trees
> To reach out dreamily
> Wall and lane over,
> Till in fresh groves are heard,
> In the green clover,
> Warbling their lays each bird
> Over and over.

Two other writers in this clutch, both of them also versifiers in a bloodless Victorian way, were Behramji Malabri (1853–1912), a Parsee, and a western Indian, Nagesh Wishwanath Pai (1860–1920). The first continued Ram Mohan Roy's effort to reconcile East and West, the second, in *Stray Sketches in Chakmakpore* (1894) showed occasional welcome touches of humour and observation decidedly lacking in this period of vague abstraction and genteel attenuation of feeling.

Lest these remarks – the burden of which is that there is no more than a limited, historical interest in Indian nineteenth-century English verse should be thought too peremptorily dismissive, I give the view of an Indian critic and poet, Adil Jussawalla.

> If the writing of poetry implies a particular kind of
> sensitivity to language and a willingness to tax and stretch
> the language, the best poetry in English has been written
> by Indian novelists. No Indian poet writing in English has
> equalled the kind of verbal dexterity we find in Raja Rao's
> *Kanthapura* or G. V. Desani's *All About H. Hatterr*
> . . . though Indian poetry in English is supposed to
> have its roots in the 1820s, it is reasonable to expect its
> earlier practitioners to have been regarded with a familiar

mixture of colonial condescension and drawing-room
tact. . . . Michael Madhusudan Dutt (1827–73), Sarojini
Naidu (1879–1949), and Sri Aurobindo (1872–1950) were
doubtless rather fine people but they wrote some atrocious
verse. And it needed saying when they wrote it. . . .[1]

Genuine Indian poetry in English really began in the nineteen-fifties,
and the reader of today who is strictly interested in poetry can ignore,
except for historical purposes, earlier versifying. This is true of the
English version of the Bengali poetry of Tagore admired by Yeats, and
of the English verse of the distinguished thinker and spiritual luminary,
Sri Aurobindo. His *Savitri*, for example, a work on the relation of
Spirit to Matter, unwinding through twelve books and some 24,000
lines, is a vast onion of a poem of which the layers gradually pull away
to reveal nothing.

To start with I want to concentrate on the work of two contemporary Indian poets whose work seem to me to have an intrinsic
distinction and illustrate in different ways the problem of writing
poetry in a language different from one's mother tongue. And by way
of introduction I shall quote the rather xenophobic stricture of another
Indian critic on the whole undertaking. This is what the caustically
vigorous Buddhadeva Bose writes in P. Lal's enthusiastic but too
inclusive *Modern Indian Poetry in English.*

The best of Indian English verse belongs to the nineteenth
century, when Indians came nearest to 'speaking, thinking
and dreaming in English'. In authenticity of diction and
feeling Sri Aurobindo far outshines the others, but Toru
Dutt's charming pastiche still holds some interest. As for
the present-day 'Indo-Anglians', they are earnest and not
without talent, but it is difficult to see how they can
develop as poets in a language which they have learnt
from books and seldom hear spoken in the streets or even
in their own homes, and whose two great sources lie
beyond the seven seas. As late as 1937, Yeats reminded
Indian writers that 'no man can think or write with music
and vigour except in his mother tongue'; to the great
majority of Indians this admonition was unnecessary, but
the intrepid few who left it unheeded do not yet realize
that 'Indo-Anglian' poetry is a blind alley, lined with curio
shops, leading nowhere.[2]

To this, Nissim Ezekiel (b. 1924), the first of the two poets I shall
consider here, replied:

The tone and implied attitudes of Mr. Buddhadeva Bose's article are distasteful to me. . . . He begins, for example, by pretending to be surprised that 'Indians should ever have tried to write verse in English'. What is so surprising about it? Is Mr Bose completely devoid of a sense of history? Does it not occur to him that since English was introduced as a medium of higher education in India, some Indians *naturally* took to writing verse in it, just as other Indians wrote political commentaries, philosophical essays, sociological surveys, economic studies, and so on? Historical situations create cultural consequences. . . . To write poetry in English because one cannot write it in any other language is surely not a despicable decision.[3]

Despicable? Most certainly not. Right? That is the question. Language, we can all agree, is the supremely humanizing influence, through which there is instituted in man a second, human nature; language is the means by which the setting of the human being is immensely enlarged, and the context of his action made immeasurably more complex. It is through the sentence patterns we use, the idioms, the words and the images, that the categories of thinking, feeling, valuing which they imply are incorporated into the stuff of our being. Language is both the creator and the expression of what is most deeply and peculiarly human in us. But this is language learnt naturally, insensibly, in the very act of living and from the first moment of our dimmest awareness. A language learnt when we are fully developed seems in comparison an artificial contrivance, between us and which there exists a gap impossible to close. How can such language express our human experience with the fullness and body of poetry? Surely in a fundamental way Yeats, if not Buddhadeva Bose, must be right? And yet there are poems by Indian writers which seem by any standard to belong to the canon of poetry. There are those which seem to be the product of a natural instinct rather than an artificial taste. About Nissim Ezekiel himself we have to remember that he is an Indian Jew of Bene-Israel origin, belonging to a community long established in India and that in his own family English was indeed the language of the home, and his use of it from the earliest days was instinctive and natural. But of course it was a language disconnected from a society constantly using and changing it, a language which to a greater degree than with native speakers had to rely for enrichment on books rather than a living use. Perhaps this accounts in Nissim Ezekiel both for the quality of inhibition one sometimes detects in his verse, and the occasional oppressive sense of deliberation and control his poetry communicates. And perhaps, finally, it is this discontinuity between the private voice and public usage that explains an intermittent degree of unawareness, surprising in so alert and scrupulous a writer, of the moribund in some of his phrases. His writing slackens momentarily because the worn out metaphor still keeps for him a suggestion of life long gone for his readers. Here is an example or two of this imperviousness to rust.

> You breathe the bitter air of loneliness,
> Pretending that it does not matter when
> You close the door and switch the wireless on,
>
> ('Virginal')

> Your sad and thoughtful love I heard
> Above the tumult of despair.
> You bent your head, I touched your hair,
> The sign was timed without a word.
>
> ('Love Poem')

> You stood before me, bold and shy,
> Your sari rustled as you bent
> To kiss, the mid-day tide ran high.
>
> ('One Afternoon')

Bitter air, sad and thoughtful love, bold and shy; this limp and melted diction, evidence of a sleeping obliviousness, is certainly not characteristic either of Ezekiel's literary personality or its expression in language. The one, in fact, is dry and detached, the other firmer, cooler, more precise. Together they give the work, low-keyed and unflamboyant as it is, a marked individuality, an unusual definition.

> Perhaps there is another way
> and I will find it: concentrate,
> concentrate, make the mind a fist.
> Why should I be reconciled
> to middle-aged spread and rigmarole?
> If nothing else, I'll keep my nerve,
> refuse the company of priests,
> professors, commentators, moralists,
> be my own guest in my own
> one-man lunatic asylum,
> questioning the Furies, my patron saints
> about their old and new obscurities.
>
> ('A Small Summit')

If Ezekiel has on one side the inhibiting discontinuity of a gap

between himself and the living, used language, he has on another side
a second but very different creative discontinuity. This is constituted
by his being of Jewish descent in a Hindu culture. It is both a theme
of his poetry and a source of considerable energy in it. It performs both
functions in 'Background, Casually', 'Island', 'In India', 'Enterprise',
'Central', and at a further remove, it is an ironic infusion in other
poems like 'Healers', 'Cows', 'Yashwant Jagtap', 'Very Indian Poem
in Indian English', and 'Night of the Scorpion'. Nissim Ezekiel in the
Indian scene is a permanent expatriate, but one who has freely elected
to stay. Displaced by his own spiritual past, he is in place by an act
of the will. His eye is familiar with, but at a distance from, the object,
and his specifically Indian poetry is both inward and detached, a
combination making for a peculiar strength and validity.

> The Indian landscape sears my eyes.
> I have become a part of it
> To be observed by foreigners.
> They say that I am singular,
> Their letters overstate the case.
> I have made my commitments now.
> This one: to stay where I am,
> As others choose to give themselves
> In some remote and backward place.
> My backward place is where I am.
>
> ('Background, Casually')

One is aware of a double impulse in the poet, which on the one
hand keeps him at a distance from his environment as he clutches his
private history and aspiration, and which on the other, by means of
a free and painful act of will, reconciles him to his environment. The
first section of 'In India' makes the one point, 'Island' the other:

> Always, in the sun's eye,
> Here among the beggars,
> Hawkers, pavement sleepers,
> Hutment dwellers, slums,
> Dead souls of men and gods,
> Burnt out mothers, frightened
> Virgins, wasted child
> And tortured animal,
> All in noisy silence
> Suffering the place and time,
> I ride my elephant of thought,
> A Cezanne slung around my neck.
>
> ('In India')

Unsuitable for son as well as sense
the island flowers into slums
and skyscrapers, reflecting
precisely the growth of my mind.
I am here to find my way in it.

Sometimes I cry for help
but mostly keep my own counsel.
I hear distorted echoes
of my own ambiguous voice
and of dragons claiming to be human.

Bright and tempting breezes
flow across the island,
separating past from future,
then the air is still again
as I sleep the sleep of ignorance.

How delight the soul with absolute
sense of salvation, how
hold to a single willed direction
I cannot leave the island,
I was born here and belong.

Even now a host of miracles
hurries me to daily business,
minding the ways of the island
as a good native should,
taking calm and clamour in my stride.

('Island')

Such an accommodation, while it is absolute in the sense of having been made and accepted, can never be total and unwavering. It encourages the collected rather than the tranquil mind, and it cannot fail to keep alive, even if it mitigates, some tension between the poet and his context. That tension qualifies him to be a remarkable observer, sharp, accurate, unsentimental, and where necessary, grim, as in his caustic reporting of certain elements in the Indian scene, for example in 'In India', 'Untouchables', 'Yashwant Jagtap', 'Healers' and 'Servant'. If his Jewishness denies the poet a background he might have shared with his Indian society, his recognition of his place and status give him an assured ground under foot from which to operate with an unqualified deftness. At the same time it leaves him intensely conscious of his situation and alert to other attractions.

Fish-soul in that silent pool
I found myself supported

> by the element I lived in,
> but dragged out with the greatest ease
> by any fluttering fly
> at the end of a hook.

('Two Images')

Coolness, distaste, objectivity: these are the marks of Ezekiel's harsher notions of Indian life, as in the poem on the misused, anonymous maidservant, or the one on the grandfather in the monsoon water supporting the grandchild who has learned to sleep on his shoulder. They are also, together with a fastidious distaste for anything loud or ornate and a balancing sense of proportion and perspective, the marks of his more affectionate recording, particularly in the context of the family, where his work shows that specially Indian candour and joy in family relationships that we observe in the writings of Narayan and Raja Rao. In these poems, for example 'Cows' and 'Night of the Scorpion', the gentleness is protected by irony, the sweetness made keen by a subdued mockery. In 'Cows' the author's mother, a seventy-year-old lady, collecting money for her school, complains about the cows on the pavements:

> She knows that cows are holy,
> worshipped by the parents
> of the children in her school.
> Even gods ought not to clutter up
> the pavements – that's her view.
> She's not against beliefs: believe
> what you like, she says,
> but get out of my way.

In 'Night of the Scorpion' the mother is stung, the rationalist and sceptical father tries 'every curse and blessing,/powder, mixture, herb and hybrid' as the peasants swarm in to console her, offering medical advice of a strongly ritualistic and faith-healing kind:

> They clicked their tongues.
> With every movement that the scorpion made
> his poison moved in Mother's blood, they said.
> May he sit still, they said.
> May the sins of your previous birth
> be burned away tonight, they said.
> May your suffering decrease
> the misfortunes of your next birth, they said.
> May the sum of evil

balanced in this unreal world
against the sum of good
become diminished by your pain.
May the poison purify your flesh
of desire, and your spirit of ambition,
they said, and they sat around
on the floor with my mother in the centre,
the peace of understanding on each face.

These lines convey the lilt and cadence of the Indian voice with ease
and precision. They suggest too the ingenuous simplicity of the peasant
beliefs as well as their spontaneous human good will. At the same time
the choric *they said, they said, they said,* implies something of the
ancient, sophisticated ritual of the chanting – as against the primitive
quality of its content – just as it points up the ironic detachment of the
poet. A lighter, more bantering exercise of this near-mathematical skill
in exact reproduction of tone, idiom and voice, occurs in the gleefully
comic but unpatronizing 'Very Indian Poem in Indian English':

I am standing for peace and non-violence,
Why world is fighting fighting
Why all people of world
Are not following Mahatma Gandhi,
I am simply not understanding.
Ancient Indian Wisdom is 100 per cent correct.
I should say even 200 per cent correct.
But modern generation is neglecting –
Too much going for fashion and foreign thing.

Other day I'm reading in newspaper
(Every day I'm reading Times of India
To improve my English language)
How one goonda fellow
Throw stone at Indirabehn.
Must be student unrest fellow, I am thinking.
Friends, Romans, countrymen, I am saying
(to myself)
Lend me the ears.
Everything is coming –
Regeneration, Remuneration, Contraception.
Be patiently, brothers and sisters.

Perhaps I could pause here to make a general comment on Nissim
Ezekiel, and the reader I am sure will be able to judge its propriety

even from the verse I have quoted so far. (I exclude, naturally, the deliberately light-hearted and charming *jeu d'ésprit* 'Very Indian Poem in Indian English'.) Nissim Ezekiel's poetry is lucid, rhythmically subtle, scrupulously honest in its effort to be accurate, calm, deliberate. At the same time it is relatively less marked by resonance, imaginative vehemence or any richly metaphorical suggestiveness. Above all it is clear, not in the sense of being simply explicable or paraphrasable, but in seeming to move in an open, level, uncomplicated light. Part of this effect must be the consequence of a lack of constant connection with the living language in a society in which it is both the means and the measure of profound experience. The poetry gives the impression of seeming to operate in a world in which the doors to the subconscious are, if not wholly, almost shut. If poetry, as Coleridge said, is 'rationalized dream', then the emphasis in Ezekiel is very much on its rationality. Nissim Ezekiel's poetry, indeed, raises in a modern form the question first posed by Coleridge in *Anima Poetae* (1802):

> *Quaere*, whether or not too great definiteness of terms in any language may not consume too much of the vital and idea-creating force in distinct, clear, full-made images, and so prevent originality. For original might be distinguished from positive thought.

Ezekiel offers a characteristically self-deprecating explanation for the sense of imaginative debility one sometimes takes from his work: 'no greater curse/than a minor talent' – but this is much too modest. The quality of the talent has less to do with it than the fact of his linguistic isolation. In any case, there *are* poems endowed with vital and idea-creating force and exhibiting original rather than just positive thought. This group would include poems already referred to, like 'A Small Summit', 'Night of the Scorpion', 'Island', 'Background, Casually', as well as 'Lawn', 'Poet, Lover, Birdwatcher', 'Philosophy', 'The Visitor', 'Paradise Flycatcher', 'In the Country Cottage', 'March', 'The Seed', 'Theological', 'Central'.

In the best of these poems, and in all of them at their best, what was a certain passivity becomes a more tingling and nipping presence. The method is still that of the naturalist's observation – Ezekiel is like a poetic birdwatcher – but the observation is so alert, fresh, so intent and honest, that it becomes a creative act. The purpose of the poems appears to be the exploration of, and then the giving of shape to, some real event whether of the outer or the inner world, the movement of a bird's wing or the tense immobility of a lizard, or the drift of a soul away from existence to some cold lucidity, or the poet's scratching effort to drag himself 'with shoestring effort to a small summit'. Part of this creative observation is what the poet calls in 'Lawn', 'the gentle art/of leaving things alone', that is an interest which does not interfere with the validity of the object; and another part is attending with patience, sympathy and self-restraint. As he says in the same poem:

> You keep an eye on it
> in rapport with its secret laws,
> maintain its ritual
> of mortality.

Nissim Ezekiel's work calls to mind a remark of George Santayana: 'Art supplies constantly to contemplation what nature seldom affords in concrete experience – the union of life and peace.'[4] This poetry itself a discipline of contemplation, certainly affords to the contemplative reader what concrete experience offers to this exquisitely equipped observer – occasions for the union of life and peace. The impression the poems give is one of intense, active tranquillity.

Ezekiel's mild, unemphatic delivery, a matter of cool diction, moderate metaphor, or syntax rather than music, fits his chosen stance as vigilant observer. His effort seems to be to disturb the silence as little as possible, to keep himself concealed, to let things happen and be recorded. He joins to his alert eye a delicate acumen about the significance of what the eye shows, and the result is clear and present, undistorted by any distracting obsession with self. The modesty and objectivity of his attitude, the neutrality of the medium, the restraint of self, provide the context in which the ordinary can reveal itself to be what it is, a tissue of the mysterious. To catch the ordinary in this way requires not an exercise of will, not forcing the pace, but waiting for words to come, trusting the slow movement, letting things be and happen.

> The slow movement seems, somehow, to say much more.
> To watch the rarer birds, you have to go
> Along deserted lanes and where the rivers flow
> In silence near the source, or by a shore
> Remote and thorny like the heart's dark floor.
> And there the women slowly turn around,
> Not only flesh and bone but myths of light
> With darkness at the core, and sense is found
> By poets lost in crooked, restless flight,
> The deaf can hear, the blind recover sight.
>
> ('Poet, Lover, Birdwatcher')

The mood, of course, is not just a comfortable and passive one, the posture not easy or reclining. It would, indeed, be impossible to associate that with a temperament as scrupulous and positive as

Ezekiel's, or with poetry as intellectually complex, fastidious and austere. It is, rather, a harassed and worn acceptance of the limitations of his own self as we see in his scratchy poem 'Theological',

> Even as myself, my very own
> incontrovertible, unexceptional
> self, I feel I am disguised,

or of the limitation of art, of what can be said and what cannot be said:

> But residues of meaning still remain
> As darkest myths meander through the pain
> Towards a final formula of light.
> I, too, reject that clarity of sight:
> What cannot be explained, do not explain.

('Philosophy')

I turn now to R. Parthasarathy, one of the most engaging and gifted of the new generation of Indian poets, and a writer who has agonized over this problem of writing poetry in English, and, in fact, come, it appears, to the most radical solution possible. Parthasarathy was born in 1934 and studied at the University of Bombay, and as a postgraduate at the University of Leeds. He works in publishing. He began to learn English at the age of ten at a Christian school kept by the Don Bosco Fathers. His days at school and university were an intense infatuation with England and English literature. When he first came to England his experience was utterly different from that of Henry James, a writer with a similar feel for the country. England offered James a total environment in which he could both construct a coherent identity and develop his own powers to their fullest. James discovered a context hospitable to his nature and responsive to the peculiar demands of his genius, an economy in which the actualities and possibilities, the relations and directions of his life combine to make 'a more constituted and sustained act of living'. Parthasarathy, a talent, I hasten to say, of a very different order of significance, found nothing so favourable in what awaited him. For James 'treasures of susceptibility lay waiting to be enjoyed', and his life was a prolongation of the act of arriving in England, where a dense and richly loaded presence confronted him on all sides. Parthasarathy arrived in England in 1963 on a scholarship from the British Council, and spent his first Christmas with an old friend from Bombay in his flat at Hampstead feasting on Guinness and packets of crisps and finding with every second and every circumstance his lyrical expectations grimly deflated. Where James found literature authenticated by life, and imagination corroborated by experience, Parthasarathy saw nothing that was not alien and obscure. He says himself that he was uneasy in India and hypercritical of everything Indian. He felt Indian society to be deeply neurotic, its feet chained to a grossly exaggerated past.

> I decided that England would be my future home. And
> the English language would help me to belong there. In
> my ignorance I even hoped for fame as a poet in English.
> But events were to prove otherwise. The English autumn
> was a little too much for my hopefully expanding tropical
> petals. In England, at last, history caught up with me: I
> found myself crushed under two hundred years of British
> rule in India. I began to have qualms about my own
> integrity as an Indian. Had not Emerson said: 'India fell to
> British character'? My encounter with England only
> reproduced the now familiar pattern of English experience
> in India: disenchantment. Here was an England I was
> unable to come to terms with. The England I had known
> and loved existed nowhere, except in my mind. This *other*
> England I didn't know even existed. My disenchantment
> was total. I felt betrayed. I was no longer a 'body of
> England's breathing English air'.[5]

Parthasarathy's disenchantment with things English seems as romantic as his previous infatuation. But it was not wholly a negative experience. He discovered in the course of it a new understanding of himself and of India. He returned to India with the intention of identifying with her totally. He spent some ten years writing poetry in English. But he now found that this very exercise continued to alienate him from his own civilization. It seemed to him that he could never master English totally, could never be utterly at home in it. But can anyone, English or American? One has the feeling that Parthasarathy's discomfort is purely intellectual. His own language, his own poetry, seems a living contradiction of his own argument. Here is a poem in which he speaks of this very predicament, but speaks of it with such inwardness and certainty as to abolish or make suspect the reality of the predicament he is describing.

> *Tamil*[6]
> My tongue in English chains
> I return, after
> a generation, to you

I am at the end
of my dravidic tether,
hunger for you unassuaged.

I falter, stumble,
Speak in a tired language
wrenched from its sleep

in the *Kural*,
teeth, palate, lips still new
to its agglutinative touch.

Now, hooked on celluloid
you go reeling
down plush corridors.

This is a middling poem but wholly characteristic of the author's
spirit and procedure, in its bareness, its drily regretful feeling, its
dispassionate tone, in its rhythm derived from the nice balancing of
carefully weighted phrases, and above all in its imagist technique. Any
poem by Parthasarathy is an assembly of images, usually visual
images; but it is more than that. The difference between him and the
more old fashioned or purely imagist poets is that while their poems
tend to be collections of fragments, sets of items with every connection
suppressed, Parthasarathy is more successful, at least in his better
work, in conducting an argument or arranging a scene or managing
a situation by means of images. Like other imagist poets, he flinches
from generality and abstraction, but this does not, as with many of
them, wholly cancel the discursive element of his poetry. Here, for
example, is a poem in which the image of the stairs, collecting into
itself the notes of climbing, longing and lodging, is used to summon
a situation and realize an experience while simultaneously commem-
orating a brittle happiness and communicating a sense of the poet's
bleak recognition of his own and life's limitation.

A year ago I held
these rails, your arms,
and climbed the stairs (all
marble to my palms)

of your flesh and bone
towards some dark sphere.
It wasn't the first time
I'd been a tenant there.

Other stairs and rails
have guided me,

always with the chill promise
of a home. Only

the heart isn't hospitable anywhere.

('Stairs')

Parthasarathy, like Nissim Ezekiel, is totally without that swelling euphoria of the late romantic tradition as it manifested itself among literary Indians. A kind of melancholy is common to them both, calmer in Ezekiel, more nervy in Parthasarathy. Disappointment is his principal theme, whether with the edgy complications of love, with the insoluble problems of poetic composition or as in England in face of the actuality of what he expected. He accepts disappointment with an irritable but unprotesting glumness, a slightly morose recognition of the way things are. A proportion between his themes and his temperament makes his work a singularly faithful projection of his nature, and accounts for the absence of fabrication and externality in it.

His naturalness and honesty of feeling are helped by this delicate skill in managing an idiomatic and unpretentiously modern line and voice. The span of the instrument may not be great but the cleanness and directness of the speech actively engage the reader's sympathy and persuade him to co-operate in accepting whatever modification of line or voice is necessary for the poet's purposes. A tiny illustration of what I mean is the last line of the poem I quoted just now, 'Stairs': 'Only/ the heart isn't hospitable anywhere.' The line is cool and grey, but saved from flatness by the natural break after 'Only', and by the active and passive meanings conflated in 'hospitable'. In fact, it turns out not to be simple or flat, and to have just that degree of complexity appropriate to one brooding, not with passion but with a sort of moderate melancholy on his checked, imperfect experiences of love. A second example in which the theme joins Parthasarathy's interest in his own past to his agitation about problems of composition shows again this natural, scrupulous and restrained line, and his gift for making a contemporary idiom suggest with precision the character of his personal experience:

Much experience, they say
dulls the mind:
    the hands touch
    the lips meet
at the evocation of a word.
Only we haven't the words
to bring it off.

But stumbling on experience
I chanced on an implement,
a supererogatory silence.

('A Supererogatory Silence')

And the essential bias of that experience, it seems to me, is the fascination with the element of foreignness in his experience. He is both attracted to and frightened by what is alien and distant in his life, whether this is in India, or the England his love affair with the English language took him to, or with the India he discovers when he is away, or the strange Tamil he decides to cultivate on his return, whether it is his experiences of love or his awareness of himself.

The street in the evening
tilts homeward
as traffic piles up.

It is then I stir about:
rise from the table
and shake the dust from my eyes.

Pick up my glasses
and look
For myself uneasily.

('Complaint')

The quality of difference breaks upon him with such shock because of the cold and accurate objectivity with, he sees, a capacity responsible for the glass-like quality of his language. His imagery even when it is in the form of metaphor is essentially composed of similes, aids to clearer sight. The consciousness of what is alien or different or remote is produced by his historical situation, his education, and the special circumstances of his life. But it is also accounted for by a poetic personality which glides silently through experience observing its properties with meticulous exactitude and an uneasy sense of not being at home.

Parthasarathy's verse is slight in bulk. Sometimes the creative pulse seems faint, and occasionally there is a scratchily personal self-regard. But at its best it is the poetry of a mature and sensitive writer, bare of unorganic ornamentation, natural in its movement, and peculiarly contemporary in its tone and idiom. The feeling it communciates is one of a pure and unaffected melancholy which calls to mind the subdued grief of Collins. It would be tragic if such a genuine talent were allowed to rust unused.

Other poets untroubled by Nissim Ezekiel's double loyalties or

Parthasarathy's sense of linguistic infidelity continue to write poems in English and sometimes both in English and a mother tongue. Indeed of the poets included in Parthasarathy's own balanced and informative anthology, *Ten Twentieth-Century Indian Poets* (1976), eight are truly bilingual. (I must interrupt myself at this point to say some poets and some poems referred to in this chapter will be inaccessible to the British reader. I propose, therefore, as much as possible, to limit myself to quoting from the two anthologies already mentioned.) When we look at one of these, P. Lal's comprehensive collection, we see the general situation with all its knots and oddities set out before us. There seem to be a remarkable number of Indians engaged in writing English verse. Many are academics, a considerable number are women, many of them have been published in Britain and the United States. The volume contains the usual quantity of tedious cleverness, both literary and typographical, and the expected amount of derivation from the usual sources. There are examples of a superannuated poeticism. Not that one would not have to say much the same about a comparable collection from many other countries. These writers, it is very clear, cannot but have deep and stubborn difficulties. And yet one has to acknowledge the technical adroitness of many poets, the skill with which K. D. Katrak, Mary Ernekar, Gauri Deshpande or Arvind Mehistra follow the contours of a speech which is both contemporary and distinctly Indian. Kamala Das is the best known of several women poets. And there are poems – 'Ashes' by Kishore Theckaduth, 'Coming up for Counsel' by I. Sarthi, 'Oranges on a Table' by Simivas Rayaprol, 'The Second Man' and 'The Death of Old Adam' by Sumiti Namjoshi, 'Fresh Faces' by T. V. Dattatreyan, 'Seekers' by Sukanta Chaudhuri, 'Half Blind' by Michael Daniels, 'A Jarring Note' by D. P. Blagat, which certainly confirm the Indian conviction that Indians enjoy an unusual inwardness of understanding of the English language and possess a peculiar sympathy with it because of historical circumstances and the bent of the Indian sensibility, conditions which qualify them in an unusual way to call on real, if latent resources of the English language.

A principal aim of many of the contemporary poets was to distance themselves from the smooth passivity of their Victorian and Georgian predecessors, and the way to achieve this was to strive to generate energy in their verse, the movement which is a sign of inner life which they saw as the first and essential characteristic of their poetry. Sometimes both subject and treatment seem predestined by this purpose. For example, in Keki N. Daruwalla's (b. 1937) poem *The Epileptic* a pregnant woman, already the mother of two children, is convulsed by a savage fit. Daruwalla's harsh, plain language and his offhand objectivity of manner convey without strain the violence of the woman's

suffering and the lightening transition she undergoes from the family
and indeed from the human family to an alien world governed by
forces denuded of consciousness and control. The detail is brutal and
exact – the husband plucking out the receding tongue, the traffic
grinding to an inquisitive halt the crowd sensing a mishap before it sees
one, the people fanning her and rubbing her feet.

> She was not hysteric, she didn't
> her force was flushed, abstract, the marionette-
> head jerked from side to side, a slave
> to cross-pulls. A thin edge of froth
> simmered round her lips
> like pan-dregs left by a receding wave . . .
> Just when he said, 'She isn't shaping
> too well', she recovered, bleached
>   by the sun of her agony.
> As a limp awareness slouched
>   along her face
> I found it was the husband who
>   was shaking.

The presence of the public throughout the poem and its personally
unengaged interest, the physician and his merely professional concern
and the shift in attention from patient to husband at the end all serve
to put a firm frame around the violence concentrated in the epileptic,
enclosing the incomprehensible in a human and rational context. Violence, framed and controlled, is the theme of several of Daruwalla's best
poems whether it be natural violence or human violence, a river in
spate or the shooting of a bird or an appalling presence in life itself.

> I can smell violence in the air
> like the lash of coming rain –
> mass hatred drifting grey across the moon.

> It hovers brooding, poised like a cobra
> as I go prodding rat-holes
> and sounding caverns
> looking for a fang that darts,
> a hood that sways
> and eyes that squint a reptile hate.
> I watch my wounds but they don't turn green.
> Cross-bones I look for you!
> Death I am looking
> For that bald bone-head of yours!

Kamala Das (b. 1934) is clearly an original on the Indian scene. Her tartly honest answers to a questionnaire from the editor of *Modern Indian Poetry in English* (pp. 102–3) include the following: 'I write poetry in English because I have found writing in English a little less difficult than writing in Malaylam. . . . "Why in English" is a silly question. It is like asking us why we do not write in Swahili or Serbo-Croat. English being the most familiar, we use it. That is all . . . I feel that when a poet publishes a poem only other poets read it with interest. Poetry has no other type of audience anywhere. Unless like Evtushenko we climb the stage and roar.' And in a bibliographical note in the same volume she says 'Born 1934. Education – nothing to speak of. Married to Madhara Das, with three sons. Health – poor. I cannot think of anything else to say about myself.'

The originality of Kamala Das as a poet is in part a function of her independent, awkward personality, in part of her fundamental rejection of the traditional Hindu woman's virtues, modesty, reticence, deference, and in part of the robust and confident idiom she has worked out for herself.

> The language I speak
> Becomes mine, its distortions, its queernesses
> All mine, mine alone. It is half English, half
> Indian, funny perhaps, but it is honest . . .

It is also an idiom capable on occasion of breathtaking infelicity

> Oh sea, let me shrink or grow, slosh up,
> Slide down, go your way.

Her poetry is self-centred and unabashedly sexual although the sexuality seems more fascinating to the poet because it is hers than because it is sexual. She speaks of her sexual experience in tones which are both self-indulgent and truculent.

> Ask me, everybody, ask me
> What he sees in me, ask me why he is
>   called a lion
> A libertine, ask me the flavour of his
> Mouth, ask me why his hand sways like
>   a hooded snake
> Before it clasps my pubes. Ask me why like
> A great tree felled, he slumps against
>   my breasts,
> And sleeps . . .

A better organized and more effective poetry results when sex recedes into the background of consciousness or below it and is used as an implicity and potent symbol of a spontaneous natural life. A good example of a better inner discipline and a more fruitful use of resources is 'The Dance of the Eunuchs'

It was hot so hot before the eunuchs came
To dance with skirts going round and round, cymbals
Richly clashing and anklets jingling, jingling,
Jingling . . . There were green
Tattoos on their chests, jasmines in their hair, Some
Were dark and some were almost fair. Their voices
Were harsh, their songs melancholy; they sang of
Lovers dying and children left unborn . . .
Some beat their drums; others beat their sorry breasts
And wailed and writhed in vacant ecstacy. They
Were thin in limbs and dry; like half-burnt logs from
Funeral pyres, a drought and a rottenness
Were in each of them. Even the crows were so
Silent on trees, and the children wide-eyed, still,
All were watching these poor creatures' convulsions.
The sky crackled then, thunder came and lightning
And rain, a meagre rain that smelt of dust in
Attics and the urine of lizards and mice . . .

There is, no doubt, a certain moral limitation in the attitude of the poet, an egotistic lack of sympathy. And the phrase, 'these poor creatures' convulsions' is singularly unsuccessful in expressing the poet's or enlisting the reader's sympathy. Nevertheless the poem does enforce the distinction between a natural spontaneous energy of which sex as Kamala Das understands it is the silent, pointed image, and the frantic whirling of the eunuchs, a forced and adventitious energy, meagre and sad, calling up the smell of 'dust in attics and the urine of lizards and mice'.

Arun Kolatkar (b. 1932) is a poet altogether different from the ungainly, driving, self-intoxicated Kamala Das. He is neat, cool, fastidiously in control of his material and decently self-effacing. I use the word neat in both senses, namely tidy and pure. The curve of the line in his verse is both delicate and exact, the distribution of weight within the line varied and balanced, the image cleanly defined; at the same time the writer is free of Parthasarathy's uneasy sense of betrayal and the pull of double loyalties in Nissim Ezekiel. An integrated psyche and a unified sensibility are the marks of this unusual poetry.

There are in *Ten Twentieth-Century Indian Poets* generous excerpts from Kolatkar's two sequences of poems, 'The Boatride' and '*Jejuri*' and perhaps I can illustrate the *oeuvre* from these. Here then is a brief piece from 'The Boatride'.

> because a sailor waved back
> to a boy
> another boy
> waved to another sailor
>
> in the clarity of air
> the gesture withers for want
> of correspondence and
> the hand that returns to him
> the hand his knee accepts
> as his own
> is the hand
> of an aged person
> a hand
> that must remain patient
> and give the boy its part of time
> to catch up

In the small space of this poem there seems to be plenty of room to fix a moment of time, to fill it with movement, to define the psychological consequence of the action and to complete the temporal circle by connecting the present instance to the future. Filling but not cramming the space in a poem is an art used effectively in 'The Boatride' and in another sequence *Jejuri* which is organized around a pilgrimage to a famous temple in Western Maharashtra, although 'organized' is too oppressive a word to describe the subdued connections between the various parts of the sequence. The poet, before he fills it, has to create the space in the poem and Kolatkar does this by blending techniques of dispersal, widening the scope of reference by contrast and analogy, and concentration, by foreshortening and telescoping. For example in 'The boatride' space is dispersed across the sea by the contrast between a pair of knees streaking down the mast and the clarity of the air or between the wave of a boy's hand and the bulk of the sea; again the melancholy of farewell and loneliness is concentrated in the boy's unanswered wave to a sailor, the relations between humankind and the sea telescopes into the two sisters looking past the boatman's profile

> splicing
> the wrinkles

of his saline
face

and loose ends
of the sea

and the finality, the absolute conclusiveness of the voyage's and man's
end by what faces the boat as it sidles up to land,

and expanse of
unswerving stone
encrusted coarsely
with shells
admonishes our sight

Space in the next poem of Kolatkar I want to glance at is created
by the very idea of a pilgrimage to which the state transport bus adds
the note of shabby, ordinary life. (The poet's own attitude to the sacred
element in pilgrimage is less that of the believer with qualms and more
that of the agnostic with pangs.) Concentration in this poem is not
only a method of realization but also part of what is being realized.
Here is the poem as it develops after an opening in which we see the
bus roaring towards town, its tarpaulin flaps buttoned down over the
windows.

Your own divided face in a pair of glasses
on an old man's nose
is all the countryside you get to see.
You seem to move continually forward
towards a destination
just beyond the caste-mark between his eyebrows.

Outside, the sun has risen quietly.
It aims through an eyelet in the tarpaulin
and shoots at the old man's glasses.

A sawed–off sunbeam comes to rest
grimly against the driver's right temple.
The bus seems to change direction.

At the end of the bumpy ride
with your own face on either side
when you get off the bus

you don't step inside the old man's head.

Travelling by bus in India through the night towards dawn affords
an immediate experience of the immensity of space. There are two

observations to be made on the management of this element in the poem. First the hugeness of space is controlled and deftly directed by the poet. He translates space into distance and distance into light, diminishing and intensifying it into the little light trickling out from the bus, the image in the old man's glasses, the sunbeam resting on his right temple. The poem focuses great forces, turning them into visible and comprehensible points of light. A second and related observation is that, as in perception, our basic experience itself, in this poem the subjective and the objective flow in and out of one another, modifying, correcting and dissolving each other. Massive external realities are summoned and made subject to the author's wry vision.

> Outside, the sun has risen quietly.
> It aims through an eyelet in the tarpaulin
> And shoots at the old man's glasses.

The basic psychological truth of Kolotkar's reading of experience gives a solid support to the structure of the poem and brings a freshness and sanity to his detached and impishly humorous attitude. A pure distillation of the poet's attractively humane attitude at once disenchanted and appreciative occurs in the tiny poem, *Chaitanya*, a fifteenth-century Bengali saint revered as an incarnation of Krishna.

> 'Sweet as grapes
> are the stones of Jejusi',
> said Chaitanya.
>
> He popped a stone
> in his mouth
> and spat out gods.

Kolatkar's poems, like the temperament evinced in them, are low-toned, organized and unpretentious, with much of the quality of the English Movement poets of some thirty years ago. Shiv K. Kumar, on the other hand, has a more vivid personality, has a more strident tone and is a degree more self-conscious. His rhythms are looser and freer and his attitude, despite the plenitude of contemporary reference, more old-fashioned. There is a distinctly Victorian feeling about these lines from 'Days in New York', a characteristic blend of locality and stance.

> At night the Voices of America
> break in upon my tenuous frequency,
> intoning the same fact three times,
> till the sediment grips the Hudson's soul.
> But my soul is still my own.

Shiv Kumar is an academic, a Professor of English Literature, and like other academics he tends to depend as much on literature as on life for significance in his poems. Imagery of the kind associated with the early urban Eliot is common in his verse. Rats, bones, skulls abound, and while his experience both in India and New York may well have given him a warrant for its use, there is still a distinctly literary flavour to it. This, together with a markedly strident, even truculent tone, gives his verse peculiarly individual character. Here is the first stanza of a poem to Kali, the goddess of destruction.

> Stone eyes of a mangled street dog
> glance at my self's patina.
> The rufous tongue of a cobra
> sticks out each time
> I circle round your ebony torso,
> jabbed in the privates
> by your devotees.

Flamboyance and stridency of the kind remarked in Kamala Das and Shiv K. Kumar are uncommon in Indian poets writing in English. Indeed, in many what is most noticeable is an inner quietude, the tranquillity of tacit acceptances and certainties provided by an ancient and vital tradition of civilization and spirituality. Arvind Krishna Mehrotra and Jayanta Mahapatra (b. 1928), and different as they are from one another, are at least alike in sharing this sensibility of fundamental assurance. The poet K. N. Daruwalla writes of Mahapatra in *Two Decades of Indian Poetry, 1960–80*: 'Mahapatra's poetry is restrained and balanced. He does not indulge in verbal excesses nor does his voice turn shrill decrying the world around him. There is a built-in irony in his poetry, but it is muted, subtle and spread over a long passage so that it never really develops a sting, (p. 118)'[7] Mahapatra deals with Indian tradition and with traditional subjects and figures: the patient woman, the bazaar, the cow, the prostitute, the land – in his case the landscape of Orissa – snakes, crows, temples, rickshaw-pullers, shrines.

> I close my eyes, feeling the million prayers
> sitting on the villages across the land of my father:
> a warm memory, cry behind the deodars.
> Years have broken time into small fragments of light and
>   shadow,
> elsewhere a hawk swoops to its deep experience of hope,
> a large group of stony women in front of a shrine
> silently sit out the whole day waiting to be cured of their own
>   will.

These lines are from 'A Ritual'. Here is another poem, 'Indian Summer', in the same mode which becomes a tiny potent symbol of the Indian-ness of India.

Over the soughing of the sombre wind,
priests chant louder than ever:
the mouth of India opens.

Crocodiles move into deeper waters.
Mornings of heated middens
smoke under the sun.

The good wife
lies in my bed
through the long afternoon,
dreaming still, unexhausted
by the deep roar of funeral pyres.

Arvind Krishna Mehrotra, born in Lahore in 1947, must have been a tempestuous young man. As an undergradute he edited a magazine called *Damn You* which ran for six issues. He also founded the Ezra-Fakir Press. In P. Lal's *Modern Indian Poetry in English* he heaps Laurentian abuse on his contemporary poets: 'Indians writing in English have made no mark when it came to poetry because still the town-men are its practitioners. Nissim, you, Adil, people living in a dead, closed, soil-less world, craving for attention in the far west. Selling their little talent to see their name in print and they all dried, melted. You have turned to translation, Nissim, to writing poems about swans and editing and running after foundations begging. Adil to staying in London "close to things".'[8] And yet there is little of these adolescent fireworks in his poetry which is serious, controlled and methodic. *Ten Twentieth-Century Indian Poets* quotes Mehrotra citing *Manifesto of Surrealism*, published twenty-three years before he was born as an influence on his poetry and attributing to it what Mehrotra himself described as his 'intolerance and passionate use of the thing which is the image'. For my part this gives too much credit to the *Manifesto*, too little to the poet who used a surrealistic technique but was never the prisoner of it, whose gift of imagery was spontaneous and personal and whose use of it was neither passionate nor immoderate but rather measured and effective.

In his brilliant poem, 'The Sale', Mehrotra takes a single image and elaborates it, through the length of a substantial poem. But all the generation of energy is from within, and there is no sense of accretion, or softness or pointless extension. Life is seen as a vast saleroom crowded with natural and human products, the genuine, the fake, the odd and the ordinary. There is an intrinsic logic, the logic of language, of subject, verb, predicate in the progression of the poem which leads the listener on in his accustomed ways. (It is significant, a tribute to the naturalness of the idiom, that one says listener but not reader.) But another economy, a wholly different argument is pitched against our expectations. The disconcerting, the utterly unexpected predicates, undermine our comfortable assurance about what is to come and leave us facing strangeness and danger.

Here is the second section of the poem.

> Would you mind if I showed you
> a few more things now yours?
> Be careful, one river is still wet
> and slippery; its waters continue to
> run like footprints. Well, this is a
> brick and we call that string.
> This microscope contains the margins
> of a poem. I have a map left, drawn
> by migrating birds.
> Come into the attic.
> That's not a doll – it's the
> photograph of a brain walking
> on sand and in the next one
> it's wearing an oasis-like crown.
> I must also show you a tiger's skin
> which once hid a palace.
> On one roof you'll see
> the antelope's horns,
> on another the falling wind. These round
> things are bangles and that long one
> a gun. This cave is the inside
> of a boot. And here
> carved wheels turn through stone.

This and other moderately surrealistic poems (by moderately I mean to imply that they are supported by a clear, rational structure) bring home to us both the dramatic presence and the mystery of existence, both the force of its impact and the maturity of its identity. These – 'Remarks of an Early Biographer' and 'Between Bricks, Madness', for example – are in a strict sense existentialist poems, but unpretentiously, genuinely so. The precise subjects, the athletic verbs, the surprising predicates with which Mehrotra explores the relation between existence and identity he uses also to discover the relation – the mutual relation – between time past and time present, whether in the personal life of a dead poet or in the silent records of the natural world. Here are the closing lines of 'Remarks of an Early Biographer' which illustrates the first theme, and then the poem 'Engraving of a Bison on Stone' which illustrates the second.

First the lines:

> In his keen memory he stored
> His silence like mistresses
> And it isn't my intention
> To disturb that symmetry of holes.
> As I turn the pages of his notebook
> A few characters come apart;
> I once more prod
> The shallow vessel filled with ash
> Then return my guides to their frontiers:
> The spider to the trellis,
> The rat to the cupboard,
> The lizard to the brick.
> As a child he divided words
> With a blade, or turned them
> Inside out like caps; at death
> His mouth was open, his right hand warm
> As if it had never written.

And next the poem:

> The land resists
> Because it cannot be
> Tempted, or broken
> In a chamber. It records,
> By carefully shuffling the leaves,
> The passage of each storm, rain
> And drought. The land yields
> In places, deliberately,
> Having learnt warfare from the armies
> It fed. The land is of one
> Piece and hasn't forgotten
> Old miracles: the engraving of a bison
> On stone, for instance. The land
> Turns up like an unexpected
> Visitor and gives refuge, it cannot be
> Locked, or put away. The land
> Cannot sign its name, it cannot die
> Because it cannot be buried, it understands
> The language, it speaks in dialect.

Gieve Patel (b. 1940), a physician who works in Bombay, has a high reputation among his contemporaries. Nissim Ezekiel, the father of modern Indian poetry in English, writes of him: 'Sobriety, balance and a slow, sometimes heavy gravity, are the main qualities of Gieve Patel's verse. He is the most precise and calculating of the Indian poets writing in English. His caution and his craftsmanship are sometimes excessive.'[9] Gravity, deliberation, caution!. These are not qualities ordinarily associated with Indian verse in English which tends to be nervous, fluent, nimble. Patel, on the contrary, shows a professionally clinical care in examining the experience in his poems. As K. N. Daruwalla writes, 'An event, an outer focus triggers off an exploration in an area of the mind. One is left with a feeling that he is conducting an autopsy over every moral problem that confronts him.'[10]

Patel's poems do as a rule pose a problem and I mean *pose*, to present in a position of tension, not simply state. The problem is concerned with the balance between inner and outer in human experience or with the clash between inner and outer, particularly as these dimensions and their relationship affect the human body. Patel is preoccupied with borders, margins, divisions, limits. He is not a Hindu but a Parsee, a monotheistic religious minority of Zoroastrian origin driven out of Persia by the Muslims in the eighteenth century. I do not know whether this is of any significance, but it does mean that he does not share the Hindu sensibility in which there is a blurring of edges and limits and a liquefaction of established boundaries. In Patel's universe there are hard lines and set limits.

Crossing these lines and ignoring these boundaries means an assault on the body's integrity and the person's being. It is an invasion which Patel sees as constantly threatening whether from human or natural violence, from force or from disease. The discipline of living is a tense resistance of the body and of the self to the encroachment of otherness. In one group of poems, Patel deals with this theme particularly in respect of the body, but the body is not simply the casing, it is also the symbol and the expression of the self. Even the titles of these poems are significant. 'How do you Withstand, Body?', 'Say Torture', 'Bodyfears', 'Here I Stand'. Here are some lines from another, 'What's In and Out', in which the heavy insistent rhythm, the harsh phrasing, the unadorned directness, the brutal conclusion themselves enforce and embody the assault they describe.

> I may have known the shore.
> Water bounded by walls or sliding
> Like linen over sand. But when I think
> Of deep sea it is as though
> I were now talking of

Untouched organs – my awareness
Of liver or spleen – mute, blanketed.
Immediate, unsubtle sensation
– That's shorelike,
And I am held by unwillingness
To go beyond a lick, at most
A skinwound. Though at times of riot
I watch intently the man
Who comes to hospital with a slit belly,
Bewildered, but firmly holding
A loop of his own gut
In his hands.

I have remarked more than once on the inestimable value of a long
and vital tradition to the Indian artist, and I turn now to one who has
a most positive and personal connection with one of its most ancient
yet living versions. A. K. Ramanujan who was born in Mysore in 1929
has for many years lived in the United States as Professor of Dravidian
Linguistics at the University of Chicago. Ramanujan's poetry, nevertheless, is essentially Indian in material and sensibility. Ramanujan
explains this paradox himself in a note in *Ten Twentieth-Century Indian
Poets* (pp. 95–96): 'English and my disciplines (linguistics, anthropology) give me my "outer" forms – linguistic, metrical, logical and
other ways of shaping experience, and my first thirty years in India,
my frequent visits and fieldtrips, my personal and professional pre-
occupations with Kannada and Tamil, the classics and folklore give me
my substance, my "inner" forms, images and symbols. They are
continuous with each other and I no longer can tell what comes from
where.' If he can no longer tell what comes from where it is because
of his perfectly undivided personality in which the forms of life and
the forms of art have melted together to become indistinguishable
elements in a subtle poetic economy.

It is an economy manifesting itself in the poetry, first, as an acute
sense of nuance and distinction and a sensitive feeling for individuality
and, secondly, as a profound understanding of the way in which
manifold shades and differences are supported by and bound together
by the ultimate unity of being itself. The unique depends upon the
individual. Let me just give a single modest example of this double
discernment, the poem 'The Striders' from the 1966 volume of that
name.

And search
for certain thin-
stemmed, bubble-eyed water bugs.

See them perch
on dry capillary legs
weightless
on the ripple skin
of a stream.

No, not only prophets
walk on water, this bug sits
on a landslide of lights
and drowns eye-
deep
into its tiny strip
of sky.

The opening directions – search and see – impose upon the reader the posture of the natural historian patiently seeking and calmly observing, which in turn implies the ordinariness, the cool fact of the tiny insects' traffic across the water: no more than a deft adaptation to surface tension. But the interpolated remark

No not only prophets
walk on water

points up the 'miraculous' quality of the striders' apparent overruling of natural law. The two notes together fix the essential, indelible individuality of the strider, its very own shade of being. Then in the last lines of the poem the borders between solid, liquid, light, sky, water, fade and dissolve and all these varied existences become particles, translucent vehicles of pure being. The temperament shown in poems of this kind is a marriage of the sharply contemporary – cool, clear, exact – and a Hindu depth of understanding of the profound and metaphysical in human nature. In particular it testifies to the unifying flow and swirl of being through the myriad forms of actual existence.

Ramanujan's poetic idiom is very pure, personal and cultured, affected by his Hindu endowment, his mastery of several Indian classical languages, and literatures by Indian and British uses of English during the first half of his life and by American in the second. His idiom presents an appearance of contemplative detachment, an unruffled surface which is, however, capable of implying depths of energy and even violence. It is an idiom which itself composes a metaphor of the poet's complex attitude to experience. There are poems in which Ramanujan uses natural creatures as the means for blending force and calm: as, for example, the New England striders, or the army ants who form their dwellings from their living bodies, who

build each builder
for a brick, altar
and martyr in one

or, a favoured creature and a favoured symbol, snakes.

No, it does not happen
when I walk through the woods.

But walking in museums of quartz
or the aisles of bookstacks,
looking at their geometry
without curves
and the layers of transparency
that make them opaque,
dwelling on the yellower vein
in the yellow amber
or touching a book that has gold
on its spine,
        I think of snakes.

The twirls of their hisses
rise like the tiny dust-cones on slow-noon roads
winding through the farmers' feet.
Black lorgnettes are etched on their hoods,
ridiculous, alien, like some terrible aunt,
a crest among tiles and scales
that moult with the darkening half
of every moon.

Sometimes the poet will use an individual as the focus of the collision
of calm and violence as in the poem in *Relations* on the Hindoo who
reads his Gita and is calm at all events.

I say nothing, I take care not to gloat.

I've learned to watch lovers without envy
as I'd watch in a bazaar lens
houseflies rub legs or kiss. I look at wounds calmly.

Yet when I meet on a little boy's face
the prehistoric yellow eyes of a goat
I choke, for ancient hands are at my throat.

But the true theatre of Ramanujan's poetic experience is the family.
The family provides a full *dramatis personae*, a scene, time past, present

and to come, intimate personal history, the rut of current fears and future anxieties, shelter and feelings of every kind. In Ramanujan's Hindu family, characters who for us have dimmed and faded bristle with presence: cousins, sons-in-law, grannies, stepmothers, an uncle's nephews, uncles themselves, aunts, a great grandfather – those who in the West are shadowy or invisible are substantial and influential there. Above all, mother and father are figures both sacred and profane and influences permanent and intimate. But they are also homely, limited and sad.

> Father when he passed on
> left dust
> on a table full of papers,
> left debts and daughters
> a bedwetting grandson
> named by the toss
> of a coin after him.

He also left his 'eye-coins' when, 'being the burning type', he burned properly at the cremation, a leaning house and two lines – as yet unfound by the writer – in the inside column of a Madras newspaper.

> And he left us
> a changed mother
> and more than
> one annual ritual.

There is a vein of melancholy in the portraits of father and mother, crisper and more ironic in that of father, more deeply sorrowful in that of mother, a cogent reminder of the power of the dead to affect the living.

> I smell upon this twisted
> backbone tree the silk and white
> petal of my mother's youth.
> From her ear-rings three diamonds
> splash a handful of needles,
> and I see my mother run back
> from rain to the crying cradles . . .
> My cold parchment tongue licks bark
> in the mouth when I see her four
> still sensible fingers slowly flex
> to pick a grain of rice from the kitchen floor.

The family is a system in which nothing human is alien and even oblivion has its function. Ramanujan writes in 'Small Scale Reflections on a Great House'

> Sometimes I think that nothing
> that ever came into this house
> goes out. Things come in every day
>
> to lose themselves among other things
> lost long ago among
> other things lost long ago.

The family is a tissue of relationships and conventions. The former supplies the poet with a rich store of human feeling, the latter with a structure against which to trace and analyse it. Thus Ramanujan's poems enriched and patterned like this are both sensitive and disciplined, quiet and dramatic. 'Quiet and dramatic', in fact, is how Ramanujan describes the classical Tamil poems he has translated exquisitely in his volume The Interior Landscape. He goes on, 'In their values and stances, they represent a mature classical poetry: passion is balanced by courtesy, transparency by ironies and nuances of design, impersonality by vivid detail, leanness of line by richness of implication.[11]

There are many more Indian poets writing in English: though not, I think, many more of greater talent or achievement. At least the problem I began by describing has been resolved: the problem, that is, whether Indians ought to write poetry in English. On this subject I want to give the last word once more to Ramanujan who in a communication to P. Lal in Modern Indian Poetry in English (p. 444) writes: 'I have no strong opinions on Indians writing in English. Buddhadeva Bose has strong opinions on why they should not; you are persuaded that they should. I think the real question is whether they can. And if they can, they will.' They certainly can and they surely will.

References

1 Journal of Commonwealth Literature, No. 5 (1968), pp. 65–66.

2 Lal, P. (ed.), Modern Indian Poetry in English (Calcutta, 1969), p. 5.

3 Ibid., p. 5.

4 Santayana, G., *The Life of Reason, or the Phases of Human Progress* (New York and London, 1905), p. 174.

5 Parthasarathy, R., 'Whoring after English Gods' in *Perspectives*, ed. S. P. Bhagwat (Bombay, 1970), pp. 45–6.

6 *Encounter*, Vol. XXXIX, No. 4 (October 1972).

7 Daruwalla, K. N. (ed.), *Two Decades of Indian Poetry* (Ghaziabad, 1980), p. 118.

8 *Ibid.*, p. 304.

9 *Ibid.*, p. 139.

10 *Ibid.*, p. 138.

11 Ramanujan, A. K., *The Interior Landscape* (Bloomington and London, 1975), p. 115.

Chapter 6

India in English Fiction: Kipling, Thompson, Myers, Forster, Scott and Farrell

In this final chapter I propose to sketch the British writers' response to the experience of India – experience both real and imagined. Of course, clusters of writers, most of them commonplace, have used India as a background for romance, adventure and fiction of every sort. In his book *After the Raj* published in the United States in 1986 David Rubin, a writer with such a clear and consistent anti-British attitude that he is unlikely to mislead any reader, finds in most of this fiction 'the bitterness of contempt of the British view of India' and an attitude comparable to that of Dickens towards the United States but 'envenomed with a candid racism and often wanting in mere factual knowledge and accurate observation. . . .'[1] My own attitude, the reader will realize, is rather less heated. At the same time, in keeping with my method, I shall concentrate on a small number of truly significant writers, one or two of the greatest distinction.

In his study of the images of India to be found in English fiction,[2] Allan J. Greenberger claims that these images, reflecting the attitudes of the British towards India, can be arranged under three headings: The Era of Confidence, 1880–1910; The Era of Doubt, 1910–35; and the Era of Melancholy, 1935–60. M. Bryn Davis[3] in his comments on this division suspects that Greenberger took his cue from the popularity of Kipling in the first period and the acceptance of E. M. Forster in the second. (As for the third, we might adduce the name of Paul Scott to complete the scheme.) M. Bryn Davis points out the inadvisability of such categories since more than half of the authors of novels in which these images appear were civil servants, army officers or their wives, people whose intimacy with the life of India had been limited by a professional creed which inculcated an essential aloofness from the indigenous population.

Allan Greenberger treats all his novelists, whether they are Ethel M. Dell or Rudyard Kipling, Maud Diver or E. M. Forster, alike as providers of clinical examples for his thesis, unconcerned by differences in literary capacity or by limitation of experience or vision. Nevertheless there is a certain grip on reality in *The British Image of India* related as it is to the experience of the British and of Britain rather than of India and the Indians, and it does correspond in a general way to the development of British attitudes not only to India but to most of the outside world. The British, particularly in the early period, felt that they had a mission and a function in India. They saw themselves – M. Bryn Davis explains – as performing an essential service in setting up a Civil Service, imposing certain standards of administrative efficiency, creating a national system of railways and beginning the process of inaugurating a national sense of identity.

Firm convictions of this kind, but with their patronizing implication of intrinsic racial superiority, were certainly present either expressly or latently in the work of Kipling (1865–1936) as they would almost certainly have been in that of any British writer on an Indian subject of the period. But Kipling was not simply the repository of contemporary British beliefs and prejudices. For one thing he knew and loved India in a way no other British writer could. India was where he spent the first five perfect years of his childhood. India was the paradise against which he was to measure the misery of his five years in 'The House of Desolation' in Southsea when, according to practice, he was taken to England to begin his formal education. After another five years at school he returned to work as a journalist on a daily paper in Lahore. With this as a base he found an extensive and catholic acquaintance with the British community – particularly with its professional section, army officers, engineers, doctors, lawyers – and an even wider knowledge of the Indian population. Kipling undoubtedly shared many of the views and prejudices of these men, the administrators and the managers of the system, who stood for loyalty, conformity, efficiency, aloofness and suspicion of those of mixed blood, and preference for the martial races. But in the larger and more important sense Kipling's vision of life cannot be equated with that of officials described by Paul Scott in *The Chinese Love Pavilion* (1960) as confused by 'a sense of duty and delusions of grandeur'. Kipling knew and loved India in the absolute, unqualified way of a member of the family. More than this he was an artist with a superlative literary gift which could discern and communicate 'truths' more comprehensive and 'truer' than his conscious luggage of contemporary ideas and attitudes could contain.

Kipling's experience of India both as a child and as a young man was the most significant influence on his art. Although, according to Charles Allen, when Kipling left India in 1889 after seven years as a journalist and writer he left for good, 'India and Anglo-India remained the deepest and the freshest of many sources from which he drew inspiration for his writing, both in his verse and fiction'.[4] From India he derived the sensibility which provided his marvellous children's stories – and not only those with an Indian context – and the short stories which are the genuine expression of his authentic talent. More than half his work is directly concerned with India and the Raj and the rest is marked by a character and by feeling found under that influence. Kipling was not an amiable or sympathetic soul. He could be vain and aggressive, he could toady for acceptance, he could sneer at the newly founded Indian National Congress. But the range and the detail of his understanding and his passion for it are unquestionable. His understanding and his passion are best expressed in what was essentially the art of the short story.

Kipling carried so much of India into so much of his work. His narrative style was influenced by the stories told to him in childhood by his Catholic Goan nurse and his Hindu bearer, two of those closest to him and most loved by him. These stories were told in an idiom which mixed easy, intimate, everyday chat with ritual, symbol and myth. It was an idiom developed by Kipling to be capable of considerable subtlety. In his later work the symbolic structure became increasingly elliptical, implied and telling, and Kipling must surely be counted a significant contributor to the art and form of the short story. As for content, his journalist colleague Kay Robinson thought that half Kipling's genius lay in his power to turn every scrap of his experience into material for his stories. His reporter's eye for judging the essentials that would make a story and his journalist's gift for expressing it briefly and forcefully were refined with practice into the power to discern and embody the inner drama of even routine events and everyday characters. His work on the newspaper staff in Lahore and Allahabad fed his appetite for information of every sort and made him familiar with the vast length and breadth of India and with innumerable aspects of Indian life. All this appears in *Kim* (1901), which is a splendid display of intimate information and contemporary attitude, however much of a failure as a novel. Kim is simply Indian and British side by side and turn by turn and never an organic personality and, by a sleight of hand which enables Kipling to evade a fundamental problem, he is *really* British. Kipling, of course, was not a novelist but a short story writer and his best stories are a superb combination of true knowledge, personal experience and authentic feeling. *Plain Tales from the Hills* (1888) and the other great collections dramatize his experience at work as a reporter, his genius for reading an incident, his infallible sense for its fictional quality, his rapport with doers, soldiers, organizers, as well as his suspicion of women fostered during his leaves, his ambiguous relations at certain points with Indians, his identification with what was best in Anglo-India and his detestation for so much that was cheap and arrogant in it. When Kipling left India for good it continued to provide material for his work. It had made him famous as a young man, and it had incidentally helped to make him rich.

Kipling rendered the life and character of India and the Raj with miraculous accuracy. At the same time he recorded the intimate convictions and the stubborn prejudices (so many of which he shared) of the British of his day. In doing so, a writer of his power and popularity both exposed and enforced these attitudes for all but the most sensitive and enlightened. The British have always liked Indians and found them much more sympathetic than any of the other races whom they ruled. They also thought they had a god-given right to rule, and they thought too that they did it better than anyone else, including the Indians themselves. It would require an act of the historical imagination for even the most conservative to understand this habit of mind today. But the Edwardian attitudes of Kipling and his society cannot all be attributed to a blind and brutish Imperialism. Apart from the geo-political resources that the Indian Empire added to British power, and apart from the economic advantages it brought with it, the British genuinely felt that they had a moral duty towards India – certainly, Kipling did – and they felt no guilt or embarrassment in assuming the imperial role. It took the best part of another half century of Indian struggle and British uneasiness to sweep this attitude away.

There is of course more to Kipling's art than the defence and propagation of contemporary British views and attitudes, partial and short-sighted as these were bound to be, whether on India or any other subject. Indeed that there was a generously humane and independent moral centre to Kipling's work is strongly argued by Bonamy Dobrée, himself a scholar and a liberal-minded English gentleman. Dobrée freely acknowledges the negative elements in Kipling's nature, his unexamined certainty about Britain's imperialist role, his hysterical hatred of Britain's political enemies, his suspicion of women, his strange fascination with cruelty, his distrust of democracy, his fear of intellectuals. On the other side, he showed complete honesty, stoicism, compassion, humour, and an exuberant zest for life. What Dobrée, after Maurois, calls 'a permanent, natural contact with the oldest and deepest layers of human consciousness' underlies the values in Kipling's art.[5] Perhaps the fairest judgement on his work, especially his Indian work, comes in a comment by Angus Ross in *British and Commonwealth Literature*: '. . . most often failure comes from technique being betrayed by manner and inadequate ideas such as notions of blood, race and unquestioning obedience.'[6]

A writer as serious, gifted and prolific as Kipling frequently has some profound, quickening impulse to his work – not always consciously recognized – which expresses itself in many different ways. Henry James had a shattering vision, which he never lost, of human evil or perhaps we should say simply of evil itself. Kipling had a similar apprehension and, like James, a semi-mystical experience of it in his twenties. In Kipling's case it was an intuition of chaos that lay close to the surface of order, the horror of the unravelling of reality by disorder. His work is his effort insistently renewed to impose order upon potential chaos. In his imaginative code, pre- or non-British India stood for chaos, British India for a controlling order: as did every expression and form of the Raj, every institution, profession, technology, school, regiment, every bridge, road and railway.

Between Kipling and Edward Thompson (1886–1946), who in the nineteen-twenties and thirties wrote a set of novels about India, the attitude of the British as recorded in fiction began to undergo a deep change. The absolute self-confidence in Kipling, the certainty that the British mission in India was fundamentally a good one, began to waver and in Edward Thompson, admittedly a minor novelist, the confidence is replaced by doubt and questioning, the assurance tinctured by guilt. The sense of such a change as it strengthened among the liberal and educated classes acts as the subtext in *An Indian Day* (1927) to a tale of the relationships of the principal functionaries, British and Indian, in the unfashionable district of Vishnugrath in Bengal. The cast includes Vincent Hamer, the newly appointed English judge, a war veteran and a man out of favour with his compatriots because of his liberal attitude to Indians, impartiality in the administration of justice being regarded by the many ignorant among them as showing favour to 'babus, swarajis, seditionists, L. R. Das, Mahatma Gandhi, L. F. Andrews, the late Mr E. S. Montague and the Labour Party'; Neogyi, the Indian Collector, an educated, Westernized Indian, a man of integrity and culture; various corrupt Rajahs; some foolish British army officers; the decent Principal and teachers from the local college; the missionaries and, in particular, John Findlay whose wife and daughter are sacrificed, the one by illness, the other by suicide, to his exclusive devotion to religion; one or two women, including Hilda Mannering, the woman Hamer falls in love with and the conventional wife of the Police Superintendent. Ordinary non-official Indians hardly appear as individuals. The events unfolded are certainly such as might occur, the linkages with history are authentic, the author's attitude both to Indians and British is wholly commendable, his eye for the genuine and the bogus sharp and discriminating. In particular he has an enthusiastically appreciative response to the Indian countryside and an almost lyrical feeling for the birds, trees and flowers.

Moreover, he is capable of shrewd observation of a sociological kind. British officials could not be bribed to arrange an election as can the Raja of Kenduti and his mother, with the approval of the equally corrupt Indian Commissioner, Deogharia. But they could be bribed obliquely. Honours might be awarded for large contributions to good causes by venal petitioners, and without the slightest offence in law or stain on the conscience.

Again the humanist Thompson gives a perceptive account of the work of the missionaries. He understands their motives, values their disinterestedness, admires their energy, altruism and the admirable example of neighbourliness they offer. They stand for an essential social morality. But they can, like John Finlay, become so immersed in their spiritual activity as to become oblivious to other and equally valid ends. Moreover, while they rescue some from servitude to false gods they can be the occasion of other kinds of enslavement. Thompson gives a devastating example. Finlay's large compound was packed, its corners in an intolerable condition, the well threatened with contamination.

> They were a community gathered by a predecessor, who with the stupidity that seemed to have marked most of the proceedings of the older generation of missionaries – men who now lived in England and wondered why 'the work' was not progressing as in their rosy memories it had done in their day – had collected them from their homes and had amassed them round his own house. He had thus killed three birds with one stone – he had ensured their absolute and parasitic dependence on the missionary, he had taken away all chance of a strong Christian belief and practice growing up amidst opposition, and he had effectively prevented any further spread of Christianity in the village from which they came. (pp. 82–83)

An Indian Day has a certain historic significance in that it is among the first to register the new British mood towards India, the beginnings of the process of disentanglement from the Raj. But in spite of Edward Thompson's humane attitudes and enlightened opinions, or possibly in part because of these, the reader is left in the end with the feeling that he has been reading an illustrated moral thesis. The novel shows a fundamental deficiency in the art of the novelist. I am not referring simply to technique, although such phrases as 'We digress' or 'We must return to Vishnugrath' certainly suggest the absence of an inward, organic propulsion. It is rather that comment overwhelms action and opinion constantly slides across the edge of realization. It is a weakness manifest in the characterization which is wooden and stereotyped, except possibly in the case of Hamer who speaks for the author and the minor but realized figure of Neogyi, the Indian Collector. It is in the treatment of women and the relationship of Hamer and Hilda Mannering that Thompson appears firmly fixed in the social and personal conventions of his period. Some of the scenes between Hilda and Hamer have the passion and poetry of a combined Ethel M. Dell and Dornford Yates. And yet that a high-minded sentimentalist capable of such treatment should feel such an uneasy conscience about the British view of another people and a different civilization makes evident the strength and decency of Thompson's deeper human instincts.

However historically foreshortened, however unfair to India's ancient, complex culture and religions, Kipling's use of India in his art was at least active and contemporary. Quite different is the 'use' of the Indian scene as the romantic background to Thompson's tales; and even more substantially different, more philosophically at odds with both, is its use by L. H. Myers (1881–1944) in his tetralogy, *The Near and the Far*, first published as a single volume in 1940. It is made up of *The Near and the Far* (1929), *Prince Jali* (1931), *The Root and the Flower* (1935) and *The Pool of Vishnu* (1940). As Myers himself explained in a foreword:

> This is not a historical novel although the action is placed
> in the time of Akbar the Great Mogul (who was a
> contemporary of Queen Elizabeth's), nor is it an attempt
> to portray oriental modes of living and thinking. I have
> done what I liked with history and geography as well as
> with manners and customs. . . . In choosing sixteenth-
> century India as a setting my object was to carry the
> reader out of our familiar world into one where I could –
> without doing violence to his sense of reality – give
> prominence to certain chosen aspects of human life and
> illustrate their significance.

However unreal this may be in contrast to Kipling's contemporary world of soldiers, engineers and colonists, it does stress other truths, and probably richer truths about India, the length of its past, the height of its civilization, the complexity of its religion and culture, the significance of its art and courts, the intellectual and spiritual problems with which the most intelligent and advanced of its members strove. One could well imagine George Santayana having a fascinated interest in this world but hardly in Kipling's.

In the remote, mysterious and enclosed court of Akbar, Myers shows us a set of delicately discriminated characters struggling towards, or at least actively concerned with, moral and intellectual maturity. It was an aim never achieved, never begun to be achieved in the personal life of L. H. Myers. The son of F. W. H. Myers, a notable Victorian figure and a 'scientific spiritualist', L. H. detested his successful father and the class he represented. He was miserable at Eton and left Cambridge after a year when his father died in 1901. A large legacy received in 1906 enabled him to live the life of a pleasure-loving, fashionable young man of his time. He was driven about in a Rolls, he raced at Brooklands, he was a part-owner of Boulestin, had a flat in St James's and houses in the country. He also had a depressive and neurasthenic personality, and joined to an acute perception into personal relationships, a sad incapacity to sustain them. He became solitary and morose, a hater of the people he spent his life with and a Communist of the most intolerant sort in politics. And yet he was, G. H. Bantock tells us, as late as 1932 'politically conservative, though of course socially critical; and he always retained a sense of spiritual aristocracy in strong contradiction to a social one'.[7] In view of Myers's peculiarly incoherent personal development and the extraordinary difference between his beliefs and his mode of living, it is perhaps odd that the writers associated with *Scrutiny* were so attracted to this early exponent of radical chic. I have referred to G. H. Bantock. Myers was also written about by Ronald Bottrall, Geoffrey Walton, by F. R. Leavis himself, and perhaps most discerningly by the psychologist and literary critic D. W. Harding. Possibly the *Scrutiny* writers favoured Myers, in part for negative reasons, because he rejected so much that they disapproved of: the vulgarity and gross wealth of London society, aestheticism divorced from moral values, the cult of novelty, the complacency and self-admiration of intellectuals, the Bloomsbury Group, the class system and the upper classes in particular, and the sophistication of those not 'sophisticated enough to hold sophistication cheap'. On the positive side Myers was admired for reasons that made Henry James admirable; that, as D. W. Harding puts it, '. . . L. H. Myers is concerned with the theme of individual development in a civilized society, a society in which leisure and a tradition of culture make possible the practised intelligence and sensibility which he takes to be necessary conditions of development.'[8]

There are two notes or tones, a double quality, in the atmosphere of *The Near and the Far*. The first is that implied by Harding, serious, moral, intellectual, in which highly developed and potentially highly developed characters work out or compound their destinies: the Buddhist, Raja Ama, seeking to desert the quotidian universe; his Christian wife, Sita, who attempts to build a balanced and open relationship with it; the Hindu sage, Ghopal, whose lofty virtue is corrupted by sensuality; the womanizer, Hari Khan, who attempts to refine his romantic sexuality into a more inclusive love; and the precocious Prince Jali, whose life is seen as a spiritual education and a theatre of good and evil. The second note is associated with the glittering court of Akbar, where the heirs plot for power, the politicians scheme for place and influence and the courtiers gossip for entertainment and malice. L. P. Hartley reminds us in his introduction to the novel that Myers owed much on this side to Lady Murasahi's classic novel *The Tale of the Genji*, whose civilized sensibility and limpid melancholy deeply appealed to him.

Myers's habit of mind was speculative and generalizing. It seldom expressed itself with that local richness and particularizing effect so much admired by contemporary English critics. We see this generalizing characteristic in the smooth Tennysonian description of scenery, whether natural or cultivated, and in the lightly individualized *personae* of the quartet. They are not exactly types but they are characters in a larger, older sense rather than distinctive individuals. D. W. Harding with his gift of unprejudiced recognition, and a personal predilection for the concrete effect adroitly makes a point of this kind in relation to Myers's narrative manner. It is made up, he writes in *Scrutiny*, of 'quasi-musings, half soliloquy from a character and half author's commentary. . . . Myers has no interest in unveiling thoughts . . . in their dumb cradles; his characters not only speak, but think, in fluent and carefully chosen words, and this has to be accepted as a convention, as an implicit recognition of the fact that Myers as author is all the time communicating with you as reader *about* these characters that seem to be talking.'[9]

Myers's personal case was a tragic one: unable to connect, unhappy, alone. 'The live self', he says in *Prince Jali*, 'seemed to be isolated by its own inalienable nature from other live selves. It was appearances that formed the bridge between person and person' (p. 224). 'Myers', says G. H. Bantock 'wanted an escape . . . from the ever-present burden of self through the acceptance of some transcendental element . . .'[10] (How close, we note, such an aim is to the classical doctrine of the Indian sages.) Nevertheless, in spite of, perhaps in part because of, the disorder of his own psyche, Myers was a most considerable literary artist whose works and particularly *The Near and the Far* succeed 'in conveying extremely clear and sensitive insights into the conditions of adult and responsible lives in a civilized society'.[11] *The Near and the Far*, according to John Harvey, 'sometimes lacks the impact and inevitability of the very greatest novels (Myers admitted his interest waned) but it is a major work. The sheer amplitude and splendour of his recreation of Akbar's India and – in his brief appearances – its tycoon-like emperor is a tour de force.'[12] I must add to these claims for *The Near and the Far* a humbler but not unimportant one. It is rivetingly readable, a point implied by D. W. Harding in the essay I have referred to more than once when he said in a glancing allusion to Myers's thrilling intrigue and exciting denouements, 'Myers offers the curious combination of a devotion to the subtleties of social life that suggests Henry James, with the sort of plot that suggests a detective story.'[13]

Looked at from the point of view of this chapter; *The Near and the Far* represents a narrower, more intensely concentrated response to India than the larger and more inclusive range of interests in Kipling's contemporary response, and an altogether different one from the liberal anxieties of E. M. Forster's troubled soul. *The Near and the Far* is detached, philosophic and engaged largely with moral issues. It takes India with absolute seriousness as the appropriate location for treating subjects of the highest intellectual and moral quality. The art of Myers is one in which the registration of fact and event and the notation of responses are carried on a style of exceptional purity. These are the means used to resurrect the greatness of Mogul India and to show it as the fitting context for a profound kind of intellectual exploration. It is irrelevant whether or not his setting and material are historical in the strict and accurate sense because his whole treatment encloses a most significant and imaginative truth about one of the great civilizations of mankind.

For the reader, *The Near and the Far* constitutes an experience which is a liberal education, particularly for the novel reader brought up to see India as a strange product of the traditional indigenous culture and the British Raj, or more frequently now under the influence of television as a vast, impoverished member of the Third World.

In his notable essay on E. M. Forster (1879–1970) in *The Common Pursuit* (p. 269), F. R. Leavis argues that the main theme of *Howards End* (1910) concerns the contrasted Schlegels and Wilcoxes. 'The Schlegels represent the humane liberal culture, the fine civilization of cultivated free social intercourse, that Mr Forster himself represents. . . . The Wilcoxes have built the Empire; they represent the "short-haired executive type" – obtuse, egotistic, unscrupulous, cowards spiritually, self-deceiving, successful.'[14] While there are sufficient similarities between *Howards End* and *A Passage to India* (1924) – for example, the contrast in humanity represented by the sensitive old lady Mrs Moore and the good commonsense Fielding on the one hand, and the dull, callous and racist agents of the Raj on the other – to read *A Passage to India* in the same way, this would simply be a single thread in a very much larger design which it took Forster some fourteen years of painful effort to complete. For me the initiating impulse, the essential creative effort has to do with something at once simpler and harder to pin down. It is based on Forster's own experience of India, something which had a profound effect on his personality and attitudes, on his long and intense friendship for Syed Ross Masood, the first man for whom he felt a homosexual love (though it was not returned) and on years of reading and meditation on the subject. It has to do with the profound effect of India on all who live there whether they are indigenous or foreign, permanent or transient inhabitants. And by 'India' one intends to imply the powerful pressure of all that is meant by India, its physical presence, its spiritual, historical and psychological influences. That Forster himself considered India to be his theme we know from his own words. It was to this he attributed the peculiarly ambiguous and apparently violent event that did or did not take place in the Marabar Caves. The relevant passages are given in Oliver Stalleybrass's admirably helpful introduction to the Penguin edition of the novel (1985).

'In the cave,' Forster writes, 'it is *either* a man, or the supernatural, or an illusion. If I say, it becomes, whatever the answer, a different book. And even if I know! My writing mind therefore is a blur here – i.e. I will it to remain a blur, and to be uncertain, as I am of many facts in daily life. This isn't a philosophy or aesthetic. It's a particular trick I felt justified in trying because my theme was India.'[15]

He wrote this in a letter to a friend in 1924. In the same year in the *Adelphi* – the passage is also given by Stalleybrass – he writes as follows:

. . . the book is not really about politics, though it is the political aspect of it that caught the general public and made it sell. It's about something wider than politics, about the search of the human race for a more lasting home, about the universe as embodied in the Indian earth and the Indian sky, about the horror lurking in the Marabar Caves and the release symbolized by the birth of Krishna.[16]

This immense theme Forster pinned to a simple tripartite structure the first two parts of which – as well as the earlier phases of the third one – are marvellously crisp, full and pointed. Nothing could surpass the pace, vivacity and insight into human relationships with which he develops the narrative from Mrs Moore's arrival with her protegée in Chandrapore, her meeting with Dr Aziz, the preparation for the picnic, the visit to the Caves, the disaster there, the accusation, the trial, the withdrawal of the charge, the aftermath of the trial. In the latter part of the third section the structure becomes limper and we are faced with a novelist bemused by his enormous theme and reluctant or unable to bring either that or his characters to an equally crisp and natural conclusion. There are also in this section more than one of those passages of secular and sentimental mysticism the Bloomsbury enlightened were occasionally disposed to. This part of the novel seems to me the one weakness in Forster's generous and liberal masterpiece.

The strength of *A Passage to India* comes from the completeness with which Forster possesses, and is possessed by, his theme – its brilliance from the unbroken way the theme of India streams into every department of life and above all into the psychology of the rulers and of the ruled. The narrative method used by Forster to present the double and complementary psychology, mixes fact and comment, evocation and analysis in such a manner as to keep the author's personality prominent throughout. As Leavis noted with characteristic sharpness in the essay already referred to, '. . . even where actions, events and the experiences of characters are supposed to be speaking for themselves, the turn of phrase and tone of voice bring the presenter and commentator into the foreground' (p. 275). It is a point not dissimilar to that made by D. W. Harding about L. H. Myers. The difference, of course, is that Forster's personality is so much more vivacious and attractive than the remote and austere Myers.

In delineating the character of the British administrator in India at the time, Forster gives us both the finished article, the Collector, the Doctor, the Police Inspector, as well as the relative newcomer, Ronny Heslop. They are members of the middling and most populous class of bureaucrat. Suddenly these quite ordinary people are elevated to a status of exceptional grandeur, which they come rapidly to accept as no more than natural. 'India likes gods,' Ronnie Heslop at one point snaps at his mother. 'And Englishmen like posing as gods,' Mrs Moore returns. These god-like creatures Forster observes not without a touch of Cambridge-enlightened superiority, still preserve a suburban taste for a stuffy English menu and stuffier English entertainment. Not that there was much more than a trace of England in the administrative character. What struck the newcomer Adela Quested was how different they were from their fellows at home. For one thing they were constantly looking – looking for the crossing of lines and the breaking of codes. And paradoxically at the same time they cultivated a special selective blindness which prevented them, except in official relationships, from 'seeing' Indians in any serious, human sense. These remote and alien officials, the main part of whose existence was devoted exclusively to governing those with whom they had nothing in common, required as a psychological necessity, space both physical and mental, in which to live at least a passable imitation of a remembered English life. It was supplied partly by the Civil Lines but more significantly by the Club, the symbol of unoccupied space – unoccupied by Indians, that is, since Indian servants were no more than insensible extensions of oneself. And while it was true, as Forster remarked, that 'most of the inhabitants of India do not mind how India was governed', the British official was beginning to face a new, young and articulate Indian who did very much care who governed India. Any defection from duty or the tribe would be seen as cataclysmic, an unforgivable act of treachery. It would also release the supposed hysteria of a close and strained society, as it did in the Club when the decent and sympathetic Fielding refuses to accept the charge of sexual assault against Dr Aziz.

Forster viewed the British presence in India with intense distaste and his analysis of the mentality of the officials sent there to enforce it showed them to be under such internal and external strain that they were liable in a crisis to break out into a brutish, stampeding hysteria, as they do in the scenes in the Club and the Court. The Indians, or those Indians he chooses to portray who are mostly Muslims, he finds immensely attractive; he admires their physical grace, their gift for relaxation, the affectionate and open friendships, their love of poetry, even if it is of a decorative and sentimental Persian kind. The odd thing is that he shows them also to be liable, individually and as a group, to a similar sort of uncontrollable hysterical feeling. It is perhaps less heavy and brutal than the British version, more like the agitation of a flock of disorientated birds. But it is there, simmering and likely to be provoked into irrational fury by occasions both serious and frivolous. The close embrace in which rulers and ruled are locked produces a similarity of symptoms that might be expected from lovers rather than enemies.

When I said a moment ago that most of Forster's Indians are Muslims I was registering implicitly an instinct or feeling of a certain narrowness and inadequacy in Forster's representation of the Indian scene – at least in one respect. I refer to the striking insufficiency of the Hindu element in Forster's version of Indian life. Of course most of his Indian characters are Muslim, and as we know it was an old British habit to look on Muslims with greater favour than Hindus: they were thought of as more reliable, less devious, as martial and straightforward. Certainly this was how the Muslims thought of themselves. How they thought of the majority of their fellow Indians we can see from the conversation of Aziz's friends.

> 'My illness proceeds from Hindus,' Mr Haq said. Mr Syed Mohammed had visited religious fairs, at Allahmabad and at Ujjain, and described them with biting scorn. At Allahmabad there was flowing water which washed

impurities away, but at Ujjain the little river Gipra was
banked up, and thousands of bathers deposited their germs
in the pool. He spoke with disgust of the hot sun, the
cow-dung and marigold flowers, and the encampment of
saddhus, some of whom strode naked through the streets.
(p. 107)

A few silent servants, the spiteful and cowardly Dr Panna Lal, a Court-
room punkah-wallah described by Forster with lingering sensuous
admiration – 'a beautiful naked god' – and his chief Hindu figure, the
polite and enigmatic Brahmin, Professor Godbole who stands in some
ambiguous middle position between comic eccentricity and mysticism
– these hardly constitute a sufficient presence, or even a sufficient
symbol of the richness, dignity and power of Hinduism.

Perhaps after all there is a touch of condescension, a trace of inherited British assumption in Forster's reading of his Muslim and Hindu
personae. One thing is unarguable and that is Forster's gift for
communicating his own bare and tingling sense of India itself with
nothing borrowed or limply inherited from elsewhere. In fact, his
success in this seems to be the supreme achievement of the novel. To
create the effect, he uses a manifold and varied technique made possible by his characteristic blending of fact and comment. Habituated to
this, the reader is unsurprised as an interpolated reflection, a tiny
episode, a casual memory, a character analysis, a physical description
weave in and out of one another to produce the complex and irresistible result. I will give as illustration no more than a miniature sample
of what is meant. Music can be an infallible clue to the nature of a
national sensibility, and Forster makes exquisite use of this possibility
in his description of Godbole's song.

His thin voice rose, and gave out one sound after another.
At times there seemed rhythm, at times there was the
illusion of a Western melody. But the ear, baffled
repeatedly, soon lost any clue, and wandered in a maze of
noises, none harsh or unpleasant, none intelligible. It was
the song of an unknown bird. (p. 87)

If music implies sensibility, climate exerts a principal influence on the
composition of character, and Forster is fully aware of its universal and
devastating effect in India on body and mind.

All over the city, and over much of India, the same retreat
on the part of humanity was beginning, into cellars, up

hills, under trees. Afail, herald of horrors is at hand. The
sun was returning to his kingdom with power but without
beauty – that was the sinister feature. If only there had
been beauty! Her cruelty would have been tolerable then.
Through excess of light he failed to triumph, he also; in
his yellowly-white overflow not only matter, but
brightness itself long drowned. (p. 115)

And Forster makes clear the climate is as brutal for the Indians as for
the British. When the seven argumentative friends left Dr Aziz's
bungalow they felt

a common burden, a vague threat which they called 'the
bad weather coming'. They felt that they could not do
their work or would not be paid enough for doing it. The
space between them and their carriages, instead of being
empty, was clogged with a medium that pressed against
their flesh, the carriage cushions scalded their trousers,
their eyes pricked, domes of hot water accumulated under
their headgear and poured down their cheeks. (p. 115)

The catastrophe of heat, the constant wretchedness and crossness,
the feeling that there was 'no reserve of tranquillity to draw upon' as
if 'irritation exuded from the very soil', the scratching impossibility
of privacy: all this side of Forster's response to India emphasizes
the elements that are repellent and alien to him. The same impression
is given by his treatment of Hindu religious ceremonial in the later part
of the novel which is so much less understanding than the factual
record in *The Hill of Devi* (1953), unfairly stressing, as it does, the
absurdity rather than the religion and the muddle rather than the
mysticism. (We see from this why many Indian readers and critics find
Forster, for all his progressive political attitudes, distinctly less
sympathetic and much more uninformed than Kipling.)
    The notion of the alien is sunk into the economy of the novel and
becomes an organic part of the experience as it does with the Marabar
Caves. At first a simple geographical feature, it becomes under
Forster's subtlety of placement and lightness of touch more and more
invested with significance, a stony symbol of the incomprehensible and
then of the sinister and dangerous, the natural becoming a preternatural
phenomenon.

What had spoken to her in that scoured-out cavity of the
granite? What dwelt in the first of the caves? Something

very old and very small. Before time, it was before space
also. Something snub-nosed, incapable of generosity – the
undying worm itself. (p. 194)

To describe the experience in the Marabar Caves in such phrases
as these is one example of the self-indulgence Forster was sometimes
capable of, in spite of his gift for being his unaffectedly natural and
inwardly disciplined self. It is odd, too, that someone with so little
sympathy for the religious spirit and so slight a sense of evil in the
theological sense should have attributed Adela Quested's crisis to a
species of evil of a primitive and animistic sort.

There is plenty of evil of the common human sort in *The Raj
Quartet* (1966–75), Paul Scott's immense study of the last days of the
British as the rulers of India. The four volumes are packed with malice,
murder, cruelty, sexual perversion, racial violence and general human
hatred. They were published between 1966 and 1975, but they still
breathe a thirties-type intensity of colonial guilt, of the sort we recognize in Forster, although less elegantly expressed. The style and
expressive mode of each is markedly different and not in the way one
might expect. Forster's novel, which appeared more than sixty years
ago, strikes one still with its light and mobile narrative, its witty and
eliptical manner and its blend of the lyrical, reflective and personal as
quite distinctly contemporary and fresh. The narrative manner of Paul
Scott (1920–78) is over-explicit and, untouched by the poetry which
animates Forster's work, curiously dated. It reminds one of the superannuated sociological technique, Mass Observation, invented by the
poet Charles Madge, the film-maker Humphrey Jennings and the
anthropologist Tom Harrison. It was a method of social investigation
highly characteristic of the thirties. It attempted to blend art, science
and anthropology by assembling vast quantities of information which
would be so compelling as to make its case unaided by formal analysis.
There are long passages in the four volumes of *The Raj Quartet* which
might well have been extracts from Mass Observation studies. There
are also enough story lines, as many types of character, sufficient
material and reworking of the same material from different points of
view to fill another four packed volumes.

The Raj Quartet may be said to be concerned with the final phase
of the Indian Empire, with the Indian struggle for independence and
with Indian politics and parties and with a significant phase of the
World War in the Far East. Certainly these vast events compose the
context and effect the progress, events and characters of the novels.
But according to the author it is

the story of a rape, of the events that led up to it and
followed it and of the place in which it happened. There

are the action, the people and the place, all of which are
interrelated but in their totality incommunicable in
isolation from the moral continuum of human affairs.
(Vol. I, p. 9)

In this essayist's prose, employed often by Paul Scott on the more
abstract aspects of his subject, he shows himself well aware of the
difficulty in his Mass Observation technique – namely, the difficulty
of saying anything concretely or effectively if it is necessary simultaneously to say everything. Both Scott's diction and his method push
the writer towards description and generalization rather than to
immediacy and dramatization. But there is one theme or association
pervasively present in *The Raj Quartet* and all those vast historical
events and sociological pressures with which it is engaged which
always lends a sharper bite and a more edged and effective strength
to the narrative. This is that endemic characteristic of English society
as well as the peculiar obsession of the English writer whose instinctive
attitudes derive from the thirties. Whenever class is an element in the
scene – as it frequently is – Scott's narrative has more grip, his characters more bite, the whole theme more presence and edge. Let me
illustrate one or two of the ways in which class colours quite different
subjects in *The Raj Quartet*.

The wretched career of Hari Kumar in India, Harry Coomer in
England, is the germ of the personal part of *The Jewel in the Crown*.
He is the son of an Anglicized business man who is determined to have
him brought up as an English boy, which is what he becomes at his
English boarding school where he does not see himself or is not seen
by anyone else as anything but another English boy, whether at school
or at the home of his English friend, where he is just another member
of the family. The death of his father, discovered to be penniless, trans-
fers the boy at a stroke from his comfortable, 'natural' upper-class life
to one step away from the indigent existence of a kindly lower middle-
class Indian aunt. In India he comes painfully to the realization that his
father's plans for him had been based on an illusion. In India, an Indian
and an Englishman could never meet on equal terms. He did not like
Indians and they did not trust him. He spoke neither Hindi nor Indian
English. He was a displaced person in what should have been his
natural home.

The belief – often the expressed belief – throughout Scott's narrative
is that it is colour which is the ultimate cause of alienation, and in a
society composed of rulers of one colour and subjects of another,
colour is bound to be highly influential in creating division. This may
be Scott's theoretical or sociological or political view, but his artist's
intuition developed in an English society where the atmosphere was
thick with class feeling and every kind of subtlety of class division,

brings into the texture of his novels the sense that it is class which finally separates, class which is the more fundamental and pervasive influence for division. There is a kind of symmetry between the importance of caste in India and that of class in Britain. What shattered Hari Kumar on the death of his father was not colour or race but being relegated from a confident upper-class life to the most meagre life of the poorest members of the Indian lower-middle class. It was not poverty as such which disabled him but the absence of an unquestioned code, a complex of language, assumptions, signals, behaviour and agreements – the collapse of the context of class which had given his life its silent, powerful support. And when Hari's relationship with Daphne Manners opens, it is more than love which effects the revival of his dead spirit. It is also the readmittance to the class, the necessary context of living which reawakens his whole personality. So much for class as a positive influence. But Scott shows also an authentic understanding of it as a negative, malignant force. The intensity of the hatred felt by the policeman Merrick for Hari Kumar is an effect of that strange emotion – possibly unique to the English and to one class at a certain time – the jealous detestation of the ambitious grammar-schoolboy for the unfairly advantaged public-schoolboy.

Class, as a way of seeing and ordering, is used by Scott in other places in the four novels to define, to place, to imply. It is used exquisitely at the very beginning of the novel in all three ways to specify the precise kind of background and upbringing of the elderly missionary Miss Crane and to fix precisely both her character and her relationship to Private Clancy, the natural 'gentleman', the tough and sensitive leader of the group of young soldiers regularly entertained to tea by Miss Crane. To this kind of evocative analysis and in this kind of situation Scott brings a tincture of poetry to his Mass Observation manner of perception. Elsewhere his detachment and his feeling for class make him a mirror-like recorder of the intense snobbery of the English of the period, a complex set of feelings which, when carried abroad into an alien and unsettling environment, becomes almost a surrogate religion, and for many, especially the women, as Scott notes like Forster before him, religion itself. Class feeling of this kind can be vicious as we see in the treatment of Barbie, poor Miss Batchelor of Rose Cottage, by Mrs Layton, the Colonel's wife, but at a lesser intensity, as in the strange rituals and Byzantine regulations of Club life, a subject – particularly when treated in Scott's po-faced semi-solemn manner – of quite dissolving comedy.

Paul Scott's sense of reality enables him to see the comprehensive power of class, his comic sense reveals its absurdities, his detachment makes clear that a Rajput princess like Lady Chatterjee is much more at home, more essentially, *with* a member of the English upper class than she ever would be with an inferior of her own race and colour. And yet in spite of his grasp of the reality and influence of class and of his related sense of its comic and its vicious effects, there is in the long run a certain limpness and conventionality in Scott's treatment. At key junctures he seems himself subject to the very forces he castigates. And those who embody the highest values turn out to be the well-bred, the products of the best establishments and the oldest families, just as what is mean, perverse and cruel is realized in a figure like Merrick, the unworthy outsider trying to break in. The characters are representative figures of a given class, both Indian and English; with one or two 'conventional' eccentrics, for example Sister Ludmilla, the Russian self-appointed nun who trawls the alleys after dark seeking to succour the dying or the elderly and finally crazed missionary, Miss Crane, whose only originality is to struggle on in her work, despite having lost its motive, her religious faith. (Religion of every sort is not, it appears something Scott understands or can realize in fiction – a severe handicap for one dealing with an essentially spiritual universe.) Like the characters, the language is conventional, competent and clear but seldom animated by wit and rarely by poetry. It is the kind of language that needs the skill of actors to bring it to effective life, as we can see in the glittering television production of certain parts of it.

The Raj Quartet is a vast and valiant undertaking. But it is less a novel than a pantechnicon of information of innumerable aspects of life in India at the time of the conclusion of British rule. And as it is the product of a sympathetic observer of liberal instincts and immense information it can be recommended as an agreeable and educative experience, but not an authentic literary experience of a particularly significant kind.

It may surprise the reader that, after speaking in so subdued a way of The Raj Quartet, which is generally taken to be the height of Scott's production, I should go on to claim the status of a minor classic for what looks at first sight a much slighter work, namely Staying On (1977). This is without doubt a considerably finer novel than the whole or any part of The Raj Quartet. Staying On is at once a most compressed and easily flowing novel. Implicit in it is all that happens or promises in The Raj Quartet – the shifts of history, the great events and their personal consequences. And the situation that the novel develops, in which two obscure figures from one of the earlier volumes elect to stay on under the new dispensation, is an image of that baffling blend of transience and permanence – in this case the choice of the latter against the former – which is an essential mark of human experience. It is also a choice which is despairing and without effect.

The difference between The Raj Quartet and Staying On is that the first is a comprehensive historical account of one sharp section or narrow phase of the Second World War and of the transfer during it of power in India; *Staying On*, on the other hand, is an intense, tightly organized novel primarily concerned with human beings and their intricate and often contrary relationships with one another and with the world both social and physical in which they are enclosed. For all its huge historical shifts and political changes, *The Raj Quartet* is an anatomy of the past, exact, fixed and still. But *Staying On* communicates throughout a sense of life modulating from moment to moment. This is an effect produced by characters who are ordinary specimens of their time and class but specimens animated by an authentic imaginative art so that they are simultaneously straightforwardly representative and fascinatingly mysterious: genuine human characters, that is.

The decision – given the circumstances, the momentous and extraordinary decision – of Tusker Smalley and his wife Lucy to 'stay on' was taken by Tusker himself. Lucy was not consulted. This was partly because Tusker – a retired Indian army officer and failed business man – was bloody minded, hectoring and bovinely convinced that such decisions were for husbands to make, and partly because much of Tusker's life (his career in the army, for example) was arranged in so far as it lay in his power, to shelter Tusker from the bewildering threats and terrors of change. Tusker was both bull and rabbit. Lucy on the other hand, had a marvellous inner steadfastness and courage beneath her frail and lady-like exterior. She had had to earn her living as a typist and had to suffer much in terms of precedence and petty slights in the society of English officers' wives and their obsession with rank and background. Lucy in her youth also had a faint family connection with the gentry and still kept the voice, manner and tone of the English lady beneath which she lived the fantasy life of a romantic actress. The relationship between the two, each beloved of and incomprehensible to the other, is thwarted, thorny and despairing, fundamentally because of that strange remoteness of the elderly which made it more and more agonizingly difficult to communicate.

The world the Smalley couple occupy in their indigent retirement is made up of the increasingly debilitated aftermath of the Raj and the strengthening Indianization of every aspect of daily life. The Smalleys' attitude to the British past is stoic and resigned, and it is eased by the gifts and devotions of their servant Ibrahim as well as by the urbane friendliness of the successor Indian officer class, by the comfort they, particularly Tusker, derive from Mr Bhoolabhoy, the manager of the hotel which owns the Smalley bungalow (though not from his grasping, bullying wife) or the Anglo-Indian Church organist and local hairdresser Susie Williams. Above all, their poverty-stricken existence is made tolerable and even on occasion enjoyable by the intense, tactful and peculiarly Indian attention of Ibrahim, who is friend, adviser, nurse, companion, infinitely more than any servant. He is an intelligent man who has worked out a modestly comfortable way of life for himself with his meagre salary, his free meals and other small perks from the hotel, his mistress also from the hotel, and his recognized and respected role in the Smalley household. It is a mark of the achieved art of this novel that it should be able to make us grasp and sympathize with a concept so remote to the Western reader as Ibrahim's dignified and independent servitude.

In contrast to *The Raj Quartet*, *Staying On* is spare rather than voluble and dramatic rather than ruminative, and by the end of it we know more (and more deeply) about the Smalleys, the Bhoolabhoys, Ibrahim, Susie, Dr Mitra, Col. Menektara and Father Sebastian than all the elaborated, discursive portraits of *The Raj Quartet* can tell us. We are also presented with a small, tightly organized world, full of contradictions, goodwill and malice, packed with precisely defined, enchantingly individual characters, a world which implies the larger world we all recognize as the one we live in. And we also understand how Colonel Smalley comes to be lying dead on his cherished bed of crimson canna lilies, while his wife is out having her hair blue-rinsed, clutching in his hand the note from Mrs Bhoolabhoy terminating his lease of his bungalow. Above all this unpretentious, natural and most accomplished novel illumines the nature we share with the Smalleys (and the Bhoolabhoys, Ibrahim and Susie and the mali). How conventional, how orthodox, how utterly ordinary all these people are! And yet what marvels and tragedies occupy the routine of their days. Colonel Smalley wears the thick carapace of an insensitive domestic tyrant and is the grossest kind of Blimpish colonial. But he is also – probably is more – one whose nerves and feelings are incurably trapped against the bone of reality, a timid romantic made frantic by inarticulacy. He is also a clown, a comic figure like his crony Mr Bhoolabhoy, in whom the humour verges on the desperate.

There are as many contrary elements in Lucy's nature as in her husband's. Rescued from her office job and transported to the glamour of India she was still vulnerable to the snobbery of the minutely classified society of military wives. Resentment at this did not prevent her from discomfort at the proffered friendship of Susie Williams. Compared to the juvenile absurdities of Tusker, Lucy's conduct seems adult and rational, and she is clearly an intelligent and sensitive woman. And yet she is enchanted by popular music and films. In fact, she shows how the human person mixes in a most individual blend quite incompatible qualities – in Lucy's case, in particular, adolescent fantasies with a profound, courageous and forgiving love, a love incess-

antly menaced by her terror at being left penniless in a remote, alien
land.

The feeling in this relatively short and richly inclusive novel encom-
passes the lonely heroism of the bereft Lucy and humour that is broad
and homely. On one side there is the boisterous by-play of the Bhoolabhoys' love-making, or the outrageous, surrealist conduct, worthy of
the Marx brothers, of Tusker Smalley, or the more refined comedy
of Lucy and Ibrahim as they manoeuvre to manage the husband or to
replace a servant partly at the hotel's expense without Tusker's knowledge, or the splendid fun and gusto of a specially Indian-flavoured
English. On the other, there is the intensifying fear and pain of Lucy
as life, in the form of Tusker's collapsing mind and physical seizures,
rehearses what it has in store for her. It takes a novelist of exceptional
skill and touch to conclude with perfect naturalness a story so full of
comedy with such a desolate cry as that of Lucy Smalley.

All I'm asking Tusker, is did you mean it when you said
I'd been a good woman to you? And if so, why did you
leave me? Why did you leave me here? I am frightened to
be alone, Tusker, although I know it is wrong and weak
to be frightened – but now, until the end I shall be alone
here as I feared, amid the alien corn, waking, sleeping,
alone for ever and ever and I cannot bear it but mustn't
cry and must must get over it but don't for the moment
see how, so with my eyes shut, Tusker, I hold out my
hand, and beg you, Tusker, beg, beg you to take it and
take me with you. How can you not, Tusker? Oh,
Tusker, Tusker, Tusker, how can you make me stay here
by myself while you yourself go home? (p. 255)

When I spoke a moment ago of the Indian-flavoured English of the
Indian characters in the novel I had in mind the exchanges between Mr
and Mrs Bhoolabhoy, known to the hotel staff and themselves as
management (he) and ownership (she), a range of communication
which can be comic, coarse, quarrelsome or menacing (on the part of
ownership), the slightly tilted usages of Susie Williams and Father
Sebastian, the slightly dated slang of the military, and Ibrahim's
fascination with, as well as his command of, the subtlety, range and
poetry of Engish idiom. All this is evidence of what has struck one
again and again in this study, namely, the intimacy with, and the quick
and nervous understanding of, the English language which seems a gift
of so many Indians during the last two hundred years. The extraordinary thing, as I have suggested before, is that this should be so with
a language which has to be learnt at school or later, which is the *lingua*

franca of a minority and which is in a real sense – if I may put it like this – an artificial language. It is clear that there could not be, the conditions being what they are, an Indian English as there is an Australian or British or Irish or Canadian English. At least there could not be in theory. Practice, however, as so often occurs in questions of language, literature or life, seems to belie the theory.

I end this chapter with J. G. Farrell's *The Siege of Krishnapur* (1973). Farrell, who was born in Liverpool in 1935, died tragically in 1979 in a fishing accident in Ireland just as he was coming to the height of his powers. The novel is set in a town in Northern India in 1857, the year of the Mutiny. One of the vivid impressions the reader takes from reading Indian literature in English is the persistence in Indian life of the sensibility and iconography of the Victorian period – a point I made when writing of R. K. Narayan – and *The Siege of Krishnapur*, although published when Farrell was thirty-eight, has a marked Victorian flavour. J. G. Farrell uses a Victorian idiom which seems both genuine and spontaneous, true to the period, and fitting his own personality. Much of the detail in sentiment, phrasing and imagery is taken, as he tells us in an Afterword, from contemporary diaries, letters and memoirs written by eye-witnesses, sometimes with the words of the witness only slightly modified. The result is comfortable for Farrell's own temperament and wholly convincing for the reader, who finds a mass of historical material animated by a sympathetic imagination and a delicate sense of period.

The Siege of Krishnapur is a historical novel in a traditional manner, large in scope, constituting a world with authoritative ease, with a central figure and a group of realized minor characters, with an organizing theme, the whole convincingly located in time and place and in a humane context of feeling and value. The immediate subject may be the Mutiny, the larger one is the tragic incomprehension of one civilization by another and the horrors that ensue when two races and two cultures are connected in an unnatural relationship of servant and master.

In the first part of the novel, where the ground for the siege is prepared by careful suggestion tactfully placed, the Indian part of the population is almost wholly passive and nearly invisible. The British, on the other hand, are shown at every point as engaged in an explicit and confident undertaking, that of imposing their Western, alien ethos upon an ancient, profound and complicated civilization. (The immensity of the distance between the two peoples and the near lunacy of British incomprehension and patronage are shamefully evoked near the beginning in the reference to a young officer 'who had decided as a pastime to study the natives'.) The British clearly intend to prosecute their aim of imposing a new order of morals and living upon the Indians while having, if at all possible, nothing whatever to do with Indians, who exist as generalized functions and members of certain useful classes. The particularly cold, distant attitude generated by this conception of the British presence and purpose in India was complained of by Nirad Chaudhuri in the twentieth century in *The Autobiography of an Unknown Indian* but it clearly existed long before in the time of the East India Company. In the novel the silence of the British towards the Indians is only broken once when the naïve young visitor Flemy visits the local Maharajah's son, Hari, discovered 'on a chair constituted entirely of antlers, eating a boiled egg and reading *Blackwood's Magazine'*. The interview is conducted through an invisible curtain of mutual incomprehension and prickly distaste.

The British – and the Collector, the great creation of the novel – stood for efficiency, hygiene, science, respectability and Anglicanism. They will construct roads and railways, impose an impartial system of justice, and correct gross moral and social abuses. And they wish to do this from within an enclosed British system and while living in as close an approximation to Britain as conditions will allow. With their transplanted intellectual and spiritual baggage, therefore, the British have imported a complete apparatus for living. Their houses, clothes and food were positively inimical to the environment. The Collector wore a formal morning coat, the women crinolines and mounds of showy petticoats, the Collector's children, as befitted their social status, velvet, flannel and wool. Menus at dinner were enormous. A picnic included real York ham, oysters, pickles, mutton pies, cheddar cheese, ox tongue, cold chicken, chocolate, candied fruit and Abernethy biscuits. The community even has a banqueting hall modelled on the town headquarters of the East India Company.

It is the grandeur, complication and parochialism of Victorian sensibility which give the book unity and spring, and it is these qualities which are most intensely embodied in the great figure of the Collector. He is a large, handsome man, with whiskers like the ruff of a cat. He is a man of dignity, fastidiously dressed, held in awe by the European community, with a powerful sense of duty and, in private, moody and overbearing with his family. He believed in the ennobling power of literature and founded a poetry society at which the ladies of Krishnapur read their own poems. He was fascinated both by art and technology. He brought back from England numerous works of art including a sculpture, 'Innocence protected by Fidelity', and objects acquired during the ecstatic days of his visits to the Great Exhibition such as the model of a carriage which supplied its own railway, laying it down as it advanced, and a gorse-bruiser which softened the prickles to make it edible for cattle.

There is an after-dinner scene in which the conversation develops ideas dear to the Victorian Great and Good – Progress, Faith, Feeling, Science. The ardent Flemy contends that if there has been any progress in their century it has been less in material than in spiritual life. 'Think of the progress from the cynicism and materialism of our grandfathers, from a Gibbon to a Keats, from a Voltaire to a Lamartine' (p. 47). But in the opinion of Mr Rayne, the Opium Agent, progress càn only be measured by material things such as the increasę in opium revenue – paid for by John Chinaman, incidentally – which enables more to be done in a genuinely practical way. Flemy's simplicity and Rayne's breathtaking realism are magisterially reconciled by the Collector.

> My dear friends, there's no question at all of a division of
> importance between spiritual and practical. It is the one
> that imbues the other with a purpose. . . . It's the other
> that provides an indispensable instrument for the one! Mr.
> Rayne you are quite right to mention the increase of
> revenue from opium but consider a moment . . . what is
> it all for. It's not simply to acquire wealth, but to acquire
> *through wealth*, that superior way of life which we loosely
> term civilization and which includes so many things, both
> spiritual and practical . . . and of the utmost diversity . . .
> a system of administering justice impartially on the one
> hand, works of art unsurpassed in beauty since antique
> times on the other. The spreading of the gospel on the
> one hand, the spreading of the railways on the other.
> (p. 48)

The siege is long and bloody. Most of those within the Residency are wounded or killed or stricken with dysentery or cholera. The action, packed and ferocious, moves with an inner natural rhythm. A fiction with such material could easily become a mere narrative of violence and disaster but *The Siege of Krishnapur* does not do so because the events of the novel sustain the reader's interest in a more complex theme. The drama and intensity of the action allows for the evolution or rather the transformation of character which might otherwise have taken the experience of a lifetime to bring about. The transformation is the more convincing in that it is essentially the development of elements latent within the nature of the character.

Perhaps I could illustrate briefly from two or three of the most prominent figures. Flemy, the decent young aesthete and dandy, is one whose nature is tilted towards subjectivity and for him the siege is the inrush of the most brutal external reality. Under its influence he becomes a brave and competent and still sensitive fighter, the extrav-

agance of self, corrected and matured. The mild dislike felt by Dr
Dunstable, the ebullient civil surgeon, for his buttoned-up counterpart
Dr McNab expanded to near maniacal proportions during the siege and
the onset of cholera. Each has his own theory of this disease and each
his own treatment. For two doctors cholera was a dangerous subject
to differ about. There is an insane juggling match between the two in
which Dr Dunstable, having deliberately induced the disease in himself
to prove the efficacy of his treatment, is treated at the request of his
daughter by Dr McNab. He makes a succession of partial recoveries
under McNab's treatment but falls back each time when he resumes
his own treatment. In the end he does not recover. There is a species
of humour – as my term 'juggling match' suggests – in this crazy
competition, even if the humour is macabre and cruel. A less ma-
licious, more mischievous, humour is seen in the relationship of Flemy,
a fairly detached kind of theist and the Padre. He is certain that the
dangerous situation his Krishnapur flock finds itself in is caused directly
by some moral perversion or failure in belief. There is little chance of
the former in the circumstances, and he is more and more frantically
convinced that it must be provoked by the sinful lack of religious faith
in Flemy. Flemy, he regards as an intellectual and he must surely,
therefore, be susceptible to conviction by the argument from design.
He therefore pursues Flemy during the crashing of cannon and canister
advancing ever more exotic instances of the Great Designer's art.

> How do you explain the subtle mechanism of the eye,
> infinitely more complex than the mere telescope that
> miserable humanity has been able to invent? How do you
> explain the eel's eye? . . . How do you explain the Indian
> Hog? . . . How do you account for its two bent teeth,
> more than a yard long, growing upwards from its upper
> jaw? . . . Think of the stomach of the camel. . . . Think
> of the milk of the viviparous female! Think how the
> middle claw of the heron and cormorant is notched like a
> saw. . . . (pp. 156–58)

Humour, one means by which the author relieves the strain of
incessant struggle, starvation and disease, is welcome in a narrative
which might without it become a catalogue of disaster. Farrell's
humour is of the Thackeray kind, armed and disillusioned. We are
reminded, for example, that not everyone is so tragically caught-up
in the fate of the Krishnapur Residency as the besieged and the
besiegers. Many hundreds of Indians turn up daily to act as cheering
spectators of the battle. The Collector, the great central figure of the
novel, has a nature without a touch of humour, although his strange

bric-a-brac is occasionally the subject of polite mockery. He is serious, powerfully concerned and utterly committed. Frivolity and lightness are wholly distasteful to him. He has his faults: he is moody and tetchy, and something of a domestic tyrant. But he represents with unselfconscious integrity the genuine Great Victorian. He is highly intelligent, acquainted with whatever is best in the age, and inevitably affected by the narrowness of the contemporary sensibility, particularly in its attitude towards women. But there is both a romantic (severely controlled) and a deeply melancholic strain in his temperament, as well as great powers of inspiring leadership. He is also a man of action, putting into practice tactics of defence which he had studied in the writings of French military experts. He was of the opinion that a civilized man could master any subject once it has been laid up in a book.

It is not during the siege, when he sustains his part with absolute firmness and conviction, but afterwards, when he has left India for good, that he is transformed. He did not take up the glorious and interesting life that was waiting for him there. He resigned from his Fine Arts Committee and from societies for reclaiming beggars and prostitutes. He grew in upon himself and took to pacing the streets of London. One day in the late seventies he came across Flemy, now a stoutish, married, opinionated man on his way to an appointment with a young lady of a passionate disposition, who asked about his collection of sculptures and paintings. Flemy is taken aback at learning that they had long been sold.

> 'Culture is a sham,' he said simply. 'It's a cosmetic painted
> on life by rich people to conceal its emptiness.' (p. 343)

The taken-aback Flemy protests that ideas are surely part of culture and we cannot live without them. 'Oh, ideas . . .,' said the Collector dismissively.

This may be the fruit of the Collector's old melancholy turned sour. It may also be the last word delivered – ironically – by an ex-proconsul on all imperial ambitions. It is certainly connected with an experience of the Collector during the siege. He has guiltily released Hari, the local maharajah's son, and an Indian functionary who had been kept as hostages. The Indian official comes before him wholly unaffected by his treatment, by the siege, by danger, singing a religious song, his eyes sparkling. The Collector is overcome by a feeling of helplessness.

> He realized that there was a whole way of life of the
> people in India which he would never get to know and

which was wholly indifferent to him and his concerns.
The Company could pack up here tomorrow and this
fellow would never notice. . . . And not only him. . . .
The British could leave and half India wouldn't notice us
leaving just as they didn't notice us arriving. All our
reforms of administration might be reforms on the moon
for all it has to do with them. (p 226)

References

1. Rubin, D., *After the Raj* (London, 1986), p. 9.

2. Greenberger, A. J., *The British Image of India* (London, 1969), p. 5.

3. Bryn Davis, M., *Ariel* (London), Vol. I, No. 4, pp. 48–56.

4. Allen, C., *Kipling's Kingdom* (London, 1987), p. 1951.

5. Dobrée, B., *Rudyard Kipling* (London, 1967), p. 28.

6. Ross, A., *British and Commonwealth Literature* (London), Vol. I, p. 295.

7. Bantock, G. H., *L. H. Myers: A Critical Study* (London, 1967), p. 150.

8. *Scrutiny* (1934), Vol. III, No. 1, p. 44.

9. Op. cit., p. 55.

10. Bantock, G. H., op. cit. p. 156.

11. *Scrutiny*, Vol. IV, No. 1, p. 63.

12. Harvey, J., *British and Commonwealth Literature* (London, 1971), p. 386.

13. *Scrutiny*, 1934, Vol. III, No. 1, p. 62.

14. Leavis, F. R., *The Common Pursuit* (London, 1952), pp. 269–270.

15. Stalleybrass, O., Introduction to Penguin edition of *A Passage to India* (1985), p. 23.

16. *Ibid.*

Chronology

DATE	POETRY	PROSE	HISTORICAL/CULTURAL EVENTS
583– 619		*Early Travels in India,* ed. W. Foster	First English travellers in India: Edward Terry, John Mildenhall, Ralph Fitch, William Hawkins, William Finch, Thomas Caryot, Nicholas Withington
600			East India Company given Crown Charter
615– 9		*Roe's Journal and Correspondence,* ed. W. Foster	Embassy of Sir Thomas Roe from James I to Great Mogul
657			Cromwell's Charter revitalizes East India Company
1658– 1700			Aurangzeb Mogul Emperor
660– 1700			East India Company given extended powers by Charles II. Company established in Bengal and Bombay

DATE	POETRY	PROSE	HISTORICAL/CULTURAL EVENTS
1757			Battle of Plassey make Company dominant power in India
1767			Robert Clive leaves India in political chao
1772			Warren Hastings appointed Governor of Bengal
1773			East India Company Act provides for a Governor General and Council and forbids officers to trade for themselves Warren Hastings appointed Governor General of India
1795			Warren Hastings acquitted of High Treason
1820		Rammohan Roy *Precepts of Jesus*	
1829			Abolition of *suttee*
1830	Kashiprosad Ghose *The Shair and Other Poems*		
1835			Macauley's Minute on Indian Education
1857			Indian Mutiny against British Rule

DATE	POETRY	PROSE	HISTORICAL/CULTURAL EVENTS
1858			Powers of East India Company transferred to British Crown
1871		Michael Dutt *Is this called Civilisation*	
1875	Toru Dutt *A Sheaf Gleaned in French Fields*		
1877			Queen Victoria proclaimed Empress of India
1882	Toru Dutt *Ancient Ballads*		
1886			First Indian National Congress
1888		R. Kipling *Plain Tales from the Hills*	
1901		R. Kipling *Kim*	
1910		E. M. Forster *Howards End*	
1914–18			First World War
1923		Ananda Coomaraswamy *An Introduction to Indian Art*	

DATE	POETRY	PROSE	HISTORICAL/CULTURAL EVENTS
1924		E. M. Forster *A Passage to India*	
1926			Simon Commission recognizes failure of Imperial Mission
1927		Edward Thompson *An Indian Day*	
1928			Congress Party votes for Dominion Status
1929		L. H. Myers *The Near and the Far*	
1931		L. H. Myers *Prince Jali*	
1935		Mulk Raj Anand *The Untouchable* R. K. Narayan *Swami and Friends* L. H. Myers *The Root and the Flower*	
1936	Rabindranath Tagore *Collected Poems and Plays*	Mulk Raj Anand *Coolie*	Rabindranath Tagore Nobel Laureate
1937		R. K. Narayan *The Bachelor of Arts*	
1938		Raja Rao *Kanthapura*	

DATE	POETRY	PROSE	HISTORICAL/CULTURAL EVENTS
1939–45		Mulk Raj Anand *Across the Black Waters*	Second World War
1940		L. H. Myers *The Pool of Vishnu*	Congress demands British withdrawal
1945		R. K. Narayan *The English Teacher*	
1947–64			The Nehru era
1947		Raja Rao *The Cow and the Barricades and Other Stories* B. Bhattacharya *So Many Hungers*	Independence achieved India divided
1948		G. V. Desani *All About H. Hatterr*	Assassination of Gandhi
1950		G. V. Desani *Hali*	Constitution outlaws untouchability
1951		Nirad C. Chaudhuri *The Autobiography of an Unknown Indian*	
1952		R. K. Narayan *The Financial Expert*	
1953	Nissim Ezekiel *Sixty Poems*	Attia Hosain *Phoenix Fled and Other Stories* E. M. Forster *The Hill of Devi*	

DATE	POETRY	PROSE	HISTORICAL/CULTURAL EVENTS
1956		R. P. Jhabvala *To Whom She Will*	
		Khushwant Singh *Train to Pakistan*	
		R. P. Jhabvala *The Nature of Passion*	
		Santha Rama Rao *Remember the House*	
1957		Mulk Raj Anand *The Private Life of an Indian Prince*	
1958		R. P. Jhabvala *Esmond in India*	
		R. K. Narayan *The Guide*	
		B. Rajan *The Dark Dancer*	
1959		Nirad C. Chaudhuri *A Passage to England*	
1960	P. Lal *The Parrot's Beak*	Kamala Markandaya *A Silence of Desire*	
	D. Moreas *Poems*	P. Scott *The Chinese Love Pavilion*	
1961		Attia Hosain *Sunlight on a Broken Column*	
		B. Rajan Too Long in the West	
		Ved Mehta *Walking the Indian Streets*	

DATE	POETRY	PROSE	HISTORICAL/CULTURAL EVENTS
1962	Adil Jussawalla *Lands-End*	Ved Mehta *John is Easy to Please*	
		K. R. S. Iyengar *Indian Writing in English*	First comprehensive study of Indian literature in English
1963		Manohar Malgonkar *The Princess*	Chinese invasion
1964			Nehru's death
1965		Nirad C. Chaudhuri *The Continent of Circe*	War with Pakistan
		Anita Desai *Voices in the City*	
1966	A. K. Ramanujan *The Striders*		Indira Gandhi Prime Minister 1966–77
1966–75		P. Scott *The Raj Quartet*	
1967	Kamala Das *The Descendants*		
1968		Raja Rao *The Serpent and the Rope*	
1971	A. K. Ramanujan *Relations*	Santha Rama Rau *The Adventuress*	India now the most populous State in the World
1972	Saleem Peeradina (ed.) *Contemporary Indian Poetry in English*	Ved Mehta *Daddyji*	War with Pakistan over foundation of Bangladesh

DATE	POETRY	PROSE	HISTORICAL/CULTURAL EVENTS
1973	Pritish Nandy *The Poetry of Pritish Nandy*	J. G. Farrell *The Siege of Krishnapur*	
1974	Arun Kolatkar *Jejuri*	R. K. Narayan *My Days*	India explodes atomic device
1975		R. P. Jhabvala *Heat and Dust* Salman Rushdie *Grimus*	
1976	Nissim Ezekiel *Hymns in Darkness* Arvind K. Mehrotra *Nine Enclosures* Adil Jussawalla *Missing Person*		Target of 7½ million vasectomies reached. Leads with other misuses of power to electoral defeat for Mrs Gandhi
1977		R. K. Narayan *A Painter of Signs* Kamala Markandaya *The Golden Honeycomb* P. Scott *Staying On*	
1978		Kamala Das *My Story*	
1979	Shiv K. Kumar *Woodpeckers*	Ved Mehta *Mamaji*	
1980		Anita Desai *Clear Light of Day* Ved Mehta *Portrait of India*	Indira Gandhi Prime Minister 1980–84
1981		Salman Rushdie *Midnight's Children*	Rushdie wins Booker Prize

DATE	POETRY	PROSE	HISTORICAL/CULTURAL EVENTS
1982	Nissim Ezekiel *Latter Day Psalms*	Kamala Markandaya *Pleasure City*	
1984	Arvind K. Mehrotra *Middle Earth*		
1987		Nirad C. Chaudhuri *Thy Hand Great Anarch*	
1988		Shashi Deshpande *That Long Silence*	

Select Bibliography

(Place of Publication, London, unless otherwise stated)

(i) General

Basham, A. L. (ed.):   *A Cultural History of India* (1975) – A full collection of authoritative essays.

Briggs, Asa: *The Age of Improvement* (1959) – Essential study of the Britain from which the Raj came.

Brown, Judith M.:   *Gandhi's Rise to Power: Indian Politics 1915–22* (1972); *Men and Gods in a Changing World* (1980); *Modern India: The Origins of an Asian Democracy* (1985) – The general history, inclusive, fair, accurate.

Campbell, Joseph (ed.):   *Myths and Symbols in Indian Art and Civilisation* (1957) – Clear treatment of an essential and complex subject.

Chaudhuri, N. C.:   *Hinduism* (1979) – Subjective but most perceptive.

Conze, Edward: *Buddhism, its Essence and Development* (1959).

De Schweinitz, Karl: *The Rise and Fall of British India: Imperialism and Inequality* (New York, 1983) – An American view.

Forster, E. M.:   *The Hill of Devi* (1953).

Foster, William (ed.):   *The Embassy of Sir Thomas Roe to India* (1926) – Essential to understanding foundations of British India.

Furber, Holden: *John Company at Work* (1931) – Intimate and picturesque portrait of life before the Raj.

Garratt, G. T. (ed.):   *The Legacy of India* (Oxford, 1937) – Set of excellent individual studies by eminent authorities.

Gokhale, B. G.:   *Indian Thought through the Ages: A Study of Some Dominant Concepts* (1961).

Greenberger, Allen J.:   *The British Image of India* (1969).

Griffiths, Percival: *The British Impact on India* (1952) – A traditional, confident and pro-British view.

Hardy, P.:   *The Muslims of British India* (Cambridge, 1972) – Clear study of key Indian religion.

Heimsath, C. H.:   *Indian Nationalism and Hindu Social Reform* (Princeton, 1964) – The connection of politics and religion.

Ingham, K.:   *Reformers in India 1793–1833* (Cambridge, 1956) – Christian Missionaries and Social Reform.

Kramrisch, Stella: *The Art of India* (1954).

McCully, B. T.:   *English Education and the Origins of Indian Nationalism* (1940) – The influence of education on politics.

McLane, J.:   *Indian Nationalism and the Early Congress* (Princeton, 1977).

Moon, P.:   *Gandhi and Modern India* (1968).

Moraes, F.:   *Witness to an Era: India 1920 to the Present Day* (1973) – A personal and readable Anglo-Indian account of a revolutionary era.

Nanda, B. R.:   *Mahatma Gandhi* (Boston, 1958).

Radhakrishnan, S.:   *The Hindu View of Life* (Oxford, 1954) – A profound study by an eminent philosopher.

Roberts, Paul: *History of British India* (1952) – Clear and straightforward summary.

Singh, Khushwant: *A History of the Sikhs*, 2 Vols (1963) – Essential to the understanding of a structural modern predicament.

Spear, P.:   *India: A Modern History* (1961) – Admirably clear and vivid study; *The Nabobs: A Study of the Social Life of the English in Eighteenth Century India* (1988).

Stokes, E.:   *The English Utilitarians and India* (1959) – The Britain out of which India grew. *The Peasant and the Raj* (1978) – A sympathetic account of the life of the Indian masses during British rule.

Wolpert, Stanley A.:   *A New History of India* (New York, 1977) – Balanced, synoptic American view.

Yalland, Zoë: *Traders and Nabobs, 1765–1857* (1988) – Fascinating background to life of East India Company and Raj.

(ii) Fiction

Anand, Mulk Raj: *Untouchable* (1935); *Coolie* (1936); *The Village* (1939); *Across the Black Waters* (1941); *The Big Heart* (1945); *The Private Life of an Indian Prince* (1953).

Cowasjee, Saros and Kamar, Shiv K.:   *Modern Indian Short Stories* (1983).

Deshpande, Shashi:	*The Dark Holds No Terrors* (1980); *Roots and Shadows* (1983).
Desai, Anita:	*Voices in the City* (1965); *Cry the Peacock* (1963); *Bye-Bye Blackbird* (1971); *Fire on the Mountain* (1977); *Clear Light of Day* (1980); *The Village by the Sea* (1982).
Desani, G. V.:	*All about H. Hatterr* (1948) – New edition: Penguin (1970).
Ganguli, J. M.:	*When East and West Meet* (1960).
Ghose, Zulfikar:	*The Murder of Aziz Khan* (1967); *Don Bueno* (1983).
Hosain, Attia:	*Phoenix Fled and Other Stories* (1953); *Sunlight on a Broken Column* (1961).
Khanna, K.:	*A Nation of Fools* (1984).
Kipling, R.:	*Plain Tales From the Hills* (1888); *Kim* (1901).
Kumar, Shiv K.:	*The Bone's Prayer* (1979).
Markandaya, Kamala:	*Nectar in a Sieve* (1954); *Some Inner Fury* (1956); *A Silence of Desire* (1960); *A Handful of Rice* (1966); *The Coffer Dams* (1969); *The Golden Honeycomb* (1977); *Pleasure City* (1982).
Mokashi-Punekar, S.:	*The Pretender* (1967).
Namjoshi, Suniti:	*Cyclone in Pakistan* (1977).
Narayan, R. K.:	*An Astrologer's Day* (1964); *Swami and Friends* (1935); *The Bachelor of Arts* (1937); *The Dark Room* (1938); *The English Teacher* (1945); *Mr. Sampath* (1949); *The Financial Expert* (1952); *Waiting for the Mahatma* (1955); *The Guide* (1958); *The Man-Eater of Malgudi* (1962); *The Sweet Vendor* (1967); *The Painter of Signs* (1977); *The Talkative Man* (1986).
Perera, Padma:	*Birthday, Deathday and Other Stories* (1974).
Rao, Raja:	*Kanthapura* (1938); *The Cow and the Barricades and Other Stories* (1947); *The Serpent and the Rope* (1960); *The Cat and Shakespeare* (1963); *Comrade Kirilov* (1976); *The Policeman and the Rose* (1977).
Rajan, B.:	*The Dark Dancer* (1959).
Ray, David and Amritjit Singh:	*India: Anthology of Contemporary Writing* (1983).
Ray, Satyajit:	*Stories* (1987).
Rushdie, Salman:	*Grimus* (1975); *Midnight's Children* (1981); *Shame* (1983).
Sahgal, Nayantara:	*A Time to be Happy* (1958); *Storm in Chandigarh* (1969); *The Day in Shadow* (1971); *Plans for Departure* (1986); *A Situation in New Delhi* (1977); *Rich Like Us* (1985).
Santha, Rama Rau:	*Remember the House* (1956).

Sidhwa, Bapsi: *Ice-Candy-Man* (1988).

Thompson, Edward: *An Indian Day* (1927)

(iii) Poetry

Anthologies: *Ten Twentieth-Century Indian Poets*, ed. R.
                    Parthasarathy (Delhi, 1976); *Contemporary Indian
                    Poetry in English*, ed. S. Peeradina (Bombay, 1972).

Aurobindo, Sri: *Poems* (Hyderabad, 1941); *Collected Poems and Plays*
                    (Pondicherry, 1942); *Savitri, A Legend and a Symbol*
                    (Pondicherry, 1950–51).

Coomaraswamy, A. K.: *Three Poems* (1920).

Daruwalla, K. N.:   *Two Decades of Indian Poetry, 1960–80* (1980).

Das, Kamala: *The Descendants* (Calcutta, 1967).

Derozio, H. L.:   *Poetical Works* (1871).

Dutt, G. C.:   *Cherry Blossoms* (1887).

Dutt, Michael   *Visions of the Past* (1849).
Madhusudan:

Dutt, Toru: *A Sheaf Gleaned in French Fields* (1875); *Ancient
                    Ballads and Legends of Hindustan* (1882).

Ezekiel, Nissim: *Time to Change* (1951); *Sixty Poems* (Bombay,
                    1953); *The Third* (Bombay, 1959); *The Unfinished
                    Man* (Calcutta, 1960); *Hymns in Darkness* (Delhi,
                    1976).

Furtadi, Joseph: *Poems* (Calcutta, 1901); *A Goan Fiddler* (Calcutta,
                    1927); *Songs in Exile* (Calcutta, 1938); *Selected Poems*
                    (Calcutta, 1942).

Ghose, Amitav: *The Circle of Reason* (1986).

Ghose, Manmohan: *Love Songs and Elegies* (Delhi, 1898); *Songs of Love
                    and Death* (Oxford, 1926).

Ghose, Zulfikar: *The Contradictions* (1966); *The Violent West* (1972).

Gokhale, Namita: *Paro Dreams of Passion* (Boston, 1984).

Honnalgere, Gopal: *A Wad of Poems* (Calcutta, 1971).

Jacob, Paul: *Alter Sonnets* (Calcutta, 1969).

Joshi, Arun: *The Foreigner* (1968).

Jussawalla, Adil: *Land's End* (Calcutta, 1962); *Missing Person*
                    (Calcutta, 1975).

Kabir, Humayun: *Poems* (1932).

Kolatkar, Arun: *Jejuri* (Calcutta, 1974).

Krishnamurti, M.:	*Love Sonnets and Other Poems* (Oxford, 1937).
Kumar, Shiv K.:	*Articulate Silences* (Calcutta, 1970); *Woodpeckers* (Calcutta, 1979).
Lal, P.:	*Draupadi and Jayadratha* (Calcutta, 1967); *Yakshi from Didarganj* (Calcutta, 1969).
Mahajan, Ashok:	*Goan Vignettes and Other Poems* (Calcutta, 1986).
Mahapatra, Sitakant:	*Quiet Violence* (Calcutta, 1970).
Mahapatra, Jayanta:	*The False Start* (Calcutta, 1980); *Relationship* (Calcutta, 1980); *Life Signs* (1983).
Malik, Keshav:	*Poems* (Delhi, 1971).
Mehrotra, Arvind K.:	*Nine Enclosures* (Calcutta, 1976); *Middle Earth* (Calcutta, 1984).
Modayil, Sujatha:	*Crucifixions* (1976).
Mohar, Kshitij:	*Ashes of Gold and Other Poems* (Calcutta, 1976).
Moraes, D.:	*Poems 1950; Poems 1955–65* (1966).
Naidu, Sarojini:	*The Golden Threshold* (1905); *The Bird of Time* (1912); *The Broken Wing* (1917); *The Sceptred Flute* (1928).
Nandy, Pritish:	*Rites for a Plebeian Statue: An Experiment in Verse Drama* (Delhi, 1960); *Riding the Midnight River: Selected Poems* (Delhi, 1975).
Narayan, R. K.:	*The Ramayana: A Version*, London, 1973.
Pant, Ghuri:	*Weeping Season* (1971).
Parthasarathy, R. (ed.):	*Ten Twentieth-Century Indian Poets* (Delhi, 1976).
Patel, Gieve:	*Poems* (Bombay, 1966); *How Do You Withstand Body* (Bombay, 1976).
Peeradina, Saleem:	*Contemporary Indian Poetry in English: An Assessment and Selection* (1972); *First Offence* (Bombay, 1980).
Sergeant, Howard (ed.):	*Pergamon Poets 9: Poetry from India* (1970).
Singh, Paran:	*Unstrung Beads: Prose and Poetry from the Punjab* (1923); *Seven Baskets of Prose Poems* (1928).
Tagore, Rabindranath:	*Gitanjali* (1912).
Vivekananda, Swami:	*Poems* (Calcutta, 1947)

(iv) Non-Fiction and General Criticism

Akademi, Sahitya:	*Who's Who of Indian Writers* (Delhi, 1961 and 1983).
Amar, G. S. (ed.):	*Readings in Commonwealth Literature* (Delhi, 1985).

Amirthanaya, Guy (ed.):   *Writers in East-West Encounter* (1982).

Buckland, C. E.:   *Dictionary of Indian Biography* (1906).

Butcher, Maggie: *The Eye of the Beholder* (1983).

Chaudhuri, Nirad C.:   *The Autobiography of an Unknown Indian* (1951) – A classic work by a brilliant and contentious writer.

Dasgupta, Subhoranjan: *Pritish Nandy* (Delhi, 1976).

Desai, S. K.:   *Santha Rama Rau* (New Delhi, 1976).

Dutt, Romesh Chunder: *The Ramayana and the Mahabharata* (1900) – Introduction by Max Muller.

Foster, William (ed.):   *Early Travels in India* (1921).

Gandhi, M. K.:   *Young India, 1919–1922* (1924); *Hind Swaraj (Indian Home Rule)* (1964); *The Story of My Experiments with Truth* (1957) – His autobiography. An ethical and political classic.

Ghose, Zulfikar: *Confessions of a Native Alien* (1965) – An interesting study of the phenomenon of cultural displacement.

Goyal, Bhagwat: *Culture and Commitment: Aspects of Indian Literature in English* (Meerut, 1984).

Iyengar, K. R. S.:   *Indian Writing in English* (1984) – The latest edition of a most useful, patient work, rather old-fashioned in critical method.

Jha, Rama: *Gandhian Thought and Indo-Anglian Novelists* (Delhi, 1983).

Karkala, J. B.:   *Indo-English Literature in the Nineteenth Century* (1970) – Writers generally of historical significance.

Karkala, John A. and Leena: *Bibliography of Indo-English Literature* (Bombay, 1974) – Essential for the research worker.

Locke, J. C. (ed.):   *The First Englishman in India: Letters and Narratives of Sundry Elizabethans* (1930) – Excellent introduction to the earliest of British traders and visitors.

MacDonald, K.:   *Rajah Rammohan Roy* (1877) – Useful contemporary account of a founder of Indian English prose.

Mahle, H. S.:   *Indo-Anglian Fiction* (Delhi, 1985).

Mohan, Ramesh (ed.):   *Indian Writing in English* (Delhi, 1978) – A collection of useful essays.

Mukherjee, M.:   *Realism and Reality: The Novel and Society in India* (Delhi, 1985).

Mukherjee, Sujit: *Towards a Literary History of India* (Madras, 1975).

Naik, M. K.:   *A History of Indian English Literature* (Delhi, 1982); *Dimensions of Indian English Literature* (Delhi, 1984); *Perspectives on Indian Prose in English* (Ghaziabad, 1982).

Nandy, Pritish: *Indian Poetry in English, 1947–1972* (Calcutta, 1972).

Narasimhaiah, C. D.: *Jawaharlal Nehru: A Study of His Writings* (Simla, 1960) – A literary study of an eminent political figure: unusual and enlightening; *Literary Criticism: European and Indian Tradition* (Delhi, 1966); *The Swan and the Eagle* (Simla, 1969) – Vigorous essays on the Indian prose tradition; *Indian Literature of the Past Fifty Years* (Delhi, 1970).

Narasimhaiah, C. D. (ed.): *Awakened Conscience* (Delhi, 1978) – A large collection of varied interest and quality; *The Swan and the Eagle* (Simla, 1978) – Important essays on the Indian Prose tradition, including studies of Ram Mohan Roy and Vivekananda.

Narayan, R. K.: *Gods, Demons and Others* (1964) – The legend and myths which lie beneath so much Indian poetry, art and fiction; *The Mahabharata* (1978) – An accessible even homely version of the best-known Indian classic.

Nehru, J.: *An Autobiography* (1936).

Prasad, Hari Mohan: *Indian Poetry in English* (1986).

Rajan, B.: *Literatures of the World in English*, ed. Bruce King (1974) – A cultured and perceptive essay.

Ramakrishna, D.: *Indian-English Prose* (Delhi, 1980).

Ramanujan, Molly: *G. V. Desani, Writer and Worldview* (1984).

Rau, Santha Rama: *Home to India* (1945); *East of Home* (1950) – An accomplished practitioner of the autobiographical form, rarely used in India.

Seton, Marie: *Panditji, A Portrait of Jawaharlal Nehru* (1966).

Sharma, K. K. (ed.): *Indo-English Literature* (Ghaziabad, 1977).

Sinha, Krishna Nandan (ed.): *Indian Writing in English* (New Delhi, 1979).

Srinivas, M. N.: *The Remembered Village* (Delhi, 1976) – An intimate study of the place closest to the sensibility of most Indians.

Srivastava, R. K.: *Perspectives on Bhabani Bhattacharya* (Ghaziabad, 1982) – A collection, and varied in quality.

Venagopal, C. V.: *The Indian Short Story in English* (Delhi, 1976).

Walsh, William: *Commonwealth Literature* (Oxford, 1973).

Walsh, William (ed.): *Readings in Commonwealth Literature* (Oxford, 1973); *R. K. Narayan* (1982).

Warwick, Ronald (ed.): *India: Review of National Literatures* (New York, 1979).

Williams, H. M.: *Studies in Modern Indian Fiction in English* (1973).

Individual Authors

Notes on biography, major works and suggested further reading

ANAND, MULK RAJ (1905–   ), was born in Peshawar and educated at Lahore, London and Cambridge Universities, after which he spent many years in England writing and engaged in left-wing causes. His best work includes his earliest novels, *Untouchable* (1935), *Coolie* (1936), *Two Leaves and a Bud* (1937), *The Village* (1939) and *Across the Black Waters* (1940). *The Private Life of an Indian Prince* (1953) was a later distinguished addition to his early fiction. He has also written a vast number of other books including non-fiction. His fundamental standpoint is a Marxist variant of humanism although it is one in which the rigidities of Socialist categories are softened by other gentler convictions and by a genuine generosity of feeling. Nevertheless the preachy, propagandist note is always likely to break through. Anand is unusual among Indian novelists in having been influenced by the great Russian writers, not least in respect of his astonishing fluency and candour of feeling. Since 1970 he has been the President of the Lokayata Trust, the purpose of which is to create a culture village centre near Delhi. He is universally recognized as one of the founders and more distinguished practitioners of the Indian novel in English.

See: Iyengar, K. R. S., *Indian Writing in English* (Simla, 1962).
       Cowasjee, Saros, 'Princes and Proletarians' in *Journal of Commonwealth Literature* (Leeds, July 1968).
       Sharma, K. K. (ed.) *Perspectives on Mulk Raj Anand* (Ghaziabad, 1978) Helpful and varied in viewpoint.

AUROBINDO, SRI (1872–1950), was born in Calcutta to a wealthy family. His father was a well-known surgeon, his mother the daughter of R. D. Bose, a leading figure in the nineteenth-century Indian cultural Renaissance. His father had a passion for English education and so in 1879 brought his children to England. Autobindo was first privately tutored in Manchester, then sent to school at St Pauls, and to university at King's College, Cambridge, where he took a first in the Classical Tripos. He returned to India in 1893 to the Civil Service of the State of Baroda and then to the College where he taught French and English. During this time he became steeped in the Indian classics and religion. He wrote a great deal of verse and several plays and an early draft of his poem 'Savitri'. Indian critics take a serious view of his work of this period but for a modern English reader its portentous abstraction and Victorian sentiment make it almost unreadable. He was the editor of a paper which brought him into conflict with the political authorities and he was arrested and acquitted more than once. In 1910 he went to Pondicherry where he stayed for the rest of his life, editing journals and composing treatises of a religious and mystical kind. In 1942 his *Collected Poems and Plays* was published and his philosophico-religious volume, *The Life Divine*.

See: for a quite different and well-argued view, Iyengar, K. R. S., *Indian Writing in English* (Simla, 1962).

Ghose, S. K., *The Poetry of Sri Aurobindo* (1969) – A sympathetic study of a writer whose interests and sensibility are now very remote.

Joshi, V. C., *Sri Aurobindo: An Interpretation* (Delhi, 1973) – A sympathetic Indian view of a philosopher and theologian often impenetrable to the British reader.

CHAUDHURI NIRAD CHANDRA (1897–   ), was born into a middle-class family. His father, who practised criminal law, gave the family its tone – serious, high-minded and self-improving. At the same time the family atmosphere was informed by traditional religion, intimately in touch with the classic Indian epics and poems and refreshed from time to time by dramatic religious festivals. He was educated at home and the University of Calcutta. A brilliant undergraduate, ill-health forced him to give up his graduate studies and closed for him any possibility of the university professorship he seemed in every respect ideally suited for. He was active in political work for the Gandhi cause in the nineteen twenties. Later he worked at a variety of jobs as journalist, broadcaster, civil servant. He developed an extraordinarily full and detailed knowledge of English life and letters and art. He began writing his first book, *The Autobiography of an Unknown Indian* (1951), in 1947 – an unabashedly egotistic work and perhaps the greatest single work produced by the clash of British and Indian civilizations. *A Passage to England* (1959) was the product of a visit to Britain sponsored by the BBC. It is a quirky and affectionate response to a country known only till then in literature. *The Continent of Circe* (1965) is a characteristically erudite and scornful account of Hindu culture. For the last twenty years Chaudhuri has lived in Oxford working on *Thy Hand Great Anarch* (1987), an idiosyncratic and scornful study of English thought and educational values.

DARWALLA, KEKI N. (1937–   ), was born in Lahore to a Zoroastrian family. English and Gujarati were the languages spoken at home. His father was a Professor of English. He went to various schools and completed his education at the University of Punjab. He lives in New Delhi, and the landscape of Northern India figures frequently in his verse, as does a deep sympathy for peasants and country folk. His main works are *Under Orion* (1970), *Apparition in April* (1971), and *Closing of Rivers* (1976). His poems have also appeared in *Poetry Australia* (Sydney), and *TriQuarterly* (Evanston, USA).

See: King, Bruce, *Modern Indian Poetry in English* (Delhi, 1987).

DAS, KAMALA (1934), was born in Kerala. Her mother is Balamani Amma, a well-known Malayali poet. She was educated at home and at a Catholic boarding school. She was married when she was fifteen. She writes in both Malaylam (short stories) and English (poetry). She has published two volumes of poetry in English, *The Descendants* (1967) and *The Old Playhouse and Other Poems* (1973). Her poems have appeared in *New Writing in English India* (London, 1974) and *Young Commonwealth Poets* (London,

1965). Her autobiography, *Mr Story*, was published in 1975. Her poems
are mostly concerned with sexual love, a subject she writes about with
unusual candour – for an Indian writer – and with considerable power.

See: Rahman, Anisur, *Expressive Form in the poetry of Kamala Das* (Delhi,
       1981) – A rather doctrinaire study of a writer not really susceptible
       to this treatment.

DESAI, ANITA (1932–   ), was born in Delhi to a Bengali father and a German
       mother. She was educated in Delhi. She is married, has four children and
       lives in Bombay. She has written several books for children. Her works
       include *Clear Light of Day* (1980), which was nominated for the Booker
       Prize, *Fire on the Mountain* (1977) for which she received the Royal Society
       of Literature's Winifred Holtby Prize and the 1978 National Academy of
       Letters. She has also published a volume of short stories, *Games at Twilight*
       (1982). She is a Fellow of the Royal Society of Literature and a member of
       the National Academy of Letters in Delhi.

See: Stivastava, R. K., *Perspectives on Anita Desai* (Ghaziabad, 1984).

DESHPANDE, SHASHI (1943–   ), was born in Dharwad, the daughter of an
       eminent Sanskrit scholar, Shriranga. She was educated at the universities of
       Bombay and Bangalore and she has degrees in economics and law. The
       early years of her marriage were devoted to two young sons. She has been
       a journalist. She has written short stories, four children's books and four
       previous novels – *The Dark Holds No Terrors* (1980), *If I Die Today, Come
       Up and Be Dead* and *Roots and Shadows* (1983) which was awarded the prize
       for the best Indian novel in English of 1982–83. Her husband is a
       pathologist and she lives in Bangalore.

DUTT, TORU (1856–77), was born to a rich, cultivated and well-educated
       family in Calcutta. Her father at first and then her mother were converted
       to Christianity. Toru and her sister Aru were educated at home. In 1869
       the family came to Europe where their cousin Romesh Chunder Dutt was
       preparing for the Civil Service examination in London. (He afterwards
       became a successful civil servant, President of the Indian Congress, Dewar
       of Baroda and wrote scholarly volumes on Indian history.) The girls
       attended a convent in Nice and then the family moved to Cambridge,
       attended the Higher lectures for women started by Henry Sidgwick and
       other liberal dons. In 1873 the Dutts returned to Calcutta. Toru published
       a volume of poems *A Sheaf Gleaned in French Fields* (1875) which was
       admired by Edward Gosse and is hardly readable here. It was, however,
       notably successful in its period as was her French novel, *Le Journal de
       Mademoiselle d'Arvers* (1879). Toru Dutt, like her sister and mother, died of
       tuberculosis.

EZEKIEL, NISSIM (1924–   ), was born in Bombay to a Jewish family long
       resident in India. He was educated at Antonio D'Souza High School and
       Wilson College, University of Bombay. He teaches American and English
       literature at the university. He is also Director of the Theatre Unity,
       Bombay. His poems have been published in *Encounter, London Magazine*
       and *The Spectator*. He was visiting professor at Leeds University in 1964
       and lectured in the United States in 1967. His principal publications are *A
       Time to Change* (1952), *Sixty Poems* (1953), *Three Plays* (1969), *Hymns in*

Darkness (1976). He is the senior and most respected of contemporary Indians writing poetry in English.

See: Taranath, Rajeev and Belliappa, Meena, *The Poetry of Nissim Ezekiel* (Calcutta, 1966).

FARRELL, JAMES GORDON (1935–79), was born in Liverpool and educated at Rossall and Brasenose College, Oxford. Farrell's first novel *A Man from Elsewhere* (1961) was published when he was twenty-eight. His second, *The Lung* (1965), has as its central figure a polio victim who is hemmed in by strange, obsessive fellow patients. In *A Girld in the Head* (1969), the chief character, himself an exotic stranger, is oppressed by people of mind-numbing ordinariness. In *Troubles* (1971), set in a once grand now shabby hotel, the Major, a relic of the Great War, stares in harassed detachment at a collection of old ladies while around rage 'the Troubles' of the twenties. It is a structural pattern reflected in *The Siege of Krishnapur* (1973), where again he deals with the contemporary world but in an oblique and deflected manner made all the sharper and more affecting by the minute accuracy with which the historical situation – its analogue – is observed. Farrell was the recipient of literary prizes in his relatively short life and his death (in a fishing accident) as he was just coming to the height of his power, was a severe blow to literature.

FORSTER, EDWARD MORGAN (1879–1970), was born in London and educated at Tonbridge School and King's College, Cambridge. He lived in Greece and Italy and spent two periods in India, one in 1912 and another in 1922: places which provided the background for his early stories and his two novels *Where Angels Fear to Tread* (1905) and *A Room with a View* (1910) and for *A Passage to India* which was published fourteen years later in 1924. His earlier work contrasted the natural vitality and unaffected feeling of Italy with British convention and gracelessness. His work in India as a Private Secretary to the Maharajah of Dewas gave him a vivid feeling for Indians and Indian sensibility which he expressed in the memoirs *The Hill of Devi* (1953) and in his masterpiece *A Passage to India*. He had been influenced at Cambridge by G. E. Moore and by Lowes Dickinson and he was a notable member of the Bloomsbury Group. In his best novels he projects an impressively individual vision of liberal democracy, cultivated feeling and a non-religious humanism which has touched generations of readers. His writing is also marked by the limitation of a purely secular humanism to which a religious conception of existence is incomprehensible. His last years were spent as an honorary Fellow of King's where he died full of honours and recognized as one of the greatest contemporary English writers.

See: Trilling, L., *E. M. Forster* (London, 1944) – Finest American Criticism.
       Beer J. B., *The Achievement of E. M. Forster* (1962) – Cool, comprehensive and helpful.
       Stalleybrass; O., Introduction to Penguin edition of *A Passage to India* (1985) The most sympathetic and perceptive of essays.
       Leavis, F. R., 'E. M. Forster' in *The Common Pursuit* (London, 1952) – Lucid and authoritative analysis.

GANDHI, MOHANDAS KARAMCHAND (1869–1948), was born at Porbander, studied law in London and practised in Bombay. He moved to

South Africa in 1893 and stayed until 1914, becoming the leader of the Indian community, both Hindu and Moslem and the originator of passive resistance to the discriminating laws. He returned to India and became leader of the Indian Congress Party in 1915. He was imprisoned in 1922 as an agitator and again in 1930. His autobiography, *The Story of My Experiments with Truth* was written during imprisonment. He came to London in 1931 and made a profound impression on the British. He was arrested again in 1933 and interned in 1942. He co-operated with the British in seeking agreement on Independence and accepted, against the wishes of Congress, the partition of India and the State of Pakistan. He was assasinated in Delhi in 1948.

JHABVALA, RUTH PRAWER (1927–), was born in Cologne of Polish parents. In 1939 she was brought to Britain as a refugee. She was educated at Hendon County School and the University of London. She became a naturalized British subject in 1948. In 1951 she married C. S. Jhabvala and went to live in India. She has three children. She is one of the most distinguished novelists to come out of India, even if not herself an Indian by birth. As a European, and one with a complex European background, living in India with an Indian family she writes from a singular, even a unique viewpoint. Her fiction combines the unblurred perception of the outsider with the intimate familiarity of the inhabitant. Her first work *To Whom She Will* was published in 1956 and she has continued publishing novels and short stories, all of an impressively, even high, quality ever since. She has written for the films and some of her own novels have been dramatized. She is much concerned with the experience of a non-Indian member of the Indian community, with the insights and strains this brings with it and with a curious blend of East and West in the Indian middle class, whom she treats often with considerable perception and sometimes with a sardonic and less than admiring crispness.

See: Gooncratme, Yasmine, *Silence, Exile and Cunning: The Fiction of R. P. Jhabvala* (Delhi, 1983).
Williams, H. M., *The Fiction of Ruth Prawar Jhabvala* (1973).

KIPLING, RUDYARD (1865–1936), was born in Bombay, son of art teacher and sculptor. He returned to England in 1871 to live a miserably solitary life with elderly relatives. He was sent to the United Services College, the background of *Stalky & Co.* (1899). He returned to India to work as a journalist from 1882 to 1889. His stories of soldiers, engineers and administrators embodied the mystical concept of the law by which the higher breeds are governed. His work also shows a neurotic suspicion of women, hostility to Americans – his wife was an American – and distorting conceptions of blood and race. He also exhibits a profound sympathy with Indians and extraordinary skill in reproducing the life of work, the codes by which people live and the Indian landscape. His reputation collapsed after his death, but there is now a more discriminating view of his highly original and creative contribution to the short story.

See: Rutherford, A. (ed.), *Kipling's Mind and Art* (London, 1964) – Catholic and balanced collection.
Dobrée, B., *Rudyard Kipling* (London, 1967) – Sound general introduction.
Eliot T. S., (ed.), *A Choice of Kipling's Verse* (London, 1941) – Begins a new phase in Kipling's reputation.

KOLATKAR, ARUN (1932–), was educated in Bombay and holds an Art Diploma. By profession Kolatkar is a graphic designer in an advertising agency. Poems have appeared in *New Writing in India* (1974) and *The Shell and the Rain* (1973). He writes in both English and Marathi, his mother tongue, and he also translates from Marathi into English. His best-known work is *Jejuri* (1974), a long poem in thirty-one sections, which has been strongly influenced by the incantatory and imagist qualities of classical Indian verse.

See: Peeradine, Saleem (ed), *Contemporary Indian Poetry in English: An Assessment and Selection* (1972).

KUMAR, SHIV K. (1921–), was born in Lahore and educated at Dayanand Anglo-Vedic High School and Forman Christian College, and at Fitzwilliam College, Cambridge. He lives in Hyderabad and is Professor of English at Hyderabad University. Kumar's father was a headmaster and both Hindu and English were spoken at home. Kumar is also a novelist but his reputation rests on his poetry which is unusual in Indian poetry in English for its ironic and bantering tones. He has been a visiting professor at Yale and Cambridge, and his poems have been published in *Ariel* (Leeds), *Meanjin Quarterly* (Melbourne), *The New York Times,* *Quest* and *Western Humanities Reviews* (Salt Lake City). His books include *Articulate Silences* (1970), *Cobwebs in the Sun* (1974), *Subterfuges* (1976) and *Woodpeckers* (1979).

LAL, P. (1931–), was born in Kapurthala in the Punjab and educated at St Xavier's, Calcutta, is a poet, translator and publisher, a man who has put considerable capacities and energies at the service of poetry and poets. He himself is the author of five books of poetry in English and two books of translation from Sanskrit; *Sanskrit Love Lyrics* (1966) and *Sanskrit Plays in Modern Translation* (1967). He has lectured in American and British universities. By his work as a publisher he has given English language readers access to many new modern Indian poets and given the poets a wide, international audience. By profession he is an academic at the University of Calcutta.

MALGONKAR, MANOHAR (1913–), was born in Bombay and educated at Karnatati College, Dharwar, and Bombay University. Served in the Armed Forces in the Marathi Light Infantry (1942–52) and retired as Lieutenant-Colonel. He was also a big-game hunter and a Cantonment Executive Officer of the Government of India (1937–42). His novels, written in lively and colloquial English, which is his first language, are stories of romantic action informed by a traditional, conservative spirit. The principal ones are *Distant Drum* (1960), *Combat of Shadows* (1962), *The Princes* (1963), and *A Bend in the Ganges* (1964).

See: Dayananda, James, *Manohar Malgonkar* (Boston, 1934).

MARKANDAYA, KAMALA (1924–), was born in India and educated at various Indian schools and the University of Madras. She has worked as a journalist in India and Britain. Kamala Markandaya is a novelist who continually extends the range of her material. Her first novel, *Nectar in a Sieve* (1954), is concerned with Indian village poor; *Some Inner Fury* (1956), with an educated girl and her Indian lover in the midst of the Independence campaign; *A Silence of Desire* (1960), with marriage problems; *A Handful of Rice* (1966), with the indigent city dweller; *The Coffer Dams* (1969), with contemporary industry. Her later works show a comparable extension of interest and an increasingly impressive skill in adding to sensitive character construction a fine grasp of context.

See: Prasad, Madhusudan, *Perspective on Kamala Markanadaya* (Ghaziabad, 1984).

MEHROTRA, ARVIND KRISHNA (1947–), was born to a middle-class medical family in Lahore and educated at Allahabad and Bombay universities. He is a lecturer in English Literature at Allahabad. In 1967 he had a volume, *Woodcuts on Paper*, published in England, and he worked in the United States in 1972. His poems have been published in *The American Review* (New York), *Modern Poetry in Translation* (London) and *New Writing in English* (1974). He has been influenced by *Manifesto of Surrealism* (1924). His *Collected Shorter Poems* was published in 1971.

MEHTA, VED (1934–), was born in Lahore to a doctor's family. He had a happy and affectionate home life. But he was stricken with blindness as a child and his father sent him to a blind school in Bombay which had some success in making blind children independent and capable of earning a living – essential, his father thought, in India where handicapped children were often abused. At fifteen he went to the United States where he attended another blind school and later took a university degree. He read history at Oxford and Harvard. He contributed to journals in Britain, the United States and India, and in 1960 became a member of staff of *The New Yorker* (see the collection *John is Easy to Please* (1971)). He is a prolific author who has written on modern philosophers, theologians and historians, several biographical studies of members of his family *Daddyji* (1971), *Mamaji* (1973) See also *Vedi* (1982) and *The Ledge between the Streams* (1984). His books are widely translated. His mature work is marked by acute intelligence, wit and a crisp athletic English style. He has, however, a gift for illuminating original and significant contemporary issues and minds.

MYERS, LEO HAMILTON (1881–1944), came of an intellectual family. His father, F. W. H. Myers was a Victorian poet and essayist and with Henry Sidgwick a co-founder of the Society for Psychical Research. L. H. Myers was educated at Eton and King's College, Cambridge. He was for a while on the edge of the Bloomsbury Group but reacted angrily against its self-centred and superior spirit. A large legacy in 1906 enabled him to lead the life of a very rich and self-indulgent man. His first novel, *The Orissers*, was published in 1922; the best, a lighter work, *The Clio*, in 1925. His masterpiece is *The Near and the Far*, a tetralogy on medieval India composed between 1929 and 1940. Myers was a very early example of champagne socialist, combining wealth and an ostentatious manner of life with a passionate and quirky communism – even with an admiration for Stalin. He suffered from ill-health and neurasthenia and led an increasingly isolated and embittered life. He died from an overdose of veronal in 1944.

See: Bantock, G. H., *L. H. Myers: A Critical Study* (London, 1967); *Scrutiny*, Vol. XVI (Cambridge, 1949) – Both these *Scrutiny*-type studies represent a highly favourable view from an unexpected source.

NAIDU, SAROJINI (1879–1949), was born to a high-caste gifted Bengali family. To avoid what her parents considered an unfortunate marriage to a man of lower caste and another region, she was sent to England with a scholarship to be educated at King's College, London, and Girton College, Cambridge. Both her lively personality and her romantic verse were admired by Edward Gosse, Arthur Symons and other members of the Rhymers' Club. She returned to India in 1898, married the man her parents had objected to and continued to write verse of a banal and sentimental sort. Her first collection, *The Golden Threshold* (1905), enjoys a considerable vogue. In later years she was engaged in the nationalist struggle and earned a remarkable reputation among its leaders. Her death in 1949 was saluted as that of a national figure by Nehru, the Prime Minister himself. Like Toru Dutt she is significant for what she stood for rather than for what she wrote.

See: Dwivedi, A. N., *Sarojini Naidu and Her Poetry* (Allahabad, 1981).
Khan, Izzat Yar, *Sarojini Naidu: The Poet* (Delhi, 1983).
Naravane, Vishwanath S., *Sarojini Naidu* (Delhi, 1980).

NARAYAN, RUSIPURAM KRISHNASWAMI (1907–   ), was born in Madras of pure Brahmin stock but brought up by his grandmother and uncle in Mysore – vividly described in *My Days* (1974) a set of autobiographical sketches. He graduated – just, after an extra year – and worked as a reporter for a Madras newspaper. His English style was influenced by the writers in his favourite magazine *The Strand*, Conan Doyle, P. G. Wodehouse, W. W. Jacobs and Arnold Bennett. His first novel, *Swami and Friends* (1935), was published with the help of Graham Greene, who remained a devoted admirer. Narayan went on to become a professional writer of a most prolific kind and has a world-wide audience. The novels are those of a natural story-teller, brought up on classical Indian tales and Vedic poetry, and one for whom everything that happens is material for his fiction. He is concerned with the middle class, with the family, with the life and work of the town, Malgudi. The novels are intensely local but also magically representative. Narayan is a fastidious artist who blends myth and realism, the natural and the grotesque, and whose work is at every point sustained by humour that is both light and wise.

See: Walsh, William, *R. K. Narayan: A Critical Appreciation* (London, 1982).
Naik, M. K., *The Ironic Vision: A Study of the Fiction of R. K. Narayan* (Delhi, 1983).
Pontes, H., *R. K. Narayan: A Bibliography* (New Delhi, 1983).
Iyengar, K. R. S., *Indian Writing in English* (Simla, 1962).
Ram, Atma (ed.), *Perspectives on R. K. Narayan* (Ghaziabad, 1981) – An uneven compilation ranging from excellent to indifferent.
Gilra, S. K., *R. K. Narayan: His World and His Art* (Delhi, 1984).

NEHRU, PANDIT JAWAHARLAL (1889–1964), was born in Allahabad, son of a wealthy lawyer. Educated at Harrow and Trinity College, Cambridge, and in 1910 called to the Bar. He practised law in India, and became an activist in the Indian National Congress. He was elected President in 1929, having spent 1921–22 in prison and 1926–27 abroad. He spent other periods in prison, some nine years, before Independence. He became Prime Minister of Independent India in 1947 and remained throughout his life devoted to Gandhi, although he was as a politician more moderate and flexible. He was the leader of the Third World until his death in 1964. His *An Autobiography*, a candid exposition of his personality and of the politics of his time, was published in 1936.

PARTHASARATHY, RAJGOPAL (1934–   ), was born in Tamil Naidu at Tirupparai and educated at Don Bosco High School, Bombay University and Leeds University. The languages spoken at home were Tamil and English. His father was an accountant. He was for ten years a lecturer in English Literature at Bombay. In 1971 he became Regional Editor of The Oxford University Press at Madras. His poems have been published in *Encounter, The Times Literary Supplement, Quest* and *Poetry India*. He has, with J. J. Healey, edited *Poetry from Leeds* (1968). His long poem, *Rough Passage*, written over a period of fifteen years, was published in 1976. At one time he gave up writing verse in England for his native Tamil, but has begun again to write in English. He is a spare, fastidious, highly respected poet in India and the English-speaking world.

PATEL, GIEVE (1940–   ), was born in Bombay. His parents were Parsees. The languages spoken at home were English and Gujarati. He was educated at St Xavier's College, Bombay, and he qualified as a medical practitioner at Grant Medical College. He spent three years at a Primary Health Centre in rural India and now practises medicine in Bombay. He began writing at an early age, and he is also a painter, an actor and playwright. His works include *Poems* (1966) and *Princes*, a play performed in 1970. He has had several one-man shows of his paintings. His poems have appeared in *The Illustrated Weekly of India, New Writing in India* (London, 1970), *Young Commonwealth Poets* (London, 1965), *Ten Twentieth-Century Poets* (Delhi, 1976), and *Contemporary Indian Poetry in English* (Delhi, 1972).

RAJAN, BALACHANDRA (1920–   ), was educated in Indian schools and at Cambridge. Fellow of Trinity College and University Lecturer in English. He is a scholar, critic and novelist. He has written on Milton's *Paradise Lost* and Jonson and the Seventeenth Century Reader (1947), on W. B. Yeats, *A Critical Introduction* (1965), and two well-known novels, *The Dark Dancer* (1959) and *Too Long in the West* (1953), which deal in a cultivated way with the predicament of the expatriate. He has held academic appointments at Cambridge, Delhi, London, Ontario, as well as being Indian representative at the United Nations.

RAMANUJAN, ATTIPPAT KRICHMASWANI (1929–   ), was born in Mysore and educated at D. Bhanumaiah's High School and Maharaja's College, Mysore. He spent eight years as a lecturer in English Literature at various Indian universities. In 1962 he was appointed to the University of Chicago where he is now Professor of Linguistics and Dravidian Studies. His principal works are *The Striders* (1966), *Relations* (1971), and *Selected Poems* (1976). His poetry is known in India and on both sides of the Atlantic and he is regarded as one of the best modern poets in the English language. Although he has lived in the United States for some twenty years, his poetry is saturated with Indian scenes and a pure Indian sensibility.

RAO, RAJA (1909–   ), was born in Mysore, South India, and educated at Nizam College, University of Madras. He completed his studies at the University of Montpellier and the Sorbonne. He has spent much of his life in France, and has been Professor of Philosophy at the University of Texas, Austin. His first novel was *Kanthapura* (1938) in which a village grandmother relates the events following the arrival of Gandhism. It is told in rich and vigorous peasant speech. *The Serpent and the Rope* (1960) is a metaphysical novel, a dramatic meditation on the nature of existence. It is opulent in thought but meagre in action. *The Cat and Shakespeare* (1963) is a more vivid and active blend of philosophical speculation and human drama. Raja Rao's fiction, lucid and magical in style, provides access not only to Indian sensibility but also to the difficult and evanescent world of Indian metaphysics.

See: Narasimhaiah, C. D., *Raja Rao* (Delhi, 1968) – Vigorous, sympathetic and perceptive study.
Naik, M. K., *Raja Rao* (Aurangabad, 1972).
Rao, K. R., *The Fiction of Raja Rao* (Aurangabad, 1980).
Sharma, R. K. (ed.), *Perspectives on Raja Rao* (Ghaziabad, 1980) – A useful and balanced compilation.
Bhattacharya, P. C., *Indo-Anglian Literature and The Works of Raja Rao* (Delhi, 1983) – Raja Rao's place in the canon of English Indian literature.

ROY, RAM MOHAN (1772–1833), was born in Calcutta of a Brahmin family. As a young man he showed an unusual gift for languages, learning not only Bengali and Hindustani but also Sanskrit, Persian and English. He developed his command of English during service with the East India Company where he showed uncommon qualities of capacity, tact and energy. He left the Company and founded in Calcutta in 1814 a movement for a more eclectic religion which would incorporate the best elements of Islam, Christianity and Hinduism. In his weekly paper, *Sambad Kamaudi*, he argued for the rights of women, especially of the outrageously treated widows, for the impoverished, for a free press and against prejudice and reaction. He was one of the first Indian thinkers to rediscover the *Upanishads*, which had been neglected or known only in quotation, and to find there a critique of superstition and a strong case against caste and other forms of discrimination. In 1831–32 he worked in England where his reputation was deservedly high, advising Ministers and Civil Servants on education, and other Indian issues. Roy was a man of intellect, of extraordinary energy and liberal passion. He was also the pioneer of Indian prose in English and the originator of the literature of thought.

See: Allen, J., Haig, W. and Dodwell, H. H., *The Cambridge Shorter History of India* (London, 1934) – An essential contextual study.
Ghosh, J. C., Vernacular Literature in *The Legacy of India* (Oxford, 1937).
The English Works of Raja Rammohun Roy, eds K. Nag and D. Burman (Delhi, 1945–51) – Key documents for the library.
Singh, Iqbal, *Rammohun Roy* (Delhi , 1958) – A modern view of the Victorian thinker.

RUSHDIE, SALMAN (1934–), was born in Bombay, educated at Cathedral School, Bombay, Rugby and King's College, Cambridge, and is married to the American writer, Marianne Wiggins. He now lives in London. In an earlier career he worked in an advertising agency as a copywriter. He has written scripts for the cinema. He is a member of the Production

Board of the British Film Institute, a Fellow of the Royal Society of Literature and the advisory board of the Institute of Contemporary Arts. His principal works are *Grimus* (1975), *Midnight's Children* (1981), *Shame* (1983) and *The Satanic Verses* (1988). *Midnight's Children* won the Booker Prize and The James Tait Black Memorial Prize, and *Shame* the Prix Meilleur Livre Etranger.

SAHGAL, NAYANTARA (1927–), was born in Allahabad, educated in India and at Wellesley College, USA, 1943–47. She was married in 1949 and has three children. She was divorced in 1967. Mrs Sahgal was born into an aristocratic family, and has lived always at the top of Indian society. Her uncle was Nehru, her mother an Indian ambassador, and from her earliest days she has mixed with politicians, the diplomatic service, the wealthy and the powerful. She has preserved in this heated atmosphere a remarkable coolness, independence and capacity for detached criticism. Her shrewd and liberal judgements of character and situation in *A Time to be Happy* (1958), *This Time of Morning* (1965), *Storm in Chandigarh* (1969) and *The Day in Shadow* (1971) are delivered from a cultivated moral standpoint. Mrs Sahgal, who is an active journalist, has also written two volumes of autobiography, *Prison and Chocolate Cake* (1954) and *From Fear Set Free* (1963).

SCOTT, PAUL (1920–78), was born in London and educated at Winchmore Hill Collegiate School. He served in the army for six years in the Second World War, chiefly in Malaysia and India, where much of his fiction is set. He had a head for figures and legalities and after the war worked as a Company Secretary in publishing firms. He became a Director of the distinguished literary agency, David Higham Associates in 1960. He reviewed fiction for the serious press and himself wrote thirteen novels. In 1976 he was a visiting lecturer in the University of Tulsa, Oklahoma. *Staying On* was awarded the Booker Prize in 1978. This was adapted for television, and the four novels of *The Raj Quartet* (1966–75) became a celebrated television series, *The Jewel in the Crown*. Both the Malaysian and the Indian worlds are accurate in detail and evocative in atmosphere. They are concerned with the end of empire the emergence of new kinds of Englishmen, the deep and fierce oppositions of class and the tragedy of those lost or displaced by changes in civilization. Most of his novels are deliberate and ruminative in the telling, and somewhat dry and jagged in the handling of the prose. Exceptions to this limiting observation are *The Chinese Love Pavilion* (1960) and his finest work, *Staying On* (1977). Paul Scott died in 1978.

SINGH, KHUSHWANT (1915–), was born in Hadali, then in India, now in Pakistan. Educated at Delhi, Lahore and King's College, London, he was called to the Bar in 1938. He practised law in Lahore, 1939–47, and then joined the Indian Foreign Service, working as a Press Attaché in London and Ottawa. He served in Paris in UNESCO 1954–56. He has been a visiting lecturer at Oxford, Princeton, Rochester and Hawaii. He is also a working journalist-editor of *The Illustrated Weekly of India* and a historian of distinction who has made many valuable contributions to Sikh studies, including *A History of the Sikhs* in two volumes (1963), a definitive study. He is the author of *Train to Pakistan* (1956), still one of the best half-dozen novels by an Indian writer in English.

TAGORE, RABINDRANATH (1861–1941), poet, painter, educator – a model of the classical guru. Born in Calcutta, he paid several visits to England. W. B. Yeats much admired translations of his Bengali poems, and his most famous work *Gitanjali*, published in England in 1913, was awarded the Nobel Prize. It is difficult to appreciate the English versions of his poems which, concerned as they are with 'the infinite within the finite', are lacking in the density and concreteness we expect from poetry. He established an educational establishment in 1901 which became a university in 1921. His autobiography, *My Reminiscences*, was published in 1917.

THOMPSON, EDWARD JOHN (1886–1946), was the eldest son of Rev. John Moses Thompson. Both father and mother were Wesleyan Missionaries. Mrs Thompson was widowed in 1894 and with six children struggled against extreme poverty. Edward was ordained and sent to the Wesleyan College at Benkuna, Bengal, in 1920, where he taught literature. He became a military chaplain in 1916 and went through the Mesopotamian and Palestine campaigns. After the war he returned to Benkuna and became more and more convinced of the necessity of self-government for India. He returned to England to Oxford to lecture in Bengali. His reputation was high in India and he was a friend of both Gandhi and Nehru. He was not only a novelist but a poet of religious and romantic subjects. His verse, however, is hardly readable today. He is a minor novelist but his experience of India and his fascination with its life and scenery, his liberal principles and his deeply religious nature helped him to an intimate sympathy and understanding of Indian character. His best novels are *An Indian Day* (1927) and *The Youngest Disciple* (1938), a novel about Buddhism.

VIVEKANANDA, SWAMI (1862–1902), was a relatively modern example of the sage and guru in the classical Indian tradition. He began as a disciple of the illiterate mystic Ramakrishna (1836–86), a man subject to trances and, according to Vivekananda, a man of grace and goodness. Vivekananda was educated both in Sanskrit and English so that he had both a means to the mastery of Indian spiritual thought and a logical language in which to express it. His aim was to purify Hinduism, to purge it of superstitions, accretions and to give it a stronger ethical content. He composed luminous commentaries on the Vedas and gave innumerable lectures, addresses and sermons and wrote countless letters. These he collected in *The Complete Works of Swami Vivekananda* (1924–32) and published in Calcutta in seven volumes. In 1957 this work had gone into a tenth edition. In his early career, Vivekananda had wandered as a mendicant preacher across the face of India preaching a purer and more rigorously moral Hinduism. In later life he travelled extensively abroad and addressed enormous audiences, in England (1896), in New York (1894–95), in Chicago (1893–94), in Harvard (1896) and San Francisco (1900).

Index

Across the Black Waters by Mulk Raj
    Anand, 65–8, 191
Adelphi, 169
After the Raj by David Rubin, 159
Age of Improvement, The by Asa
    Briggs, 27
Akbar, 165–7
Ajanta, Caves of, 15, 63
Alema, 13
All about H. Hatterr by G. V. Desani,
    95–6
Anand, Mulk Raj, 62–8, 205
Area of Darkness, by V. S. Naipaul,
    5–6
Argument Without End by Ved Mehta
    (*New Yorker* article), 60
Art of India & Pakistan, 13–16
Ashoka, 14
Aspern Papers, The by Henry James,
    123
Attlee, Clement, 23
Atman, 8
Aungier, G, 19
Aurobindo, 38, 40, 127, 205
*Autobiography of an Unknown Indian,
    The* by N. C. Chaudhuri 21–2,
    45–53, 182

Bachelor of Arts, The by R. K.
    Narayan, 75
Badami, 15
Balzac, Honoré de, 81
Bantock, G. H., 166, 167
*Battle Against the Bewitchment of our
    Intelligence* by Ved Mehta (*New
    Yorker* article), 60
Becket, S, 17
Bend in the Ganges, A., by Manohar
    Malgohkar, 101
Bengal Magazine, The, 126
Bentham, J, 31

Bentinck, Lord William, 31
Bevin, E, 13
Bhagavad, Gita, The, 8
Bhattacharya, Bhagani, 101
Bianca novel by Toru Dutt, 126
Blagat, D. P., 141
Big Heart, The by Mulk Raj Anand, 64
Bose, Buddhadeva, 127
Bottrall, Ronald, 166
Brahman, 8
Brahminism, 33
Briggs, Asa, 27
Briggs, M. S., 15
British and Commonwealth Literature,
    ed. David Daiches, 162
British Image of India, The by Allan J.
    Greenberger, 159
British Impact on India, The by
    Percival Griffith, 7
Brown, Judith M., 6–7, 13, 24, 28, 42
Bryn Davis, M., 159–160
Buchan, John, 101
Buddha, The, 10, 12, 14, 37
Burgess, Anthony, 95
Burke, E., 27
Byron, George Gordon Lord, 123

Calcutta, 25, 50–1
Carlyle, Thomas, 73
Caste, 4–5
Cat & Shakespeare, The by Raja Rao,
    72
Charles II, 19
Chatterji, Bankim Chandra, 48
Chaucer, Geoffrey, 95
Chaudhuri, Nirad C., 2–4, 21, 27,
    45–53, 182, 206
Chaudhuri, Sukanta, 141
Child, Sir Joshua, 20
Chinese Love Pavilion, The by Paul
    Scott, 160

Clapham Sect, The, 31
Clear Light of Day by Anita Desai, 113–5
Clive, R., 52
Coffer Dams, The by Kamala Markandaya, 115
Coleridge, Samuel Taylor, 104, 124
Common Pursuit, The, essays by F. R. Leavis, 168
Comrade Kirillov by Raja Rao, 72
Concise History of Indian Art by Roy Craven, 14
Congress Party, The, 28–9, 39–44
Constantine, 14
Continent of Circe, The by N. C. Chaudhuri, 2–4
Coolie by Mulk Raj Anand, 64, 67
Cow of the Barricades, The by Raja Rao, 73
Craven, Roy, 14
Cromwell, O., 19
Cry The Peacock by Anita Desai, 111
Cultural History of India, A by Dr. Sarvepalli Radhakrishnan, 12
Curzon, Lord, 28

Daddyji, by Ved Mehta, 57
Daiches, David, 97
Daniels, Michael, 141
Dark Dancer, The, by Balachandra Rajan, 100–1
Daruwalla, Keki N., 141–2, 206
Darwin, C., 60
Das, Kamala, 143–4, 206
Dattatreyan, T. V., 141
Davis, M. B., 159
Dell, Ethel M., 165
Derozio, Henry, 125
Desai, Anita, 101, 111–15, 206
Desai, Mahinder, 39
Desani G. V., 95–6
Deshpande, Gauri, 141
Deshpande, Shashi, 101, 117–9, 206
Dickens, Charles, 63, 121
Distant Drum, The by Manohar Malgonkar 101
Diver, Maud, 159
Dobrée, Bonamy, 162
Donne, John, 112
Dutt, Aru, 123
Dutt, Michael Madhusudan, 48, 125
Dutt, Romesh Chunder, 126
Dutt, Toru, 125, 126, 207
Dyer, General, 27

East India Company, The Hon., 10, 19–20, 32
Eliot, Thomas Stearns, 119
Ellis, Havelock, 76
Ellora, 15
English Teacher, The by R. K. Narayan, 55, 75
English Works of Ram Mohan Roy, The, 32
Ernekar, Mary, 141
Esmond in India by Ruth Prawer Jhabvala, 108
Evtushenko, Yevgeny, 143
Experience of India, An, by Ruth Prawer Jhabvala, 16–7
Ezekiel, Nissim, 127–136, 144, 207
Face to Face by Ved Mehta, 57
Farrell, J. G., 181–6, 207
Financial Expert, The by R. K. Narayan, 74
Fly and the Fly Bottle by Ved Mehta, 57
Forster, E. M., 9–11, 20, 63, 100, 101, 168–174, 208
Francis Xavier, St., 12
Freud, S., 60
Future Poetry, The, Essay by Autobindo, 38

Gaitskell, Hugh, 23
Gandhi, Indira, 22, 23, 29
Gandhi, Mahatma, 23, 28–9, 39–43, 208
Gandhi, Sanjay, 22
Ganesha, 53
Gellner, Ernest, 60
Get Ready for Battle by Ruth Prawer Jhabvala, 108
Ghose, Aurobindo, 38, 126
Ghose, Kashiprosad, 125
Gibbon, E., 183
Godard, 17
Gokul Ashtami, 10
Golden Honeycomb, The, by Kamala Markandaya, 116–7
Gordon, Mr – Correspondent of Ram Mohan Roy, 33
Gorky, Maxim, 63
Gourd and the Sickle, The by Mulk Raj Anand, 64
Greenberger, Allan J., 159
Greene, Graham, 54
Griffith, Percival, 7
Grimus by Salman Rushdie, 119–120

Guide, The by R. K. Narayan, 76
Gujarati School, 15

Hali by G. V. Desani, 95
Handful of Rice, A by Kamala
    Markandaya, 115
Hanuman, 56
Harding, D. W. 166–8, 170
Harrison, Tom, 174
Hartley, L. P., 167
Harvey, John, 167
Hastings, Warren, 27
Heat and Dust by Ruth Prawer
    Jhabvala, 109
Heber, Bishop, 12
He Who Rides the Tiger by Bhagani
    Bhattacharya, 101
Hill of Devi, The by E. M. Forster,
    9–11, 173
Hinduism, 2–3, 6–11, 13, 49
Hosain, Attia, 101–3
Householder, The by Ruth Prawer
    Jhabvala, 118
Howards End, by E. M. Forster, 168
Human Cycle, The. Essay by
    Aurobindo, 38

Ideal of Human Unity, The. Essay by
    Aurobindo, 38
In Custody by Anita Desai, 111–13
Indian National Congress, 28, 36, 41
Indian Writing in English by K. R. S.
    Iyengar, 102
Inquiring Spirit ed. K. Coburn, 124
I Shall Not Hear the Nightingale by
    Khushwant Singh, 99
Islam, 12–3, 14
Ivory, James, 109
Iyengar, K. R. S., 102

James, Henry, 45, 59, 81
James I, 19
Janism, 11, 12, 14
Jennings, Humphrey, 174
Jewel in The Crown, The First volume
    of *The Raj Quartet* by Paul Scott,
    175
Jhabvala, Ruth Prawer, 16–7, 18,
    105–11, 208
Jinnah, M., 28
John is Easy to Please by Ved Mehta,
    57
Journal de Mademoiselle D'Avers, Le,
    Novel by Toru Dutt, 126

Joyce, James, 95
Jussawalla, Adil, 126

Kanthapura by Raja Rao, 62
Katrak, K. D., 141
Keats, J., 100, 183
Kim by Rudyard Kipling, 161
King Lear by William Shakespeare, 22
King, Ursula, 36–37, 39
Kipling, Rudyard, 95, 160–3, 209
Kolatkar, Arun, 144–8, 209
Krishna, 8, 10, 53
Kumar, Shiv K., 209

Lakshmi, 74
Lal, P., 12, 76, 149, 157, 210
Lamartine, 183
Lawrence, D. H., 149
Leavis, F. R., 168, 170
Lectures From Colombo to Almora by
    Vivekananda, 35
Ledge Between the Streams, The by
    Ved Mehta, 57
Life Divine, The. Essay by
    Aurobindo, 38
Lok Sabha, The, 22
Love Songs & Elegies by Romesh
    Chunder Dutt, 126
Luther, M., 52

Macaulay, Lord, 31
Madge, Charles, 174
Mahabharata, The, 8, 48
Mahapatra, Jayanta, 148–9
Malabari, Behramji, 126
Malgonkar, Manohar, 101
Mamaji by Ved Mehta, 57
Man Eater of Malgudi, The by R. K.
    Narayan. 79–88
Manifesto of Surrealism, 149
Man With the Dog, The by Ruth
    Prawer Jhabvala, 110
Marabar Caves, The, 169, 173–4
Markandaya, Kamala, 101, 115–7, 210
Marx, K., 44, 60, 72
Masani, R. P., 4–5
Masood Syed Ross, 168
Mass Observation, 174, 176
Masters, John, 101
Mehistra, Arvind, 141
Mehrotra, Arvind Krishna, 149–51,
    210
Mehta, Ved, 25, 56–61, 210–211
Menon, Krishna, 23

Merchant, Ishmael, 109
Middle Years, The by Henry James, 59
Midnight's Children by Salman Rushdie, 120–22
Mill, John Stuart, 31
Milton, John, 73
Modern Indian Poetry in English, ed. P. Lal. 127, 157
Mohun, Ras, 58
Montaigne, 108
Moore, Thomas, 125
Mother Theresa, 23
Mr. Sampath by R. K. Narayan, 9, 75
Mulk Raj Anand and the Thirties Movement in England by Gillian Packham, 63
Murasahi, Lady, 167
Muslim League, The, 28
Mutiny The, 20
My Days by R. K. Narayan, 53–6
My First Marriage by Ruth Prawer Jhabvala, 109
Myers, F. W. H., 165
Myers, L. H., 165–8, 170

Naidu, Sarojini, 211
Naik, M. K., 68
Naipaul, V. S., 5–6, 16, 20, 26
Namier, L., 60
Namjoshi, Sumiti, 141
Narasimhaiah, C. D., 34
Narayan, R. K., 15, 53–6, 211
Nature of Passion, The by Ruth Prawer Jhabvala, 108
Near and The Far, The by L. H. Myers, 167–69
Nectar in a Sieve by Kamala Markandaya, 115
Nehru, J., 23, 29, 43–5, 212
New Yorker, The, 59, 60
Notes of a Son and Brother by Henry James, 59

One Out of Many by V. S. Naipaul, 26

Packham, Gillian, 62–3
Pai, Nagesh Wishwanath, 126
Paramahamsa, Ramakrishna, 34
Parliament of Religions, Chicago, 1893, 35
Parthasarathy, R., 136–140, 141, 212
Parsees, 11
Passage to England, A by Nirad C. Chaudhury, 45

Passage to India, A by E. M. Forster, 168–74
Passion by Ruth Prawer Jhabvala, 109
Patel, Gieve, 152–3, 210
Pater, Walter, 43
Philosophical Investigations by Wittgenstein, 59
Phoenix Fled by Attia Hosain, 102
Plain Tales from the Hills by Rudyard Kipling, 161
Ponni Amnan, 53
Possession by Kamala Markandaya, 115
Princely Order, 21
Princes, The by Manohar Malgonkar, 101
Private Life of an Indian Prince, The by Mulk Raj Anand, 65–7

Rabelais, 95
Radhakrishnan, Sarvepalli 12, 39
Raj Quartet, The by Paul Scott, 174–8
Rajan, Balachandra, 100–1, 213
Ramanujan, A. K. 153–7, 213
Ramayana, The, 8, 48
Ramu by Attia Hosain, 102
Rao, Raja, 67–73, 213
Rau, Santha Rama, 103–4
Rayaprol, Simivas, 141
Religion of Man, The, Rabindranath Tagore, Hibbert Lectures 1930, 36
Rich Like Us by Nayantara Sahgal, 104–5
Rise and Fall of British India, The by Karl de Schweinitz Jr., 25
Robinson, Kay, 161
Roe, Sir Thomas, 19, 20
Ross, Angus, 162
Roy, Ram Mohan, 31–34, 48, 126, 213
Raja Ram Mohan Roy, English Works of, ed. Jogandra Chander Ghose, 32
Rubin, David, 157
Rukoji Rav III, H. H. Sir, 9
Rushdie, Salman, 119–23, 214
Russell, Bertrand, 43, 60, 63
Rutherford, Anna, 64–5
Ryle, Gilbert, 60

Sahgal, Nayantara, 103–5, 214
Sanchi, 14
Santayana, George, 165
Sarthi, I., 141
Savitri, by Sri Aurobindo, 126

Schweinitz Jr., Karl de, 25
Scott, Paul, 20, 174–80, 214
Scrutiny, 166
Serpent & The Rope, The Raja Rao, 71–2
Shakespeare Wallah by Ruth Prawer Jhabvala, 109
Shame by Salman Rushdie, *122–3*
Shastras, 34
Shiva, 7
Siege of Krishnapur, The by J. G. Farrell, 181–86
Sikhism, 11
Silence of Desire, A by Kamala Markandaya, 115
Singh, Khushwant, 98–100, 215
Small Boy and Others, A by Henry James, 59
So Many Hungers by Bhagani Bhattacharya, 101
Some Inner Fury by Kamala Markandaya, 115
Spiritual Call, A by Ruth Prawer Jhabvala, 110
Stalleybrass, Oliver, 169
Staying On, by Paul Scott, 177–80
Stendhal, H., 108
Storm in Chandigarh by Nayantarah Sahgal, 104
Stray Sketches in Chakmakpore by Nagesh Wishwanath Pai, 126
Street of the Morn, The Attia Hosain, 102
Study of History, A by Arnold Toynbee, 60
Sunlight on a Broken Column by Attia Hosain, 103
Suttee, 22, 31, 33
Swadeshi, 42
Swami and Friends by R. K. Narayan, 62
Sweet Vendor, The by R. K. Narayan, 15, 89–95
Synthesis of Yoga, The Essay by Aurobindo, 38

Tagore, Rabindranath, 38, 48, 215
Tale of the Genji, by Lady Murasahi, 167
Tenets of the Veda Essay by Aurobindo, 38
Ten Twentieth Century Indian Poets, ed. R. Parthasarathy, 141, 149

That Long Silence by Shashi Deshpande, 117–9
Theckaduth, Kishore, 141
This Time of Morning by Nayantara Sahgal, 104
Thomas St., 12
Thompson, E. 163–5, 215
Time is Unredeemable by Attia Hosain, 102
Times, The, 22
To Whom She Will by Ruth Prawer Jhabvala, 108
Toynbee, Arnold, 60
Train to Pakistan by Khushwant Singh, 99–100
Trevor–Roper, Hugh, 60
Turn of the Screw, The by Henry James, 123
Two Leaves & A Bud by Mulk Raj Anand, 62

Untouchable by Mulk Raj Anand, 63–4

Veda, The, 8
Vedanta, 3
Vedi by Ved Mehta, 57
The Village by Mulk Raj Anand,
Vivekananda, Swami, 34–8, 40, 215
Vivekananda, Swami: Complete Works of 34
Voices in the City by Anita Desai, 111
Voltaire, 183
Voss by Patrick White, 82
Waiting for the Mahatma by R. K. Narayan, 43, 75
Walking the Indian Streets by Ved Mehta, 61
Walton, Geoffrey, 166
Wells, H. G., 63
White, Patrick, 82
Widow, The by Ruth Prawer Jhabvala, 109
Wilde, Oscar, 43, 95
Wittgenstein, 59, 60
Wodehouse, P. G., 95
Woolf, Virginia, 100
Words & Things by Ernest Gellrer, 60

Yates, D., 165
Yeats, William Butler, 127